No More Takeout!

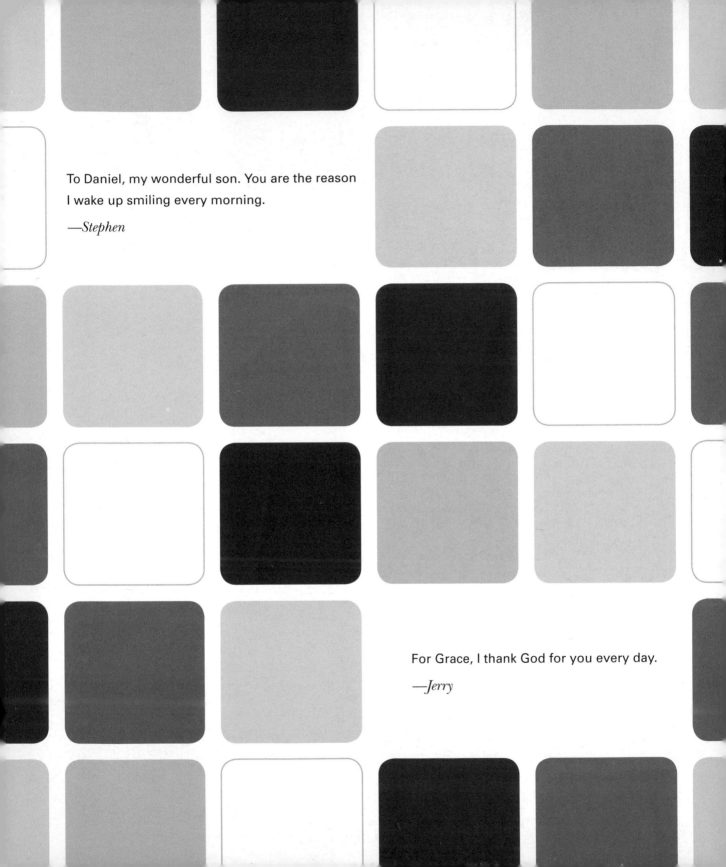

To Daniel, my wonderful son. You are the reason I wake up smiling every morning.

—*Stephen*

For Grace, I thank God for you every day.

—*Jerry*

NO

A Visual Do-It-Yourself Guide to Cooking

MORE

Stephen Hartigan & Jerry Boak

TAKEOUT!

WILEY

JOHN WILEY & SONS, INC.

Photographs © 2009 by Michael Filosa

Published by John Wiley & Sons, Inc., Hoboken, New Jersey

Published simultaneously in Canada

For general information on our other products and services or for technical support, please contact our Customer Care Department within the United States at (800) 762–2974, outside the United States at (317) 572–3993 or fax (317) 572–4002.

Wiley also publishes its books in a variety of electronic formats. Some content that appears in print may not be available in electronic books. For more information about Wiley products, visit our web site at www.wiley.com.

Library of Congress Cataloging-in-Publication Data:
    Hartigan, Stephen.
No more takeout : a visual do-it-yourself guide to cooking / Stephen Hartigan & Jerry Boak.
  p. cm.
Includes index.
ISBN 978-0-470-16998-8 (cloth)
1. Cookery. I. Boak, Jerry. II. Title.
TX651.H37 2009
641.5--dc22
         2008019001
Printed in the United States of America

10 9 8 7 6 5 4 3 2 1

CONTENTS

Acknowledgments   vi

Introduction   vii

Getting Set Up   viii

Ready, Steady, Prep!   xviii

THE BASIC BASICS   1

Waking Up to Breakfast Anytime   2

Spectacular Salads   24

Quick Bites and Simple Snacks   32

Easy Main Dishes   40

Simple Sides   70

Basic Basics Desserts   76

Level 1 Menus   82

RAISING THE BAR   87

Savory Starters   88

Soups and Stews   96

Elegant Salads   104

Marvelous Main Dishes   110

More Sides   134

Delicious Desserts   142

Level 2 Menus   150

NOW YOU'RE COOKIN'!   155

Hors d'Oeuvres   156

Elegant First Courses   168

Sophisticated Main Dishes   174

Stylish Sides   192

Delectable Desserts   200

Level 3 Menus   210

Index   214

Acknowledgments

From Stephen: I'd like to thank my grandmothers, Siobhain and Maureen, who were instrumental in raising my early interest in the beauty and comfort of food; Mum and Dad, for teaching me invaluable lessons in life that couldn't be learned in college or culinary school; Trish, for introducing me to the culinary industry at an early age and for being a great sister; Niall O'Neill, advisor, solicitor, counselor, and best friend; Caroline Mulcahy, for her continuous love, support, and friendship over the years; Tracy Nugent, for being a wonderful mum and a great cook; and all my wonderful friends and family who have supported me throughout my career, and even tested recipes for *No More Takeout*.

A huge thank-you to Mr. and Mrs. Allen J. Grubman, for giving me their continuous support, encouragement, and the time to complete this project; to Larry Shire (G.I.S.) for being a great attorney (and accepting meatloaf for payment); and to Marion O'Neill for all her behind-the-scenes work.

Des McDonald, Mark Hix, Jeremy King, and Chris Corbin: the best restaurateurs I have had the pleasure to work with.

To Jerry Allen, Geoff Du Feu, Seamus Forde, Paul Gaylor, Malcolm Gee, Gray Kunz, Andy Magsdon, Liam Noonan, Gerald Redican, Ollie Sullivan, and Jean-Marc Tsai, who all have given me some of their knowledge, inspiration, and skills to help me along the way to do what I do every day, "cook great food."

From Jerry: A big thanks to my über-helpful recipe testers: Hope Breiding, Nancy Byrne, Terry Byrne, Tish Byrne, Deb Cluverius, Jake and Jennie Cluverius, the Dubishar family, Sam Earle, Holly Frederick, Marcia Frederick, Andy Goodman, Reid Goodman, Jill Lamar, Betsey Nadle, Noah Raizman, Ken Rock, Robin Shoemaker, Dorian Singh, and Maegan Skinner.

In memory of my dear mother, who first taught me how to cook, "bon appétit!" And with unending appreciation to my lovely wife, who put up with so much during the long process of bringing this book to print.

From both of us: Thank you to our agent, Katherine Cluverius, for being a great agent, friend, and supporter; to our editor, Linda Ingroia, for believing in our dream and making it a reality; to Charleen Barila, for all her hard work, dedication, and 2 a.m. e-mails to keep us on track; and to the rest of the hard-working team at Wiley: production editor Amy Zarkos; copyeditors Suzanne Fass and Shannon Egan; designer Nick Anderson; marketing manager Michael Friedberg, and publicist David Greenberg. Special thanks to Lizzie Grubman for all her support and hard work and for fitting us into her busy schedule to make this book a success.

A heartfelt thank-you to Mickey Filosa for jumping on board this project and producing amazing photography to illustrate our goal for a visual do-it-yourself guide, and to Andy Varela for all expertise in photography, lighting, setup, food styling, and cooking, and for still smiling at 6 a.m. after a 12-hour shoot.

Mr. and Mrs. Fred Shuman, thank you for letting us take over your beautiful kitchen for our photos; to Devon Graham for introducing us, for all her hard work on the book, and to all her friends who kindly tested recipes for us—too many to mention! You know who you are.

Introduction

Are you tired of your weeknight #8 General Tso's Chicken special? Your favorite local dinner spot is getting a bit stale, isn't it? If you're faced with empty cabinets and a fridge stocked only with bottled water and last night's pizza, then *No More Takeout* is your answer.

The idea of cooking a meal can seem daunting after a long day at work. But before you reach for the phone to call for a delivery of moo shu, consider this: It really is easier—and much more fun than you think—to *learn to cook*. And *No More Takeout* will show you how.

You will learn how to make delicious meals, from simple weeknight dinners to more sophisticated cocktail parties, and develop your own cooking and entertaining repertoire that will be sure to impress your friends and loved ones. Most important, you will discover how to think outside the box and learn how to cook (almost) anything.

HOW TO USE THIS BOOK

This is a comprehensive, easy-to-follow cooking instruction manual for those of you who don't know a spatula from a whisk, but are ready to learn. Get started by reading the essentials at the beginning, including a guide through basic cooking principles and techniques.

The book is divided into three levels, to guide you step-by-step as you build skills (and comfort!) in the kitchen. Every recipe comes complete with detailed how-to photos to demonstrate complex steps and techniques, and with tips and sidebars to help you solve everyday cooking problems simply and effectively. Each level culminates in three menus that include a Plan of Work to walk you through the process of putting a meal on the table.

Getting Set Up

The Gear Essentials

You have probably been inside houseware stores packed with every conceivable kitchen tool and gadget. Intimidating, isn't it? But what do you really need to get started?

Every recipe in the book lists the gear you'll need to make the recipe successfully, and alternatives are given for those harder-to-find tools.

Start with these basics as a minimum investment, then work your way toward building up your arsenal.

The lists here are divided into two categories:

Gotta Have It: the things you really need while preparing these recipes. Many of these items can be bought as part of a large set—a very cost-effective way to outfit your kitchen.

Helpful Add-Ons: noncritical tools or equipment that may come in handy now and again.

KITCHEN GADGETS

Gotta Have It . . .

○ Food processor
○ Hand-held mixer
○ Blender

Helpful Add-Ons . . .

○ Immersion blender
○ Electric stand mixer
○ Slow cooker

YOUR KITCHEN TOOL BELT

Gotta Have It . . .

- ○ Potato masher or ricer
- ○ Wooden spoon
- ○ Spatulas (narrow, medium, and wide)
- ○ Ladles (one small, 2 ounces; and one medium, 6 ounces)
- ○ Whisk
- ○ Tongs
- ○ Heatproof silicone or rubber mixing spatula
- ○ Slotted spoon
- ○ Box grater
- ○ Can opener
- ○ Instant-read thermometer
- ○ Pepper mill
- ○ Pastry brush

- ○ Bottle opener/wine bottle opener
- ○ Meat mallet
- ○ Vegetable peeler
- ○ Stainless-steel mixing bowls (small, medium, large)
- ○ Salad spinner
- ○ Fine-mesh sieve (6-inch stainless steel)
- ○ Wood cutting board or butcher block
- ○ Plastic cutting boards
- ○ Colander
- ○ Rolling pin
- ○ Kitchen timer
- ○ Ruler
- ○ Mixing bowls (small, medium, large)

Helpful Add-Ons . . .

- ○ Fine-mesh conical sieve
- ○ Mandolin
- ○ Melon baller
- ○ Microplane grater

- ○ Plastic scouring brushes
- ○ Ring molds
- ○ Small prep bowls

And Don't Forget . . .

- ○ Aluminum foil
- ○ Cotton dish towels
- ○ Oven mitts and/or potholders
- ○ Paper towels

- ○ Plastic wrap
- ○ Resealable plastic bags
- ○ Resealable plastic or glass containers (microwave-safe)

COOKING GEAR

Gotta Have It . . .

- ○ Roasting pan with rack
- ○ Rectangular glass baking/casse-role dish (3-quart)
- ○ Ovenproof glass baking dish (8 x 8)
- ○ Stockpot (8-quart)
- ○ Dutch oven
- ○ Small saucepan with lid (1½-quart)

- ○ Small nonstick skillet/fry pan (8- or 9-inch)
- ○ Sauté pan
- ○ Large skillet/fry pan (10-inch or larger)
- ○ Medium saucepan with lid (3-quart)
- ○ Vegetable steamer

Helpful Add-Ons . . .

- ○ Cast-iron skillet
- ○ Cast-iron grill pan
- ○ Sauté pan with lid (4-quart)
- ○ Wok (10- to 16-inch)

- ○ Nonstick French skillet/omelet pan (8-inch)
- ○ Oval enameled cast-iron baking dish (14-inch)

The most important thing to consider is the pan's weight. The heavier the better; flimsy pans won't stand up to heavy use and don't retain heat uniformly.

Stay away from ultra-light, ultra-economy aluminum and stainless-steel pans, which can burn more than they cook because of uneven heating qualities with notice-able hot spots. Nonalloy aluminum pans are unfit for use with acidic foods like tomato sauce.

Nonstick Pans
These are great for dishes involving delicate or sticky ingredients (like fish or eggs). Replace the pan if the nonstick coating becomes damaged or begins to peel or flake off.

Mid-Weight Stainless-Steel and Aluminum Pans
Many stores sell complete sets of mid-weight stainless-steel and aluminum alloy pans and pots with lids for a relatively modest price.

Multi-Clad Stainless Steel or Aluminum Alloy
Many chefs and experienced home cooks swear by this heavyweight cookware, made of layered, bonded mate-rials for maximum heat retention and distribution.

Enamel-Coated Cast Iron
Best known for its heat retention, these pans require no seasoning or extra care, can be used on a stove top or in the oven.

USE NONSTICK COOKWARE FOR:

- Eggs and pancakes
- Fish and shellfish
- Stir-frying
- Breaded cutlets (chicken, veal)
- Reheating pasta
- Low-fat or no-fat cooking
- Baking

USE STANDARD COOKWARE FOR:

- Steak and chops
- Chicken dishes with sauce
- Making a sauce or gravy
- Searing meats
- Roasting, braising, and stewing

BAKING GEAR

Gotta Have It . . .

- Muffin pan
- Square pan (8 x 8)
- Rectangular pan (9 x 13)
- Rimmed baking sheet/jelly roll pan
- Wire cooling rack
- Ramekins (5-ounce)
- Flour sifter
- Parchment paper
- Round cake pan (9-inch)
- Springform pan
- Cookie/baking sheet

Helpful Add-Ons . . .

- Metal loaf pan
- Pie plate
- Tart pan
- Pastry scraper

MEASURE UP

Gotta Have It . . .

- Measuring spoons (⅛- to 1-teaspoon)
- Glass measuring cups (1- and 2-cup)
- Dry measuring cups (¼- to 1-cup)

BASIC KNIVES

Gotta Have It . . .

○ Kitchen shears/scissors
○ Paring knife (3½-inch)
○ Chef's knife (6- to 10-inch)
○ Serrated bread knife (8 inches)

Helpful Add-Ons . . .

○ Santoku knife (7-inch)
○ Boning knife
○ Carving knife
○ Sharpening steel

WHAT TO BUY

You don't need to be a sushi chef (or a surgeon) to appreciate the value of high-quality cutlery. But before you go spending hundreds of dollars for a state-of-the-art set of professional cutlery, think about what tasks you need the knives for.

LOOKING SHARP

Take care of your knives, and you'll be rewarded with many fine cuts. A few things to keep in mind:

- Protect your blade's edge by never *ever* scraping the surface of a cutting board or cutting on stainless-steel or granite counters.
- To test your knife's sharpness, try slicing into the skin of a tomato; if the blade travels through it with minimal force, it's sharp. If not, you'll need to sharpen it yourself.

The best way to sharpen your knife is to use a steel (also called a honing steel). Use a steel with a guard or plastic cuff at the top of the handle to protect your fingers. If you're right-handed, hold the steel in your left hand (or vice versa for lefties) and draw the knife down the blade of the steel at an angle of 25 to 30 degrees using considerable pressure, almost all the length of the knife of the blade or the steel (from heel to tip), four to five times per side. This will align the sharp edge (burr) of your blades.

STORING

- Wall-mounted magnetic holding strip
- Hardwood storage block
- In a drawer (keep sheaves on)—the least preferable method

WASHING

- Wash individually in hot water with dish soap and a soft sponge
- Don't put them in a dishwasher
- Don't let them sit in soapy water
- Don't use abrasives
- Dry immediately with a cotton dish towel
- Keep clean between use

See "Prep 101" (page xviii) for more information on how to use your knives and other basic prep techniques.

The Ingredient Essentials

To be a good cook, at the very least, you'll need a kitchen stocked with basic ingredients—those everyday staples you should always have on hand. These versatile ingredients will quickly become your go-to items for fast and easy cooking. And having a well-stocked pantry will save you time (and money) at the grocery store.

The key to a well-stocked kitchen is to keep track of frequently used ingredients. Don't stock up on items you rarely use, or they'll just go to waste. Use the following lists to get you started, or create your own list of go-to ingredients.

EVERYDAY STAPLES

In the Fridge

- ○ Cheese (cheddar or Swiss; blue; and Parmesan for grating)
- ○ Dijon mustard
- ○ Eggs
- ○ Ketchup
- ○ Mayonnaise
- ○ Milk
- ○ Salted butter
- ○ Unsalted butter

In the Pantry

- ○ All-purpose flour
- ○ Baking powder
- ○ Baking soda
- ○ Balsamic vinegar (aged)
- ○ Boullion cubes
- ○ Bread crumbs (unseasoned)
- ○ Coffee
- ○ Confectioners' sugar
- ○ Extra-virgin olive oil
- ○ Light brown sugar
- ○ Long-grain white rice
- ○ Pasta (shapes are up to you)
- ○ Red wine vinegar
- ○ Satay paste (or spicy peanut sauce)
- ○ Sesame oil
- ○ Soy sauce (natural soya is best)
- ○ Sugar
- ○ Tabasco sauce
- ○ Tea
- ○ Teriyaki sauce
- ○ Two 28-ounce cans chopped tomatoes (or four 14-ounce cans)
- ○ Two 6-ounce cans tomato paste
- ○ Vanilla extract
- ○ Vegetable oil (canola or corn)
- ○ White wine vinegar
- ○ Worcestershire sauce

YOUR SPICE RACK

ON THE RACK

Pepper

I prefer to use freshly ground.

- **Black pepper**—the most versatile and widely used (and most frequently used in this book).
- **White pepper**—especially used for cream sauces. Not as robust as black pepper.
- **Green peppercorns**—usually come in a jar in brine or vinegar, and traditionally used in steak sauce.

Hot Stuff

- **Red pepper flakes**—Good for adding heat to tomato sauces or fish stews.
- **Paprika**—There are many variations, made from different varieties of ground sweet or pungent peppers.
- **Chili powder**—A mixture of ground ingredients, including ground hot chiles combined with spices like garlic, cumin, and oregano.
- **Cayenne pepper**—A ground hot chile. Different brands vary greatly, especially in degrees of heat.

Salt

Valuable for seasoning, brining, and preserving. But all salt is not alike.

- **Kosher salt**—Dissolves well, imparts great flavor, and is easy to measure. Use less of this salt because its crystals are larger than table salt.
- **Sea salt**—Good for finishing a dish, especially seafood. It can be expensive, depending on the variety.

Other Dry Seasonings

- **Cinnamon sticks**—These add flavor without leaving a grainy residue like ground cinnamon.
- **Nutmeg**—Buy whole nutmeg and grate directly over a bowl or a dish using a Microplane grater.

Fresh vs. Dried Herbs

Whenever practical and available, use fresh herbs rather than dried; you'll be happier with the end result. The flavors in dried herbs are more concentrated, so be sure to adjust your measurements accordingly:

- **Fresh Herbs:** use as directed in the recipe
- **Dried Herbs:** use half the amount called for in the recipe

Aromatics

Aromatics are vegetables that infuse a persistent flavor, depth, and character throughout the cooking process. I mostly use fresh garlic, onions, and/or shallots. Keep some of each on hand, since you'll be using them often. Store them on the counter or in a basket away from direct sunlight. Scallions, chives, and leeks should be kept cool in the fridge.

THE ESSENTIAL AROMATICS

Garlic

Sold by the head, which is a cluster of smaller cloves, encased in a tough skin. Remove the skin of the cloves before using.

Onions

Great for adding depth, color, and heartiness to a dish. Different varieties are used for specific purposes. When necessary in a recipe, I specify which variety is preferred.

- Red onions
- White onions
- Yellow onions
- Spanish onions
- Scallions
- Chives

Others

- **Shallots**—Taste like a cross between garlic and onion. Sweeter than onions, they are great for browning in butter as a sauce base.
- **Leeks**—Use only the white part and about an inch of the light green leaves. They can be dirty inside, so slice them lengthwise, fan them open, and soak in cold water before using.

Perishables

Meat

This includes beef, veal, lamb, and pork. If you're going to freeze the meat, ask the butcher to vacuum pack it for you to avoid freezer burn. Keep meat frozen for 3 months, maximum. Otherwise, buy fresh meat, fish, and poultry when needed, and only keep a day or two. Look for:

Freshness Check dates on packages: The "sell by" date should never be more than four days away, as a general guideline.

Color Bright red for beef (though some cuts will be darker, especially if they're aged or prime); for pork and veal—think pink, never gray.

CUTS OF BEEF

You should familiarize yourself with the different cuts of steak:

Filet Mignon
8-ounce center-cut filet mignon; the meat should be bright red and steaks evenly sized to ensure consistent cooking time.

Sirloin Steak or NY Strip
10 ounces, excess fat trimmed off; should be bright red, with small flecks of fat, evenly distributed. This "marbling" keeps meat tender and moist during cooking. The rim of fat should be firm: brittle in texture, creamy white in color. Cut should be thick (about 2 inches).

Rib Eye or T-Bone
Unless otherwise stated, ask butcher for a center cut.

Rib eye—the eye should be half of the steak. Avoid cuts with excess fat or ask butcher to trim.

T-bone—includes the tenderloin and the strip cut. Again, look for a thick cut with lots of marbling.

Poultry

This includes chicken, turkey, and precut poultry parts. Look for:

Freshness The middle breast bone should be pliable. As with meat, check the "sell by" dates on packages.

Color Skin should be white for free-range chickens, yellow for corn-fed ones.

Feel Look for a nice plump breast; the flesh should be firm. To test it, push in the flesh with your finger. If it stays sunken, put it back. Skin should be unbroken.

Fish and Shellfish

There are three main groups of fish:

White fish: sole, halibut, hake, cod, haddock, snapper

Oily fish: salmon, bluefish, herring, sea bass, sardines, mackerel

Deep ocean fish: tuna, swordfish, marlin, and mahi mahi; great for nice steaks or thick fillets

Shellfish: lobster, mussels, clams, oysters, shrimp, crab

If you need to make a recipe substitution, choose another fish from the same category. Make sure the fishmonger has cleaned the fish (removed guts and scales) and extracted unwanted bones. Look for:

Freshness On whole fish, eyes should be bright, clear, and full, the gills should be red. If it's a fillet, look for firm flesh and edges that do not look dry.

Smell Fresh fish has a very clean sea scent, almost odorless. If the fish smells fishy, *do not buy it.*

Feel The flesh should bounce back when you touch the skin. If whole, there should be plenty of scales prior to cleaning.

Produce

Here are some guidelines for buying fresh produce.

Lettuce Look for bright green, crisp leaves with no bruises.

Tomatoes Look for bright red and soft (but not squishy) flesh. With beefsteak or traditional red tomatoes, the smaller the fruit, the better the taste; big ones can be watery and flavorless.

Herbs Smell will determine freshness. Basil should have bright green leaves without holes or black marks. Tarragon should be soft to the touch but not limp. Rosemary should be green, not brown. Thyme should be dark green and have most leaves intact. Parsley is sold in two varieties, flat-leaf (Italian) and curly. I always call for flat-leaf.

Mushrooms Look for minimal dirt, dry and not slimy. White mushrooms should be free of dark bruises. Stay away from packaged pre-cut mushrooms, as they dry out quickly and lose their flavor.

Potatoes If skin is soft or the flesh too pliable, it isn't fresh. If it has sprouted eyes, it definitely isn't fresh. Yukon Gold are higher in moisture and sugar and are the best all-around potato for baking, mashing, and roasting. Idaho or Russet potatoes are high in starch, making them light and fluffy and great for frying. Store in a cool, dry place (*not* in the fridge).

Bell peppers Choose peppers that are firm, full, and free from blemishes or bruises. Whether you are buying green, yellow, or red, look for a solid, deep color.

Broccoli Look for tops and stalks that are firm to the touch, not rubbery, and with florets that are tight and bright green (never yellow).

Squash Uniform firmness is a sign of freshness.

Fruit

As a general rule, look for firm flesh that's neither too soft nor too hard, especially with citrus (lemons, limes, oranges, and grapefruits). Skin shouldn't be loose or rubbery. Same goes for peaches, apples, or pears. With citrus and melons, you can judge the fruit's ripeness by its smell. Bananas can be purchased slightly green; store them in a paper bag for a day or two to speed up ripening.

Most berries are sold in cartons. Examine the package, particularly on the bottom, to see if any of the berries have begun to rot. The same is true for grapes.

Eggs and Dairy

Freshness is most important, so keep your eye on expiration dates. Buy organic or local if possible. Always open the egg carton and inspect the eggs for any cracks or breaks before buying.

The Food Shopping Trip

The key to organizing your shopping trip is understanding how items are organized in the store.

Fresh and perishable items, like meats, fish, dairy, fruits, and vegetables, are usually located around the outside edges (perimeter) of a grocery store.

The center aisles usually contain packaged goods, snacks, condiments, and seasonings, and everyday items like paper towels.

Start with the center aisles first, so your fresh ingredients don't spend too much time sitting in your shopping cart.

Try to break down your shopping list into six categories:

1. Meat
2. Fish
3. Vegetables, fruits, aromatics, and fresh herbs
4. Dairy and eggs
5. Dry and canned goods
6. Bakery

Remember to always use fresh, quality ingredients whenever possible. *Fresh is best.*

REMEMBER: SAFETY FIRST!

It's important to take food safety very seriously. **Keep hot food *hot* and cold food *cold*. If it's not in use, fridge it!**

Keep chilled foods under 40°F and hot foods over 140°F. Everything in between is in the *danger zone*.

- Wash your hands thoroughly after each handling of different ingredients, particularly meat and poultry.
- Wash cutting boards, knives, and work surfaces thoroughly with hot soapy water after use.
- Look for "sell by," "use by," and "best before" dates on products.
- When preparing food, minimize its time at room temperature.

When in Doubt, Throw It Out!

Proper storage and handling of food is essential to keeping a safe environment in your kitchen. Perishable like meat, seafood, poultry, dairy products, and eggs go bad far more quickly than fruit or vegetables.

Don't leave unrefrigerated for more than two hours:

- All raw meats, poultry, and seafood
- Raw eggs
- All dairy
- All prepared foods (including salad ingredients and smoked foods)
- Discard foods left out at room temperature for more than 2 hours.

Other commonsense actions:

- Don't keep cooked proteins at room temperature for more than one hour.
- Never place cooked food on the same surface that held raw food without washing the surface first.
- Place leftovers in shallow containers and refrigerate or freeze immediately.
- Thaw frozen foods in the refrigerator only.
- Frozen foods that have been thawed need to be cooked as soon as possible, especially proteins.
- Don't cross-contaminate foods during prep: Keep raw meats or seafood away from raw vegetables and herbs. Wash your hands with soap and hot water before moving between food types or handling other items.

For more information, please go to:

USDA

http://www.fsis.usda.gov/factsheets/Safe_Food_
Handling_Fact_Sheets/index.asp

Ready, Steady, Prep!

Now that you have your essential gear and ingredients, you're ready to get in the kitchen and start cooking.

Always remember these basic steps: 1) read each recipe thoroughly; 2) do all your prep before you start cooking; 3) figure out how long it will take you to get it all done (timing is everything!).

SET UP YOUR COMMAND AND CONTROL CENTER

The French term *mise en place* means having all your gear and ingredients washed, prepped, and ready. If you have everything laid out in an orderly fashion, you'll be relaxed and enjoy the process so much more.

Think of your counter or workspace as a conveyer belt, moving from left to right, or the opposite direction if you find it more comfortable:

Raw ingredients unprepped --> on board for prep --> prepped and ready for cooking --> cook --> finish

---

Prep 101

"Prep" encompasses everything from kitchen setup and correct refrigeration to vegetable chopping and general preseasoning. Proper preparation will make your cooking go a lot more smoothly.

First, Pick Up Your Knife . . .

Before you start cutting, you must first learn how to properly hold and use your knife. Safety and proper technique are important, so keep the following guidelines in mind:

Rule #1: Be aware of your fingers. Always watch where they are, and where your knife is; you don't want any accidents!

Rule #2: Hold your knife properly. Fingers should be relaxed, but have a firm grip on the knife. Slide fingers upward from the handle. Place thumb and index finger on the blade for balance, thumb on one side and index finger curled behind the other side. Your remaining three fingers should grasp the handle.

Rule #3: Use your free hand to hold the food and guide it under your knife. Place fingers on the food using a claw-like grip, fingers tucked under. This will prevent the food from slipping and allow you to control your cutting motion as you protect your fingers.

Rule #4: Cut away from the edge of the work surface; *never* slice toward your hand.

Rule #5: When peeling and chopping vegetables, clear your surface of debris as soon as you've finished.

Rule #6: When not in use, lay your knife down flat next to your cutting board.

Rule #7: Be careful when washing the blade and drying it with a towel. Never approach the sponge or towel with the sharp edge, but work from the back (spine) of the blade.

Rule #8: Never leave knives in a sink of soapy water.

Prepping Fruits and Vegetables

Avocado

Pit It: Using a chef's knife, cut the avocado in half, then twist the two halves apart. Use a spoon to scoop out the pit, or use the heel of your knife to gently whack the pit and remove it.

Score It (A)

Score It (B)

BASIC TYPES OF CUTS

Slice

Chop

Dice

Mince

Grate

Shred

Score It: Using the tip of your knife, make three to four vertical cuts into each half of the avocado flesh. Then make three to four horizontal cuts across. Use a spoon to scoop out the flesh.

Slice It: Place each half of the avocado flat on the cutting board, flesh side down. Using a paring knife or your fingers, gently remove the skin. Cut lengthwise into slices.

Broccoli

Trim It: Rinse broccoli thoroughly under water. Lay flat on the cutting board. Use a chef's knife to remove the stalks and discard. Split apart by the stem into smaller pieces if too thick.

Cut Florets: Using a paring knife, trim broccoli clusters into small florets. Trim and discard stems.

Carrots, Potatoes, and Other Root Vegetables

Slice It (A)

Slice It (B)

Slice It: Rinse carrot under water. Remove the skin using a vegetable peeler. Using a chef's knife, trim off the ends. Slice on the diagonal or make straight vertical slices. To make matchstick (or julienne) slices, cut the carrot lengthwise in half or smaller. Make lengthwise vertical cuts, then stack the slices and cut vertically again.

Dice It: Stack matchstick pieces flat on the cutting board. Cut across evenly to make fine cubes.

Fresh Herbs

Chop It: Prep just before using to prevent browning. Rinse and dry whole sprigs or leaves. Remove the leaves and discard the stems. Chop leaves to desired size.

Mince It: Chop leaves to desired size, then continue to mince into fine pieces.

Garlic

Slice It: Peel the clove with a paring knife or use your fingers. Cut it into thin planks in one direction.

Dice It: Stack slices, a few at a time (so bottom is flat) and cut into thin strips; slice across the strips to create small dice.

Mince It: Same as dicing, but cut into thinner slices and strips, then smaller dices.

Crush It: Use the heel of your chef's knife to lightly press each clove of unpeeled garlic against the cutting board. Remove the peel and mince finely.

Mushrooms

Clean It: Use a damp paper towel and gently wipe the dirt off each mushroom, one at a time.

Trim It: Use a paring knife or small chef's knife to cut off stems and discard.

Slice It: Stand mushrooms upright on the cutting board. Using a chef's knife, make thin vertical slices.

Onions

Chop It: Use a chef's knife to cut off the stem and the root end. Cut the onion in half from the root

Slice It (A)

Slice It (B)

to the top. Lay each half flat side down on the cutting board. Without cutting through the root, make three or four horizontal cuts parallel to the cutting board, starting near the bottom and working upward. Holding the slices together, cut across, making six or seven vertical cuts. Discard the root.

Slice It: Use a chef's knife to cut a peeled onion in half diagonally, slicing through the middle, leaving the root and top untouched. Lay each half flat side down on the cutting board. Divide each half again, cutting through the root and top. Turn each quarter flat on its side, and slice to desired thinness. Discard root and top ends.

Peppers

Trim It: Using a chef's knife, remove the top and bottom pieces. Discard the ends.

Seed It: Using a paring knife, gently remove seeds and discard.

Slice It: To make ring-shaped slices, trim the pepper, then lay it flat on the cutting board. Make horizontal slices across. Remove the ribs, core, and seeds, and discard. To make sticks, stand the whole pepper upright on the cutting board. Using a chef's knife, slowly make four vertical slices, one on each side. Discard stem, core, and seeds. Lay slices skin side down on the cutting board. Make vertical or crosswise slices.

Dice It: Stack slices flat on the cutting board, and cut crosswise into cubes.

Tomatoes

Seed It

Dice It

Slice It: Use a serrated knife or chef's knife to cut the ends off the tomato and discard. Make thin vertical slices.

Seed It: Using a serrated knife or chef's knife, cut the tomato in half, in wedges, or in slices. Scoop the seeds using a small spoon, or trim with the tip of a paring knife, and discard.

Dice It: Cut the tomato in half. Place each half flat side down on the cutting board and make thin vertical cuts into slices. Hold the slices together and cut crosswise into smaller cubes.

Winter Squash

Peel It

Seed It

Dice It

Trim It: Rinse squash thoroughly under water. Use a chef's knife to trim off the stem and discard.

Seed It: Using a chef's knife, cut the squash in half lengthwise. Scoop out the seeds using a spoon and discard.

Peel It: Use a vegetable peeler to trim away outer skin, or use a chef's knife if skin is too tough. Or, cut squash in half and seed before peeling.

Dice It: Cut squash in half, seed and peel as directed above. Lay halves flat side down on the cutting board. Using a chef's knife, make thin vertical cuts into slices. Hold the slices together and cut crosswise into smaller cubes.

Measure for Measure

It's important to learn how to accurately and efficiently measure ingredients, regardless of what type of cooking you're doing. Make sure you have the proper tools to get you started.

Dry Ingredients

Liquid Ingredients

Brown Sugar

Pinch

Dry Ingredients: Use dry measuring cups. Take a small spatula and gently run it across the top of the dry ingredient to smooth and level it.

Liquid Ingredients: Use a glass measuring cup or measuring spoons. If using a measuring cup, be sure to bend down and face the measuring cup at eye level to ensure accuracy.

Brown Sugar: Use dry measuring cups. Brown sugar needs to be packed into the measuring cup firmly, using a spoon or a small spatula, until it is level.

Pinch: Use your thumb and forefinger to pick up a small amount of seasoning. A pinch is equal to approximately $\frac{1}{16}$ of a teaspoon.

Separating Eggs

Gently (but firmly) tap the egg against the edge of a bowl or your work surface to crack it open. Turn the egg so it's standing vertically in your hand. Using both hands, slowly pull apart the top half, revealing the yolk and whites inside. Working over a bowl, slowly pass the egg yolk from one shell half to the other; the egg whites should fall into the bowl below. Be careful not to get any shell pieces in the yolk or the whites.

Crack Open

Separate Shell

Pass Yolk

Cooking Methods 101

The skills in this book may be new to you, but with practice (and patience) you'll be able to apply them to any recipe you cook. As always, be sure you have the proper tools before getting started.

On the Stove

Boiling

Use a medium saucepan or large stockpot. When rapid bubbles appear, the liquid has reached the *boiling* point (212°F at sea level). Many dishes require that you heat water (or other liquid) until it reaches a boil, before you can add ingredients to cook.

Simmering

Bubbles in a *simmer* are much smaller than in a boil, and turn over less vigorously and with less force. You will often be instructed to bring a liquid to a boil only to then turn down the heat until it is just simmering. The thicker a liquid, the quicker it will boil and the lower the heat will need to be to maintain a simmer.

Blanching

Blanching allows vegetables to retain their color and flavor without becoming overcooked. Use this technique for vegetables such as carrots, broccoli, or sugar snap peas. In a medium saucepan, bring water to a boil over medium heat. When boiling, add the cut vegetables and cook until just tender (time varies depending on the vegetable). Vegetables should be cooked but still crisp. Using a slotted spoon, remove the vegetables from the water and immediately plunge them into a bowl of ice water. Then drain in a colander over the sink.

Pan-Frying

The most commonly used method in this book, *pan-frying* means to cook something in a wide flat-bottomed pan (like a fry pan or a sauté pan) using oil, butter, or another type of fat to brown and crisp food.

Sautéing

The French word for "jump," *sauté* means to quickly pan-fry over medium heat without a lot of oil or fat. A bit of stirring and tossing is involved when using this method. You can use a plain fry pan, a sauté pan, or a wok; an open shallow surface is necessary so you have room to stir the ingredients.

Searing

Searing means to cook quickly over high heat to seal and brown all sides of a piece of meat, poultry, or hearty fish. Searing items until lightly browned on all sides (unless otherwise specified) also helps hold in the juices. Use a fry pan or sauté pan with very little oil. To ensure a golden brown crust, pat your food dry with a paper towel, even if you've marinated it first. Wait until the pan is hot before you add your oil: Test with a drop of water—if it sizzles, you're ready to go. Pour in a little oil and swirl it around to coat the pan, but don't let it start to smoke. Use tongs to place the food in the pan and let it sit until the underside is brown. Use tongs or a spatula to flip. (And don't forget to sear the sides, too.)

Sweating

To *sweat* means to cook vegetables in a covered pan over medium heat, using just enough fat to release moisture and soften the vegetables without overcooking or browning them. This method is mostly used with aromatics like onions, or a combination of evenly diced vegetables like onions, carrots, and celery.

Deglazing

After searing, pan-frying, sautéing, or roasting, the protein residue (those tasty leftover browned—but not burnt—bits) that is stuck to the pan after the grease is poured off can be integrated into a sauce by *deglazing*. Place the pan with browned bits over medium- high heat and pour in a liquid, such as stock, wine, or water. Immediately scrape up and stir in the bits with a spatula, whisk, or spoon and mix thoroughly. Then strain the liquid through a fine-mesh sieve. This adds a delicious flavor and texture base to your sauce or gravy.

Reducing

Reductions are made when a sauce or other liquid is left to simmer (stirring occasionally) until the liquid level reduces (or evaporates) to a certain point as specified in your recipe. This is often (though not always)

done after deglazing. Because water evaporates in the process, the sauce thickens. Using cream, butter, pasta water, or grated Parmesan cheese will accelerate this process in certain sauces.

In the Oven

Roasting/Baking

Baking refers to the steady, consistent cooking necessary for desserts, breads, or certain egg dishes. *Roasting* refers to baking or cooking under dry heat with the addition of juices and or fats, such as roasted meats or vegetables.

Broiling

Whether you have a super-duper convection oven or a simple toaster oven, you *broil* food the same way: cooking with direct heat from above. Look inside your oven (make sure it is off!) and you'll see the coils on the top that are used for broiling. This allows the top surface to brown under direct heat while the inside (which receives no direct heat) remains tender and juicy.

On the Grill

Grilling refers to a method of cooking on a heated grid (rack, ridged cast-iron pan, etc.), often—but not always—over an open flame. This can be done on an outdoor grill or on a grill pan indoors on the stove.

Meat Matters

TEMPERATURE GUIDE
FOR AN INSTANT-READ THERMOMETER

How do you like to eat your meat? Rare? Well Done? How do you know when it's ready? There are two ways to tell when your meat is done to your liking: visual cues, like color and texture; and checking the internal temperature with an instant-read thermometer. An instant-read thermometer takes the guess work out of knowing when your food is done. Use it every time you prepare chicken, turkey, beef, veal, pork, or lamb.

	RARE	*MEDIUM-RARE*	*MEDIUM*	*MEDIUM-WELL*	*WELL DONE*
Beef, Lamb, Pork, Veal	120°F	130°F	140°F	150°F	160°F

	ROASTED
Whole Chicken, Turkey	165°F

Four-Finger Firmness Guide

Rare

Medium Rare

Medium Well

Well Done

Here is a clever trick that will help you know if your steak is done without slicing it open to look at the color:

Place your index finger against the fleshy part of your thumb on the opposite hand. Draw an imaginary line between the outside beginning of your thumb and various fingers. Now press on that fleshy point between thumb and a particular finger. The firmness at that point will replicate the basic doneness of the cooking steak as shown.

- **Rare:** Skin between thumb and index finger will be relaxed and pliable.

- **Medium Rare:** Skin between thumb and middle finger will be slightly firm but still pliable.

- **Medium Well:** Skin between thumb and ring finger will be firm.

- **Well Done:** Skin between thumb and pinky finger will be extra firm or taut.

Before You Begin . . .

The recipes that follow aren't just easy; they're versatile (and of course, they're delicious!). Remember: *No More Takeout* is about skill building. This is a theme we'll hit over and over again in *No More Takeout*: Learn the basics, apply your new cooking skills to more complex dishes, expand your repertoire, and soon you'll be able to cook whatever you want.

Read each recipe through *before* you turn on your stove, and then try to follow it as written, making substitutions when necessary. As you read each recipe, make mental (or written) notes about the skills used that are applied to other dishes you might make. For instance, you'll notice that the Eggplant Parmesan (page 116) and Veal Milanese (page 126) in Level 2 use the same breading method. This repetition is intentional. You'll find that certain methods are applied to a wide range of cooking possibilities, often with only minor adjustments along the way.

Armed with lots of tips and helpful photos to guide you, you'll be a super cook before you know it. Seriously, it is *just that easy*.

TIPS AND TIDBITS

- Use extra-virgin olive oil. Less expensive varieties are more economical to use for cooking, but stick with quality brands in salads and dressings.
- Use unsalted butter unless otherwise specified.
- Butter measurements are specified in tablespoons; you can find this on the wrapper of sticks of butter. One stick is equal to 8 tablespoons (¼ cup). Softened butter should be measured using a tablespoon or measuring cup.
- To soften butter, leave it out at room temperature for 30 minutes or microwave for 10 seconds on high—watch it carefully so it doesn't melt completely.
- Use kosher salt unless otherwise specified.
- Pepper means freshly ground using a pepper mill. When using pepper to season, think two to four solid twists of your pepper mill.

- Add ingredients "to season" by tasting the dish as you add your seasoning; stop when you reach your preference.
- *Parmesan* refers to fresh Parmigiano-Reggiano cheese that can be grated by hand.
- Herbs should always be fresh. Remember that dried herbs are far more potent than their fresh counterparts, and should be used in smaller quantities.
- Measure herbs and other chopped ingredients *after* they are chopped. If a recipe calls for "1 tablespoon chopped cilantro," remove the leaves from the stems, chop the leaves, and then measure.
- *Zesting* refers to the process of scraping the rind of a citrus fruit using a grater or microplane.
- When alternatives are listed for ingredients (and the directions only list the first option on the list), work with whichever ingredient option you have chosen.

THE

Ready to start cooking? This is the place to begin. Level 1 is an introduction to your kitchen, to your tools, and to your ingredients. We start with breakfast, the **most important meal** of the day, with everything from Super-Simple Pancakes (page 18) to Baked Frittata (page 10). Then it's on to simple salads, including the super-convenient Outta-the-Bag Salad (page 25). Having a party? Try some of the **quick and easy** appetizers, like Nachos with Guacamole and Fresh Salsa (page 34), that are perfect for any

BASIC

get-together. Main meals include hearty **comfort food favorites** like Macaroni and Cheese (page 47) and Rustic Meatloaf (page 62). And we end with delectable dessert favorites like Chocolate Chip Cookies (page 80) and Brownies (page 81).

At the end of Level 1, you'll find three menus to ease you into cooking for your friends and family. The **step-by-step** game plans and checklists will help you stay organized (and stress-free!) as you prepare for your get-together.

BASICS

Waking Up to Breakfast Anytime

I was raised in a large extended family and both of my grandmothers ruled their clans from the kitchen, teaching me early on how to please folks with good food, and how to feed many hungry mouths at the same time. And no matter the crowd, our morning always started with a hearty breakfast.

You don't need to be a professional (or a grandmother) to create a delicious morning meal. Everyone knows how to make some sort of breakfast, be it a bowl of cereal, fresh fruit, or a couple of frozen waffles pushed into a toaster. Here are some super-basic breakfast recipes and tips for making your morning meal the best it can possibly be.

IN THIS CHAPTER

In this chapter you'll find easy-to-follow recipes for:
- Fried Eggs
- Scrambled Eggs
- Soft or Hard "Boiled" Eggs
- Poached Eggs on Toast
- Mushroom and Swiss Omelet
- Baked Frittata
- Bacon, Two Ways
- Sausages, Two Ways
- Ham, Two Ways
- Super-Simple Pancakes
- French Toast
- Blueberry Muffins
- Scones
- Fruit and Yogurt

And you'll develop the skills and know-how to:
- Separate egg yolks from egg whites
- Soften butter
- Test your pan or pot to see when it's hot enough to start cooking
- Make simple flavor swaps in breakfast favorites like omelets and muffins
- Start preparing the night before, so breakfast is half done when you wake up
- Throw together a quick breakfast for guests

SERVES 2
PREP TIME 5 minutes
COOK TIME 5 minutes

Gear

- Nonstick fry pan
- Silicone mixing spatula

Ingredients

- 2 tablespoons (¼ stick) butter
- 4 eggs
- Salt and pepper

Kitchen FYI

When you crack an egg into a hot fry pan, separate the shell halves close to the pan to prevent the fat from splashing.

How Do You Like Your Eggs?

TEXTURE	COOK TIME
Sunny Side Up	30 seconds (to fully set egg whites)
Hard	1 minute
Over Easy	15 seconds (to fully set egg whites, then slide spatula underneath egg and gently turn it over)

Fried Eggs

There are a number of ways to fry your eggs—sunny side up,* fried, hard, or over easy. The secrets to excellent fried eggs are to use the freshest eggs possible, and cook them on low-medium heat for even cooking without drying out the yolks.

① Preheat the broiler. Place the fry pan over low-medium heat. When hot**, drop in the butter and melt it until it's just foamy. Swirl the butter around by tilting the handle, to coat the pan entirely.

STEP 2

② Crack the eggs and gently drop them into the pan with enough space between so they aren't touching. Add the salt and pepper to season. Cook until the whites and yolks are lightly set (not wobbly).

③ Remove the pan from heat, place it under the broiler, and cook the eggs according to the chart (left) for your preferred texture.

④ Remove the pan from the broiler and place it on a heat-resistant surface. Lift each egg with the spatula, slide it onto a plate, and serve.

*See Egg Safety (page 5) for more information on sunny side up eggs.

**Is your pan hot enough? Test it with a drop of water. If it sizzles, you're ready to cook.

LEVEL

SERVES 2
PREP TIME 5 minutes
COOK TIME 5 minutes

Gear

- Small bowl
- Whisk
- Nonstick fry pan
- Silicone mixing spatula or wooden spoon
- Optional, for add-ins: cutting board; chef's knife; box grater

Ingredients

- 4 eggs
- ¼ cup plus 1 tablespoon whole milk (for creamier eggs, substitute heavy cream or half-and-half)
- Pinch of salt and pepper
- Optional seasoning add-ins: a few drops of Tabasco sauce or a pinch of cayenne pepper (for a little punch); a pinch of grated nutmeg; 1 tablespoon chopped flat-leaf parsley, tarragon, thyme, or chervil
- 1 tablespoon (⅛ stick) butter
- Optional ingredient add-ins: 1 tablespoon sour cream; ½ cup of your favorite grated or diced cheese; ⅓ cup chopped ham or smoked salmon; ⅓ cup crumbled bacon (see page 13); ⅓ cup seeded and diced fresh tomatoes or green bell pepper; ⅓ cup diced zucchini or scallions

Scrambled Eggs

I love scrambled eggs because they're so versatile. You can add almost anything—meat, herbs, veggies, cheese—and with a quick toss of the pan, you have an excellent morning meal. The most important rule when cooking scrambled eggs is to be patient. If you rush your eggs, they can stick, become crumbly, develop a burned skin, or separate. Mix and match the optional ingredients and seasoning add-ins to customize your eggs.

1. Crack the eggs into the small bowl (discard the shells). Add ¼ cup of the milk and season with the salt and pepper. Whisk until the mixture is completely yellow, without any thick white streaks. Add your preferred seasoning add-ins to eggs, if using.

2. Place the fry pan over medium-high heat. When hot*, add the butter and the remaining 1 tablespoon milk. Swish in the pan until the mixture bubbles or gently sizzles; cook for 1 minute, until bubbles reduce and sizzling subsides. Pour in the eggs and turn down the heat to medium. Slowly stir the eggs in the pan with the spatula, in a continuous motion, scraping the bottom as you stir.

3. When the eggs start to solidify, add your preferred ingredient add-ins, if using, and continue stirring until the eggs are cooked to the desired consistency. Stirring constantly makes creamy eggs; less stirring creates looser, curd-like eggs; for solid (or well-done) eggs, continue stirring for 45 seconds more after eggs reach curd-like state. Once cooked to your liking, tilt the fry pan and slide the eggs onto a plate. Serve immediately.

STEP 2 (A)

STEP 2 (B)

How Do I . . . ?

To separate eggs, simply crack egg evenly along its widest part while holding halves above a small bowl. Gently pass the yolk between halves, allowing egg white to fall into the bowl. Continue passing yolk back and forth until all white has been separated. Discard yolks unless you have an immediate use for them.

Healthier Scrambled Eggs   For a low-fat, lower-cholesterol version of this recipe, substitute 6 egg whites plus 2 egg yolks for the whole eggs; ⅓ cup soy milk for the milk; 1 tablespoon nonhydrogenated natural margarine for the butter; and salt substitute for the salt.

Is your pan hot enough? Test it with a drop of water. If it sizzles, you're ready to cook.

EGG SAFETY

Brown or white, large or extra large, Grade A or Grade AA, all eggs are basically the same for our purposes here. To keep it simple, unless otherwise noted, all of the recipes here call for large eggs.

Fresh is best. When in doubt, place an uncracked egg in a cup of water. If the egg is fresh it will fall to the bottom; if it is not fresh, it will float to the top. Remember:

- Use the freshest eggs possible and gently rinse them. Avoid cross-contamination by cleaning your hands and gear with hot water and soap after use. If raw egg gets on anything, wipe it down with hot soapy water followed by a spray sanitizer made for kitchen use.
- Cook your eggs until the white is firm and the yolk begins to thicken but is not hard. For safety's sake, scrambled eggs should be cooked until no visible liquid remains. Fried eggs should be cooked on both sides until the whites are fully solid (not runny).
- Take special care when preparing foods that contain uncooked or lightly cooked eggs, in particular egg-based salad dressings and sauces. To avoid undercooking the eggs in these dishes, start with a well-stirred egg custard base that is cooked to at least 160°F.

For more safety tips, see Remember: Safety First! (page xvii).

Gear

- Medium saucepan
- Slotted spoon
- Paring knife
- 4 soft-boiled egg serving cups (2 per person)

Ingredients

- 5 eggs, at room temperature (see Kitchen FYI, below)
- ½ teaspoon salt
- Salt and pepper

Kitchen FYI

Do not put cold eggs into boiling water; it will cause the eggs to crack.

How Do You Like Your Eggs?

TEXTURE	COOK TIME
Soft	4 to 5 minutes
Medium	6 to 7 minutes
Hard	8 to 9 minutes

Soft or Hard "Boiled" Eggs

There's nothing like a simple soft-boiled egg, warm and easy to scoop up with a spoon. Serve them with tops sliced off in egg cups, with a bit of salt and pepper. Hard-boiled eggs take a bit longer, but they're worth the wait. The result is a delicious treat for breakfast or a great topping for a Niçoise Salad (page 108.)

1. Place the eggs and ½ teaspoon salt in the saucepan and fill it with enough cold water to cover the eggs by about 2 inches. Place the saucepan over medium-high heat.

2. When the water comes to a boil, turn down the heat and allow the eggs to simmer (page xxiii) gently according to the chart (left) for your preferred texture. Lift the eggs out of the water with the slotted spoon and serve.

3. For soft-boiled eggs, place each in an individual egg serving cup. Use the paring knife to gently tap and cut top ½ inch off of each egg. Serve with egg spoons (or regular teaspoons). For medium- or hard-boiled eggs, run cold water over the egg for 30 seconds to 1 minute, then gently crack the egg and peel the shell carefully. Add salt and pepper to season.

STEP 1

STEP 3 (A)

STEP 3 (B)

Gear

- 4 ramekins or shallow cups
- Medium saucepan
- Slotted spoon
- Paper towels
- Optional: timer

Ingredients

- 4 eggs
- Water
- 2 tablespoons white vinegar
- ½ teaspoon salt
- 2 slices bread (your preference), toasted
- Salt and pepper

How Do You Like Your Eggs?

TEXTURE	COOK TIME
Very soft	2½ minutes
Soft	3 minutes
Medium	3½ minutes
Hard	4½ minutes

Poached Eggs on Toast

Poaching eggs can be a bit tricky, but if you take your time, and remain patient, the results are simply delicious. I recommend cracking the eggs into cups first before pouring them into the water; the eggs are less likely to break and will cook at the same rate. These are excellent served with a nice piece of toast (to soak up the yolk), but they also go well over lightly dressed greens or a bowl of steaming pasta with Parmesan cheese.

1. Gently crack the eggs into individual cups or ramekins. Set aside.

2. Fill the saucepan with water until about 3 inches deep. Place it over medium-high heat and bring it to a bare simmer (page xxiii), then reduce heat to medium to maintain the simmer. Add the vinegar and salt. Stir the water with the spoon in a circular motion to create a whirlpool.

3. Gently slide each egg from its ramekin into the saucepan while the water is still swirling. Cook the eggs according to chart (left) for your preferred texture. Lift out each egg with the slotted spoon and gently touch the yolk with the back of a spoon to test doneness. (If it is wobbly, the texture is very soft to soft). Return to the water if not cooked enough. When eggs are done, lift out each egg with the slotted spoon and place it on a piece of paper towel to drain lightly.

4. Cut each slice of toast diagonally into 2 triangles and place 2 triangles on each plate. Slide one egg onto each piece of toast, add salt and pepper to season, and serve.

STEP 3 (A)

STEP 3 (B)

STEP 4

LEVEL

SERVES 1 OR 2

PREP TIME 10 to 15 minutes

COOK TIME 5 minutes per omelet

Gear

- Cutting board
- Chef's knife
- Box grater
- Small bowls or plastic containers for fillings
- Medium bowl
- Whisk
- Nonstick fry pan with a metal handle
- Wide spatula

Ingredients

- 2 tablespoons vegetable oil (or butter)
- ½ cup trimmed and sliced mushrooms (white, shiitake, and/or chanterelle)
- 3 extra-large eggs
- Salt and pepper
- ½ cup grated Swiss cheese

Mushroom and Swiss Omelet

There are many ways to cook an omelet, but my easy method works every time and produces a light, fluffy American-style omelet. (Think evenly cooked eggs folded around your favorite filling ingredients, and you'll hit this on the nose.)

1. Preheat the broiler if serving the omelet open-faced.

2. Place the fry pan over medium-high heat. When hot*, pour in the oil and swirl it around the pan for 1 minute. Discard oil, leaving a thin film in the pan.

3. Add the mushrooms and salt and pepper to season. Sauté (page xxiv) for 1 minute until just soft. Transfer the mushrooms to a dish or platter and set aside.

4. In a small bowl, crack open the eggs and add salt and pepper to season. Whisk eggs until smooth and well-combined. Pour the eggs into the hot pan; immediately stir in a circular motion with the spatula. Keep it moving until mixture starts to thicken, about 30 seconds.

5. Add the mushrooms. Stir once more with the spatula, then sprinkle the cheese on top. Cook for 1 minute more.

6. To finish as a closed omelet, fold the omelet in half with the spatula and cook for 2 minutes more. For an open-faced omelet, place the fry pan under the broiler and cook until cheese is melted.

7. To serve, tilt the fry pan and slide the omelet onto the plate. If serving two, cut the omelet in half and use the spatula to lift half onto a second plate.

Is your pan hot enough? Test it with a drop of water. If it sizzles, you're ready to cook.

STEP 5

STEP 6

STEP 7

BASIC OMELET AND FRITTATA FILLINGS

Cheese (grated or chopped, or crumbled if soft; about ½ cup per omelet)

- ○ Swiss
- ○ Gruyère
- ○ Goat
- ○ Cheddar
- ○ Monterey Jack
- ○ Parmesan

Meat (about ½ cup per omelet)

- ○ Bacon (cooked and crumbled; see pages 12–13)
- ○ Ham (chopped)

Veggies (about ½ cup per omelet)

- ○ Roma (plum) tomatoes (sliced or seeded and diced)
- ○ Onions or scallions (trimmed and minced)
- ○ Red, yellow, and/or green bell peppers (trimmed, seeded, diced, and pan-fried—page xxiv—in olive oil until golden brown)
- ○ Zucchini (sliced and pan-fried in olive oil until golden brown)
- ○ Broccoli florets (blanched—page xxiii—or pan-fried in olive oil until soft yet still green)
- ○ Spinach (whole leaves or chopped; steamed or microwaved with 1 cup of water, then drained, and dried with paper towels)

Fresh Herbs (leaves only, minced; about 1 tablespoon per omelet)

- ○ Chives
- ○ Parsley
- ○ Fines herbes (a mixture of equal parts tarragon, chervil, chives, and flat-leaf parsley)

Seasonings

- ○ Pinch of sweet paprika
- ○ Pinch of cayenne pepper

LEVEL

SERVES 4
PREP TIME 12 minutes
COOK TIME 15 minutes

Gear

- Medium bowl
- Whisk
- Cutting board
- Chef's knife
- Nonstick fry pan with a metal handle
- Spatula
- Optional, for filling: box grater
- Small bowls or plastic containers for filling(s)

Ingredients

- 4 eggs
- Pinch of salt
- Pepper
- 3 tablespoons olive oil
- 2 thick slices country bread, crust removed, bread cut into ¾-inch squares
- 1 tablespoon (⅛ stick) butter
- Your choice of Basic Omelet and Frittata Fillings (page 9)

Baked Frittata

A frittata is an Italian "egg pie," similar to an omelet but baked in the oven. It works nicely with numerous savory add-ins, like fresh veggies, and can be an elegant dish for breakfast or a brunch dish cut into wedges and served with a salad.

1. Preheat the oven to 375°F. Crack the eggs into the medium bowl. Whisk until thoroughly blended (no white streaks). Whisk in salt and pepper to season.

2. Place the fry pan over medium-high heat. When hot*, pour in the olive oil. Add the bread cubes and fry, stirring with the spatula, until golden brown and crisp on all sides.

3. Add the butter to the pan. When it has melted, pour in the eggs; immediately stir in a circular motion with the back of the spatula. Keep it moving until mixture starts to thicken, about 1½ minutes.

STEP 2

STEP 4 (A)

STEP 4 (B)

(4) Add filling(s) as preferred. Stir filling(s) in with the spatula briefly, allowing raw egg to settle to the bottom for even cooking. Allow to cook for 3 minutes, then transfer the pan to the oven.

(5) Bake for 10 minutes, until the eggs puff up and are firm to the touch. Remove the pan from the oven using oven mitts and place the pan on a heatproof surface or back on the stovetop (turned off). Cut the frittata into wedges and serve.

*Is your pan hot enough? Test it with a drop of water. If it sizzles, you're ready to cook.

LEVEL

SERVES 4
PREP TIME 5 minutes
COOK TIME 5 to 10 minutes
per batch

Gear

- Nonstick fry pan or two rimmed baking sheets, both the same size
- Tongs
- Baking sheet lined with a wire cooling rack or several layers of paper towels
- Glass jar with a lid or measuring cup
- Parchment paper

Ingredients

- ½ pound sliced bacon

Kitchen FYI

Don't warm bacon in a micro-wave; it will become soggy. Instead, heat up in a 400°F oven, or under the broiler for one minute, keeping each bacon piece separated.

Bacon, Two Ways

There's nothing like Sunday morning bacon, crisp and warm, served with eggs and toast or lying across silver dollar pancakes covered in maple syrup. If you make extra, just wrap the leftover strips in a paper towel, place in a plastic bag, and store in the fridge.

STOVETOP BACON

1. Place the fry pan over high heat. When hot*, separate the slices of bacon and arrange them in the pan, leaving enough room for them to cook without touching each other. Fry in batches if necessary.

STEP 2

2. Fry the bacon until sizzling and brown on one side, then use the tongs to gently flip. Continue frying to desired doneness. Using tongs, transfer slices from the pan to the cooling rack or paper towels to drain.

3. Pour off fat into the jar after each batch is cooked to use in other dishes; cover and store in the fridge. Or, when oil is cool, carefully pour it into an empty container, then discard container in the trash (see opposite page for instructions on discarding oil).

*Is your pan hot enough? Test it with a drop of water. If it sizzles, you're ready to cook.

BAKED CRISP BACON

1. Preheat the oven to 425°F. Place a sheet of parchment paper on one of the baking sheets. Separate the slices of bacon and lay them in rows, close but not touching, on the parchment paper. Cover with a second sheet of parchment paper.

2. Place the second baking sheet on top (to keep the bacon flat) and place in the oven. Bake for 5 minutes, then remove the pan from the oven and, holding the two ends of the baking-sheet sandwich with oven mitts, carefully drain off the fat from one corner by tilting into the jar or cup. Return the baking sheets to the oven, turning them around 180 degrees to ensure even cooking. Bake for 5 minutes more.

③ Remove from the oven and carefully drain off any more collected fat. Place the baking sheets on a heatproof surface and remove the top baking sheet and piece of parchment paper.

④ Using tongs, place the bacon slices on the cooling rack or paper towels to drain. Serve when crisp and golden brown.

STEP 2

STEP 3

SAFETY FIRST

Discarding Hot Oil

To safely discard oil after cooking, first wait until the oil has cooled completely. Then carefully pour it from the pan into an empty can or container, seal it with aluminum foil, the lid from the container, and rubber bands, then throw the can in the trash.

SERVES 4
PREP TIME 5 minutes
COOK TIME 5 to 15 minutes

Gear

- Nonstick fry pan or a rimmed baking sheet
- Tongs
- Optional: instant-read thermometer
- Baking sheet lined with a wire cooling rack or several layers of paper towels
- Parchment paper

Ingredients

- 2 tablespoons vegetable oil or butter (¼ stick), softened (see How Do I . . . ? below)
- ½ pound sausages of choice (about 4 links), thawed in the fridge if frozen

How Do I . . . ?

To soften butter, leave it out of refrigerator for 30 minutes before needed, or place it in a microwave-safe bowl or dish and heat it for 10 seconds per stick on high, keeping a close eye on it to make sure butter doesn't completely melt.

Sausages, Two Ways

Whether you like frozen links, patties, or butcher-made sausages, try to go as natural as possible to avoid tasteless fillers or industrial chemicals. When cooked correctly, fresh natural sausage—whether chicken and apple or spicy Italian—is an unparalleled side for any serious breakfast.

STOVETOP SAUSAGES

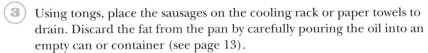

STEP 2

① Place the fry pan over medium-high heat. When hot*, add the oil or butter.

② Arrange the sausages in one layer in the pan and fry until brown on all sides (5 to 7 minutes for small breakfast sausages, or up to 15 minutes for thicker uncooked sausages), turning frequently with the tongs. To test doneness, make a discreet cut in the middle with the tip of a sharp knife (inside color shouldn't be pink), or use an instant-read thermometer (internal temperature should read 170° to 175°F for well done).

③ Using tongs, place the sausages on the cooling rack or paper towels to drain. Discard the fat from the pan by carefully pouring the oil into an empty can or container (see page 13).

*Is your pan hot enough? Test it with a drop of water. If it sizzles, you're ready to cook.

Baked Crisp Bacon (page 12) and Baked Sausages (opposite)

BAKED SAUSAGES

STEP 2

(1) Preheat the oven to 400°F. Place a sheet of parchment paper on the baking sheet. Lay the sausage on the parchment paper in rows and coat with the oil. Bake for 5 to 7 minutes, turning every few minutes with tongs, until brown on all sides.

(2) To test doneness, make a discreet cut into the middle with the tip of a sharp knife (inside color shouldn't be pink), or use an instant-read thermometer (internal temperature should read 175° to 175°F). If not done, place back in oven for 2 minutes more.

(3) Remove the pan from the oven, carefully drain off any collected fat (see page 12), and place the baking sheets on a heatproof work surface. Using tongs, place the sausages on the cooling rack or paper towels to drain, and serve.

SERVES 4

PREP TIME 5 minutes

COOK TIME 5 to 7 minutes

Gear

- Large nonstick fry pan or rimmed baking sheet
- Tongs
- Baking sheet lined with a wire cooling rack or several layers of paper towels

Ingredients

- 2 tablespoons vegetable oil or nonstick cooking spray or butter (¼ stick), softened (see page 14)
- ½ pound thick-sliced ham or Canadian bacon

Ham, Two Ways

Thick-sliced ham can be super when it's fried or baked. I don't recommend using thin-sliced deli ham as it will break apart and crumble. Also try Canadian bacon (cured pork loin), which is a smaller, lower-fat round-cut version.

STOVETOP HAM

1. Place the fry pan over medium-high heat. When hot*, add the oil or butter. Arrange the ham slices in the pan in one layer. Fry for 5 to 7 minutes, turning once with tongs, until golden brown on both sides.

2. Using tongs, place slices on the cooling rack or paper towels to drain. Discard the fat from the pan by carefully pouring the oil into an empty can or container (see page 13).

Is your pan hot enough? Test it with a drop of water. If it sizzles, you're ready to cook.

BAKED HAM

1. Preheat the oven to 400°F. Place the ham slices on the baking sheet and coat with the oil or nonstick cooking spray. Bake for 5 to 7 minutes, turning once with tongs, until brown on both sides.

2. Using tongs, place slices on the cooling rack or paper towels to drain. Discard the fat from the pan by carefully pouring the oil into an empty can or container (see page 13).

STEP 1 (A)

STEP 1 (B)

STEP 2

LEVEL

SERVES 4
PREP TIME 10 minutes
COOK TIME 10 minutes

Gear

- Medium bowl
- Whisk or hand-held mixer
- Large dish
- Nonstick fry pan
- Wide spatula
- Aluminum foil

Ingredients

- 3 eggs
- 1 cup milk
- Optional: ½ cup heavy cream
- ½ cup sugar
- 2 drops vanilla extract
- Pinch of cinnamon
- 8 thick slices bread
- 2 tablespoons (¼ stick) butter
- Optional: real maple syrup; confectioners' sugar; strawberry jam

French Toast

You can use any bread you like, but I recommend the thick-cut, fluffy egg bread called *challah*, as it absorbs the egg mixture more quickly than other breads. Or, for extra flavor, try using raisin bread. Either way, this combination of egg, cinnamon, sugar, and butter can't be beat—it's easy and delicious, and makes quite an impression!

1. Preheat the oven to 275°F. Combine the eggs, milk, cream (if using), sugar, vanilla extract, and cinnamon in the medium bowl, and beat well with a whisk or hand-held mixer.

2. Pour mixture into the large dish, add the bread slices, and soak them for 2 minutes. Turn over and leave for 2 minutes more.

3. Place the fry pan over medium-high heat. When hot*, drop in butter and melt until it's just foamy. Using spatula, lift bread slice from dish, allowing excess mixture to drip off bread, and transfer it to the pan. Repeat with additional slices as space allows.

4. Cook until underside is golden brown. Using spatula, flip slice over and cook other side until golden brown. Transfer slices to a plate and serve immediately, or cover the plate with aluminum foil and keep it warm in the oven. Repeat with remaining slices in batches.

5. Cut toast into triangles. Pour maple syrup over or dust with confectioners' sugar, if you like. Serve with a side of strawberry jam, if using.

*Is your pan hot enough? Test it with a drop of water. If it sizzles, you're ready to cook.

STEP 4

STEP 5 (A)

STEP 5 (B)

SERVES 4
PREP TIME 5 minutes
COOK TIME 10 minutes

Gear

- Medium bowl
- Whisk or fork
- Large cast-iron fry pan, nonstick fry pan, or cast-iron griddle
- Small ladle or large spoon
- Wide spatula
- Aluminum foil

Ingredients

- 2 cups packaged pancake mix
- 1 cup milk
- 2 eggs
- Optional: 1 cup fresh berries
- 1 tablespoon (⅛ stick) cold butter
- Optional, for serving: real maple syrup; butter

Super-Simple Pancakes

These light and fluffy pancakes are always welcome at my house and provide a great start to the weekend. Add fresh blueberries or raspberries for extra flavor. While I prefer using pancake mix that calls for milk and eggs, some brands only require the addition of water and/or vegetable oil, so be sure to read the ingredients list on the mix carefully.

1. In the medium bowl, combine the pancake mix, milk, and eggs and mix with a whisk or fork to eliminate lumps. The batter should be smooth and somewhat thick, not runny. Toss in fresh berries, if using.

2. Place fry pan or griddle over medium-high heat; When hot*, drop in butter and melt until it's just foamy. Pour off excess butter into the batter and stir well to combine.

STEP 1

STEP 3

STEP 4

(3) Using the small ladle or large spoon, pour batter (about ¼ cup) into the pan or griddle to form small pancakes. Add additional pancakes to the pan or griddle, leaving enough room between them so they don't touch.

(4) Cook until bubbles rise to top and pop, and the underside of the pancake is golden brown (not burned). Slide the spatula under the pancakes and gently flip them over. Cook on other side until bottom is golden brown.

(5) Transfer pancakes to a plate and serve immediately, or cover the plate with aluminum foil and keep it warm in the oven (at 225°F). Repeat in batches with remaining batter. If desired, serve with fresh butter and real maple syrup, heated in a microwave.

*Is your pan hot enough? Test it with a drop of water. If it sizzles, you're ready to cook. Before making pancakes, be sure the heat is distributed evenly throughout by adding a teaspoon of batter to the pan; if the batter begins to set right away, you're ready to go.

MAKES 12 MUFFINS
PREP TIME 10 minutes
COOK TIME 30 minutes

Gear

- 2 bowls (1 small, 1 medium)
- Whisk
- Flour sifter
- Wooden spoon
- Silicone mixing spatula
- 12-cup muffin pan
- Paper muffin cups or liners
- Wire cooling rack

Ingredients

- 1 egg
- 4 tablespoons (½ stick) butter, softened (see page 14)
- 1 cup sugar
- ¾ cup sour cream
- ½ cup half-and-half
- 2 cups all-purpose flour
- 1½ teaspoons baking powder
- 1¼ cups blueberries (fresh or frozen)
- Nonstick cooking spray
- Optional: butter; honey; jam

Blueberry Muffins

Warm from the oven, these muffins are as delightfully tasty as they are easy to make. I sometimes get up early just to bake up a batch, filling the house with the smell of blueberries. Now, that's the right way to start the day!

(1) Preheat the oven to 375°F. Whisk together the egg, butter, and sugar in the medium bowl; stir in sour cream and half-and-half. Sift the flour and baking powder into the small bowl; toss in the blueberries.

(2) Using the wooden spoon, make a well in the center of the flour mixture by pushing mixture against the sides of the bowl. Add egg mixture and fold flour and egg mixture together with spatula until batter is moist and lumpy.

(3) Spray the edges and cups of the muffin pan with nonstick cooking spray. Place the paper liners in the cups and spray the papers. Spoon batter into each liner, about ½ to ⅔ full. Be sure to evenly distribute the batter among the liners.

(4) Bake for 15 minutes, then, using oven mitts, rotate the pan 180 degrees to ensure even baking. Bake for 10 to 12 minutes more, until golden brown. To test doneness, insert a toothpick into the center; if it comes out clean, the muffins are ready. Remove pan from oven and place it on the cooling rack. Allow the muffins to cool for 5 minutes. Serve warm, alone or with butter and honey, or jam, if you like.

STEP 1

STEP 2

STEP 3

Kitchen FYI

When combining the (dry) flour mixture and (wet) egg mixture, it's important that you don't overmix because that can lead to dry, tough muffins or scones. Combine the liquid and dry ingredients just until the batter is moist all the way through but still a little lumpy.

FLAVOR SWAP

Get more out of your muffins in the morning. Try one of these delicious and seriously simple flavor substitutions:

	IN PLACE OF THE BLUEBERRIES, ADD:	HOW MUCH?
Berry Blast Muffins	Raspberries, blackberries, or chopped strawberries	1 cup
Banana-Walnut Muffins	Sliced bananas and chopped walnuts	¾ cup banana; ¼ cup walnuts
Chocolate Chip Muffins	Bittersweet or semisweet chocolate chips	½ cup
Pinapple Coconut Muffins	Fresh diced pinapple and shredded coconut for topping	½ cup pineapple; ¼ cup coconut
Apple Spice Muffins	Diceed peeled apple and brown sugar, mixed with cinnamon for topping	½ cup apple; ¼ cup brown sugar; ¼ teaspoon cinnamon

MAKES 8 TO 14 SCONES
PREP TIME 10 minutes
COOK TIME 25 minutes

Gear

- 2 bowls (1 small, 1 medium)
- Flour sifter
- Electric stand mixer or hand-held mixer
- Small whisk or fork
- Wooden spoon
- Silicone mixing spatula
- Rolling pin
- Large knife
- Round cookie cutters
- Baking sheet
- Pastry brush
- Wire cooling rack

Ingredients

- 2 cups all-purpose flour, plus ¼ cup for rolling
- 1 teaspoon baking powder
- 2 tablespoons plus 1½ teaspoons sugar
- Pinch of salt
- 4 tablespoons (½ stick) butter, softened (see page 14), plus additional for baking sheet
- 1 egg
- 1 egg yolk (see page xxii)
- ⅔ cup milk
- Optional: 3 tablespoons raisins, currants, or dried cranberries; 3 tablespoons chopped fresh strawberries or raspberries; 1 tablespoon sugar; fresh butter or whipped cream (see page 79); your favorite jam

Scones

Scones are a bit firmer than muffins and are delicious with tea or coffee. The secret to making them light and fluffy is to mix the batter as little as possible—until just moist and lumpy—after you add the wet ingredients. Your homemade versions will taste more satisfying than those from your favorite café.

(1) Preheat the oven to 375°F. In the medium bowl, sift the flour, baking powder, sugar, and salt. Add the butter. Using a mixer set on low speed, combine for 3 to 4 minutes, until the contents look thick and chunky.

(2) In the small bowl, whisk together the egg, egg yolk, and milk. Using the wooden spoon, make a well in the center of the flour mixture by pushing mixture against the sides of the bowl. Add ¾ of the egg mixture to the flour mixture.

(3) Using the mixer on low speed, combine for 1 minute or until batter is moist and lumpy. With the spatula, fold in raisins, currants, dried cranberries, or berries, if using.

(4) Dust a flat surface with ¼ cup of flour. Pour the dough onto the floured surface, dust the top of dough with flour, and begin rolling it lightly to make large 1½-inch-thick patties. Using the knife, cut patties into evenly sized triangles or squares, or use a round cookie cutter for round scones.

(5) Place the scones on the buttered baking sheet and brush with the remaining egg mixture. Dust with the extra sugar for a sweeter version, if you like.

(6) Bake for 16 to 20 minutes, until edges are golden brown. To test doneness, insert a toothpick into the center; if it comes out clean, the scones are ready. Remove pan from oven and place it on the cooling rack. Allow the scones to cool on wire rack for 5 minutes. Serve warm with jam and butter, or a dollop of whipped cream, if you like.

STEP 4

STEP 5

STEP 6

② ③
LEVEL

SERVES 4
PREP TIME 5 to 10 minutes

Gear

- Cutting board
- Chef's knife or paring knife
- 3 bowls (2 small, 1 medium)

Ingredients

- 3 cups fresh fruit in season, chopped
- ¼ lemon
- 1 quart (4 cups) yogurt
- Optional: nutmeg, cinnamon, cocoa, or mint leaves for garnish; confectioners' sugar
- Granola or cereal

FRUIT SUGGESTIONS

Summer	Blueberries, Strawberries, Peaches
Fall	Melon Balls, Pear, Raspberries
Winter	Citrus, Apples, Grapes
Spring	Mango, Bananas, Kiwi

Fruit and Yogurt

On mornings when you just want something cool and simple, try fresh fruit and yogurt. For the best results, use a good-quality yogurt (organic usually tastes superior) and the best available fruit of the season. Or mix-and-match toppings like honey, granola, or maple syrup.

①   Clean and chop fruit into bite-size pieces. Combine fruit pieces in the medium bowl. Squeeze with the lemon wedge, cover with plastic wrap, and store in fridge to allow juices to produce, about 30 minutes.

②   In a small bowl, add yogurt and stir with a spoon until smooth. Shake nutmeg, cinnamon, or cocoa on top, or garnish with a trio of mint leaves, if using.

③   Place the granola or cereal in a third bowl. Remove the fruit from the fridge and sprinkle with confectioners' sugar, if using.

④   Serve with spoons, bowls, and napkins, preferably on a platter or tray, or lay out nicely in center of breakfast table.

Fruit and Yogurt Smoothie   On the run? You can still have a quick-and-healthy breakfast to go. Simply blend your favorite fruit-and-yogurt combinations in the blender until smooth, pour into a glass or to-go container, sprinkle granola and extra chopped fruit on top, and you're all set!

STEP 1

STEP 4

Spectacular Salads

Some of the very best salads I've eaten were made simply, with the freshest of ingredients and naturally grown greens, then tossed with a basic dressing. The six salads included in this section are perfect for either a first course or as sides for any of the recipes in the book, or they can stand alone as a meal.

Always rinse your greens, even when using pre-washed salad from a bag. Drain in a colander and dry the leaves in a salad spinner or pat dry with paper towels.

To store lettuce, place inside an airtight food storage bag and keep refrigerated until ready to use. Washed-and-dried greens will last three to five days in the fridge.

IN THIS CHAPTER

In this chapter you'll find easy-to-follow recipes for:
○ Outta-the-Bag Salad
○ Spinach Salad with Honey-Mustard Dressing
○ Arugula and Parmesan with Balsamic Dressing
○ Tomatoes with Fresh Mozzarella and Basil
○ Coleslaw
○ Chilled Pasta Salad

And you'll develop the skills and know-how to:
○ Tell apart different salad greens
○ Properly wash and dry lettuce so it remains crisp
○ Create your own homemade dressings
○ Make candied walnuts

LEVEL

SERVES 4
PREP TIME 5 minutes
ASSEMBLY TIME 3 minutes

Gear

- 2 Large bowls
- Colander
- Optional: salad spinner
- Cutting board
- Paring knife
- Salad tongs or 2 large spoons

Ingredients

SALAD

- 1 bag prewashed spring lettuce mix or mixed greens
- 1 cup crumbled blue cheese (Gorgonzola or Roquefort)
- 1 fresh pear, ends trimmed, cored, then sliced or diced
- 2 tablespoons sliced honey roasted almonds
- 2 tablespoons dried cranberries

DRESSING

- Prepared Italian, balsamic, or herb vinaigrette

Outta-the-Bag Salad

Two words best describe this salad: *easy* and *fast*. All the ingredients can be purchased ready to go, so just assemble and enjoy.

1. Remove lettuce from the bag and place leaves in a large bowl filled with cold water. Soak the leaves for 4 minutes, then drain in the colander and allow to sit for 5 minutes. Dry leaves in a salad spinner or pat dry with paper towels.

2. Toss the lettuce, cheese, pear, almonds, and cranberries in a large bowl. Add dressing in a slow drizzle until all ingredients are lightly coated. Toss again, then serve.

FLAVOR SWAP

Mix-and-match ingredients to create your own delicious combo, or try one of these super-easy substitutions:

ADD TO THE LETTUCE	
½ cup	*2 tablespoons*
Red seedless grapes; walnuts; diced apple	Raisins
Diced tomatoes; feta cheese; pitted olives	Diced cucumber

STEP 2

SERVES 4

PREP AND COOK TIME
15 minutes

ASSEMBLY TIME 5 minutes

Gear

- 2 bowls (1 small, 1 large)
- Whisk or blender
- Cutting board
- Chef's knife
- Optional: salad spinner
- Nonstick fry pan
- Salad tongs

Ingredients

DRESSING
- Homemade Honey-Mustard Dressing (recipe follows)

SALAD
- 1 head Belgian endive
- 1 large bag baby spinach
- 1 recipe Stovetop Bacon (page 12), coarsely chopped
- Pepper
- Optional add-ins: 1 cup Croutons (page 99, or use packaged croutons); 1 medium-size ripe tomato, diced; 1 cup crumbled blue cheese (preferably Roquefort)

Spinach Salad with Honey-Mustard Dressing

This hearty, filling salad is great for a spring lunch or a fall starter. The sweetness of the honey paired with the sharpness of the mustard and the brininess of the bacon make for a perfect combination. Make the dressing first, then put together the salad; toss everything together, and presto, you have a beautifully light dish. Make sure the spinach is vibrant and green and the endive leaves are blemish free.

1. Make the dressing and set aside. Wash, dry, and wrap the endive and the spinach separately.

STEP 1

2. Cook bacon and set aside. When oil is cool, carefully pour it into an empty can or container, then discard container in the trash (see page 13 for instructions on discarding oil).

3. Place the spinach in the large bowl, add the dressing, and toss until the leaves are well coated. To serve, arrange the endive leaves pointing from the center of the plate outward in a star pattern. Add a handful of the spinach to the center of the plate, but don't completely cover the endive. Top with bacon, pepper, and any or all of the suggested add-ins.

Change It Up

If using cheese, spruce up the salad with a diced apple or pear.

HOMEMADE HONEY-MUSTARD DRESSING

MAKES ABOUT 1⅓ CUPS

¼ cup white wine vinegar
1 tablespoon honey
1 tablespoon Dijon mustard
½ cup olive oil

¼ cup vegetable oil
1 tablespoon whole-grain mustard
Salt and pepper

Mix the vinegar, honey, and Dijon mustard in the small bowl or blender. Slowly whisk or blend the oils into the mixture until emulsified. Add the whole-grain mustard, and whisk or pulse for 2 seconds, but no longer as you will break up mustard grains. Taste and season with salt and pepper as preferred. Cover and refrigerate until ready to use.

MAKE YOUR OWN . . .

Candied Walnuts

MAKES 1 CUP

COOKTIME   6 minutes

GEAR
Medium bowl
Measuring cups
Baking sheet

INGREDIENTS
¼ cup sugar
1 cup water
1 cup walnuts

Preheat oven to 375°F. In the medium bowl, add ¼ cup sugar. Slowly drizzle in water until a thick paste develops. Add walnuts and mix until well combined. Spread mixture evenly on the baking sheet and bake for 6 minutes, or until walnuts are glistening and golden brown. Let cool before using.

SERVES 4
PREP TIME 7 minutes
ASSEMBLY TIME 7 minutes

Gear

- Optional: salad spinner
- 2 bowls (1 medium, 1 large)
- Whisk or blender
- Salad tongs
- Vegetable peeler

Ingredients

SALAD

- 5 ounces fresh arugula (about 2 bunches, or 1 bag prewashed)
- Wedge of Parmesan cheese
- Optional: freshly ground pepper

DRESSING

- ¼ cup balsamic vinegar
- 2 teaspoons sugar
- ½ teaspoon Dijon mustard
- ½ cup olive oil
- ¼ cup corn or vegetable oil
- Salt and pepper

Arugula and Parmesan with Balsamic Dressing

Because of its simplicity, this salad will match well with any of the Basic Basics dishes. Whether you want to use mature arugula or baby leaves is up to you; buy what looks best at the store. Substitute green leaf lettuce or watercress for a French-inspired version of this same salad.

1. Wash and dry the arugula according to the instructions on page 25 and set aside.

2. Make the dressing by whisking together the vinegar, sugar, and mustard in the medium bowl or in the blender. While mixing, slowly add the oils into the mixture until emulsified. Taste, then season with salt and pepper as preferred, and set aside.

3. Place the arugula in the large bowl and drizzle with ¾ of the dressing. Use tongs to gently toss until coated. To serve, place a mound of arugula in the center of a plate. Drizzle with some of the remaining dressing. Using a vegetable peeler, shave long shards of Parmesan directly on top of arugula. Season with freshly ground pepper, if using. Repeat for each plate of salad.

Insalata Tricolore   For an elegant enhancement to this salad, try making an *Insalata Tricolore*, or "three-color salad" in Italian. Use the same cheese and dressing, but modify the lettuce by adding equal parts chopped radicchio (red) and Belgian endive (white) to the arugula.

STEP 2

STEP 3

LEVEL

SERVES 4
PREP TIME 5 minutes
ASSEMBLY TIME 5 minutes

Gear

- Cutting board
- Chef's knife

Ingredients

- 8 medium-size ripe plum or vine tomatoes
- Two 4-ounce balls fresh mozzarella cheese, drained
- 1 cup fresh basil leaves, loosely packed, well washed to remove all sand
- Extra-virgin olive oil to drizzle
- Balsamic vinegar to drizzle
- 1 teaspoon coarse sea salt
- Freshly ground pepper

Kitchen FYI

I prefer to use plastic squeeze bottles when drizzling olive oil or vinegar, or I simply place my thumb over the spout of the bottle to control the flow. However, you can achieve the same effect with a small teaspoon. Fill the spoon, then gently tilt as you move it across the salad.

Tomatoes with Fresh Mozzarella and Basil

Best known as Caprese Salad, this traditional dish from the island of Capri is the perfect summer fare. Be sure to use ripe tomatoes; moist, slightly soft, freshly made mozzarella; and smooth, fragrant basil. (*Ripe* and *fresh* are key words here.) Just slice, season, drizzle, and serve. A word of advice: To retain the full flavor of summer-fresh tomatoes, store them in a cool, dry place, not in the fridge.

1. Thinly slice equal amounts of the tomatoes and mozzarella, about five ⅓-inch-thick slices for each; discard the ends.

2. Arrange the mozzarella slices on a serving platter or individual plates. Top them with the tomato slices, followed by 1 or 2 whole basil leaves (use only the best ones from the bunch) sprinkled on top. Repeat mozzarella, tomato, and basil layers on the platter or individual plates.

3. Drizzle each plate with olive oil and 3 or 4 of drops of balsamic vinegar. For a platter, use 3 or 4 drops of balsamic on each tomato-mozzarella pair. Season with coarse sea salt and freshly ground pepper.

STEP 1

STEP 2

SERVES 4
PREP TIME 15 minutes
ASSEMBLY TIME 5 minutes

Gear

- Cutting board
- Chef's knife
- Box grater
- Colander
- 2 bowls (1 large, 1 medium)
- Mixing spoon

Ingredients

- 1 medium head cabbage
- 2 tablespoons kosher salt
- 1 large carrot, peeled and coarsely grated
- ⅛ cup sweet pickle juice
- 3 tablespoons olive oil
- ¾ cup mayonnaise
- Pepper

Change It Up

Try using this summer slaw as a topping on your grilled hamburger (page 60) or piled on top of fresh crab cake (page 94) tucked between a toasted brioche bun.

Coleslaw

A summer staple, coleslaw is the perfect accompaniment to fried chicken and barbeque. Or serve it on top of a turkey sandwich for extra punch. Try low-fat mayonnaise for a healthier alternative.

1. Cut the cabbage into quarters (through the stem end) and cut out the solid core from each quarter. Finely shred the cabbage into the colander using the box grater.

2. Add the kosher salt, toss, and let sit in the sink or over the large bowl to drain for 2 hours.

3. Place the cabbage in the medium bowl. Add the carrot, pickle juice, and olive oil and mix together. Add the mayonnaise gradually, and continue to mix until the coleslaw is liberally coated. Season with pepper to taste.

STEP 3

LEVEL

SERVES 4
PREP TIME   15 minutes
COOK TIME   15 minutes
ASSEMBLY TIME   5 minutes

Gear

- Cutting board
- Chef's knife
- Paring knife
- Box grater
- 8-quart stockpot
- Fry pan
- Blender
- Colander
- Large bowl

Ingredients

PASTA

- Kosher salt
- 1 pound fusilli
  (corkscrew-shaped pasta)

DRESSING

- ¾ cup plus 2 tablespoons
  olive oil
- 1 medium red onion, peeled,
  ½ sliced, ½ finely diced
- 1 medium red bell pepper,
  trimmed, seeded, ribs removed,
  finely and evenly diced
  (reserve odd-size scraps for
  dressing)
- 2 medium tomatoes, evenly
  diced (reserve odd-size scraps
  for dressing)
- 1 tablespoon Dijon mustard
- 1 teaspoon sugar
- ¼ cup balsamic vinegar
- 1 small carrot (or ½ large),
  peeled and grated using a
  box grater (about ½ cup)
- 2 tablespoons chopped fresh
  basil leaves plus extra whole
  leaves for garnish
- Pepper

Chilled Pasta Salad

Fast, simple, and healthy, this is great served as a main course for lunch or as a side with burgers or summer grilled fish. It also keeps well in the fridge, so double the recipe for leftovers.

1. Fill the stockpot ¾ full with water and bring to a boil over high heat. Add 1 tablespoon salt and the pasta, and cook according to instructions on the package. Drain in the colander in the sink, then plunge into the large bowl of cold water. Drain again, then set aside to cool.

2. While the pasta is cooking, make the dressing. Place the fry pan over medium-high heat. When hot*, add 2 tablespoons olive oil, the sliced red onion, and the red pepper scraps, and sauté (page xxiv) for 5 minutes.

3. Stir in the tomato scraps and cook for 2 minutes more; remove from the heat and set aside to cool for 10 minutes. Transfer the vegetable mixture to the blender. Add the mustard, sugar, 1 teaspoon salt, and the vinegar. Puree while slowly adding ¾ cup olive oil.

4. To assemble, toss the pasta with the carrot, diced onion, tomatoes, red peppers, and the chopped basil in the large bowl. Drizzle in the dressing while tossing until pasta is evenly coated. Season with salt and pepper to taste. Garnish with whole basil leaves.

*Is your pan hot enough? Test with a drop of water. If it sizzles, you're ready to cook.

STEP 2

STEP 4 (A)

STEP 4 (B)

Quick Bites and Simple Snacks

When you're rushed for time or need to entertain in a pinch, there's nothing better than the almighty snack. My snack recipes take very little energy to put together and are meant to be served on the fly. In a snap, they can also be turned into appetizers for a cocktail party (see page 211) or a late-night mini-meal. Either way, they are easy to prepare and eat, and perfect to enjoy while watching TV on game day (see page 85), hanging out on the back deck, or sipping a beer on a lazy sunny afternoon.

IN THIS CHAPTER

In this chapter you'll find easy-to-follow recipes for:
O Grilled Cheese Sandwiches
O Nachos with Guacamole and Fresh Salsa
O Potato Skins with Bacon and Cheese
O Buffalo Chicken Wings
O Satay Chicken Skewers

And you'll develop the skills and know-how to:
O Create a perfectly melted grilled cheese
O Add extra spice to your chicken wings
O Make your own yogurt dipping sauce

SERVES 6
PREP TIME 10 minutes
COOK TIME 10 minutes

Gear

- Cutting board
- Chef's knife
- Spreader knife
- Nonstick fry pan
- Medium spatula
- Aluminum foil
- Optional: round cookie cutter

Ingredients

- 12 slices white bread or country bread (all-natural bread is best)
- 8 tablespoons (1 stick) butter, softened (see page 14)
- 24 slices cheese of choice, ¼-inch thick (about 20 ounces)
- Salt and pepper

Kitchen FYI

The secrets to a perfect grilled cheese are temperature control—you need enough heat to crisp the bread but not burn it—and enough time on the heat to melt the cheese. Just keep an eye on the pan. Don't be afraid to lift one corner of your grilled cheese to check.

Grilled Cheese Sandwiches

Who doesn't like a crisp, well-made grilled cheese sandwich? Use your favorite cheese, whether it's cheddar, American, Italian Taleggio (my favorite), Gouda, or Swiss. These are great with Tomato and Basil Soup (page 99) or a simple salad, or, like the good old days (when I was a kid), with plenty of mustard or ketchup.

1. Lay out the bread on a clean work surface. Spread butter evenly on 6 slices, then turn slices upside down. Cover each slice to the edges with cheese slices. Add salt and pepper to season. Cover with the remaining 6 slices of bread and spread butter evenly on top of each sandwich.

2. Place the fry pan over low-medium heat. When hot*, arrange the sandwiches in the pan as space allows.

3. Cook until underside is golden brown. Using the spatula, flip sandwich over and cook other side until golden brown and the cheese is melted. Transfer sandwich to a plate and serve immediately, or cover the plate with aluminum foil and keep warm in the oven. Repeat with remaining sandwiches in batches.

4. To serve, cut the sandwiches into triangles, or use a cookie cutter for a unique twist on the traditional shape.

Is your pan hot enough? Test it with a drop of water. If it sizzles, you're ready to cook.

STEP 1

STEP 2

STEP 3

LEVEL

Gear

- Cutting board
- Chef's knife
- 3 bowls (1 large, 1 medium, 1 small)
- Silicone mixing spatula
- Wooden spoon
- Baking sheet
- Optional: box grater (for cheese)
- Wide spatula

Ingredients

FRESH SALSA

- 6 medium-size ripe tomatoes, diced
- 1 small red onion (or ½ of a large one), peeled and finely diced
- 3 pickled jalapeños (jarred), drained and chopped
- One 12-ounce jar marinated roasted red peppers, drained and diced
- 2 teaspoons kosher salt
- 1 teaspoon sugar
- Dash of Tabasco sauce or your favorite hot sauce
- Pinch of smoked paprika
- Pinch of cayenne pepper
- 3 tablespoons ketchup
- 2 tablespoons olive oil
- 2 tablespoons chopped fresh cilantro leaves

(continues)

Nachos with Guacamole and Fresh Salsa

The secret to good salsa is freshness—ripe tomatoes and fresh herbs—plus the right amount of heat (which depends on your taste buds, or those of your guests. When in doubt, play it safe and go for medium spicy). The jarred variety, which uses cooked tomato, is fine, but look for the fresh salsa found in your store's vegetable aisle. Or better yet, make it yourself. Fresh homemade salsa is actually better the next day, when the flavors are more saturated, so make it a day ahead, if you can. Removing seeds and interior ribs of hot peppers will reduce their "heat" content.

Unlike the salsa, this guacamole is best on the day it's made, but will keep in the fridge for another day. To keep it from turning brown while storing, toss the avocado pit back into the container, and press some plastic wrap directly onto the surface of the guacamole. A word of wisdom: Be sure to make the guacamole and salsa *first* (if using the salsa recipe below), before you pop the nachos under the broiler.

FRESH SALSA

MAKES 3 CUPS

PREP TIME 10 minutes

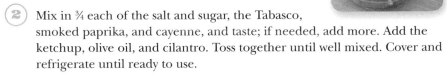

STEP 2

1. Combine the tomatoes (along with any juices), onion, jalapeños, and roasted peppers in the large bowl. Mix gently with the spatula.

2. Mix in ¾ each of the salt and sugar, the Tabasco, smoked paprika, and cayenne, and taste; if needed, add more. Add the ketchup, olive oil, and cilantro. Toss together until well mixed. Cover and refrigerate until ready to use.

Ingredients (cont'd)

GUACAMOLE

- 1 medium-size ripe tomato, diced
- ½ red onion, peeled, and finely diced
- 1 fresh red chile pepper, seeded, ribs removed, and minced
- 2 teaspoons chopped fresh cilantro leaves
- 2 ripe avocados, pitted, peeled, and cubed
- ¼ teaspoon kosher salt
- Sugar
- Pinch of cayenne pepper
- Juice of 1 lime

NACHOS

- One 16-ounce bag tortilla chips (yellow corn, blue corn, or nacho cheese)
- Pinch of cayenne pepper
- Optional: 1 can refried beans; 1½ cups Quick Chili (page 64); 1 fresh jalapeño pepper, seeded, ribs removed, and minced; ½ cup pitted black olives, drained and sliced; ¼ cup chopped fresh cilantro (leaves only); ½ cup sour cream
- 1½ cups grated cheddar cheese
- 1½ cups grated Jack cheese
- 2 teaspoons olive oil
- Salt and pepper
- Cayenne pepper
- Salsa and Guacamole, for serving

GUACAMOLE

MAKES 1 CUP

PREP TIME 5 minutes

STEP 2

1. Mix together the tomato, onion, chile, and cilantro in the small bowl.

2. Place the avocado in the medium bowl. Crush into a paste with the back of the wooden spoon. Add the tomato mixture and mix well. Season with salt, sugar, and cayenne, while gradually adding lime juice, to taste. Adjust seasoning as necessary. Cover and refrigerate until ready to use.

NACHOS

PREP TIME 10 minutes

COOK TIME 5 minutes

STEP 2

1. Preheat the broiler to high.

2. Spread tortilla chips on the baking sheet. Add toppings as preferred. Sprinkle grated cheeses onto chips, one handful at a time. Drizzle olive oil over chips, and season as preferred with salt, pepper, and cayenne.

3. Place baking sheet under broiler and cook for 5 minutes, or until cheese is bubbling. Be careful not to burn the chips. Remove baking sheet and place on a heat-resistant surface.

4. To serve, transfer the nachos to a serving platter using the wide spatula, with salsa and guacamole on the side for dipping or spooned on top as a garnish.

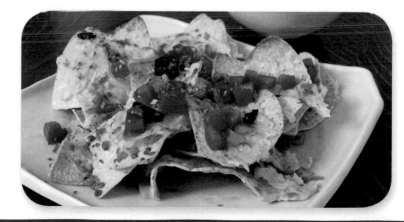

LEVEL

SERVES 6
PREP TIME 10 minutes
ASSEMBLY TIME 10 minutes
COOK TIME 1½ hours

Gear

- Cutting board
- Chef's knife
- Optional: box grater (if not using packaged cheese)
- Baking sheet
- Small spoon or melon baller
- Nonstick fry pan
- Wooden spoon
- Medium stainless-steel bowl
- Tongs
- Small bowls

Ingredients

- 6 evenly sized large Yukon Gold potatoes, or 24 round red potatoes (2-inch diameter) for finger-size snacks, scrubbed well and dried
- ½ pound bacon, chopped
- 2 tablespoons olive oil
- Salt and pepper
- Optional: pinch of cayenne pepper
- 1½ cups grated cheddar cheese
- 1 medium-size ripe tomato, diced, or 1 cup Fresh Salsa (page 34)
- 3 scallions, trimmed and finely chopped (about ⅓ cup)
- Optional: 1 cup sour cream

Potato Skins with Bacon and Cheese

This staple bar snack is easy enough to make in your own kitchen. Just be warned: Once you've learned how to do them right, you may never order skins in a bar again. Although you can use any size or shape of potato, I've found that the Yukon Gold variety cooks evenly and crisps just right on the outside.

1. Preheat the oven to 375°F. Place the potatoes on the baking sheet and bake for 1½ hours, until skin is a golden brown and a bit crinkled and crispy. Remove baking sheet from the oven, place on a heat-resistant surface, and let potatoes cool to the touch.

2. Cut the potatoes in half; scoop out ¾ of the flesh with a small spoon or a melon baller and discard. Set skins aside.

3. In the fry pan, cook bacon over medium-high heat. When crisp, transfer the bacon to paper towels and drain off the fat from the pan into the stainless-steel bowl. Add the olive oil and season with salt and cayenne pepper, if using; mix well. Using tongs, dip skins into bowl and coat with mixture.

4. Place skins on the baking sheet, cut side down. Bake for 12 to 15 minutes, until a deep golden brown. Remove the baking sheet, and flip the skins over with tongs, cut side up. Sprinkle the bacon and cheese onto each skin.

STEP 2

STEP 4

(5) Turn the oven to broil. Place the baking sheet under the broiler until the cheese melts and crisps a little, about 3 minutes. Remove baking sheet and place on a heat-resistant surface.

(6) To serve, transfer skins to a platter, and top with tomato or fresh salsa and sour cream, if using. Or, serve salsa and sour cream on the side. Sprinkle scallions on top of the skins.

FLAVOR SWAP

Want to take your skins to the next level? Try switching up the toppings with these delicious combos.

WHAT?	HOW MUCH?
Diced grilled chicken; Monterey Jack cheese; Diced red pepper	1 cup
Sautéed Bay scallops; freshly grated Parmesan cheese; sliced shallots	1 cup
Quick chili; grated cheddar cheese	1 cup

LEVEL

SERVES 6
PREP TIME 20 minutes
MARINATING TIME 2 hours
COOK TIME 40 minutes

Gear

- Cutting board
- Chef's knife
- 3 bowls (1 large, 1 medium, 1 small)
- Plastic wrap
- Vegetable peeler
- Roasting pan

Ingredients

CHICKEN WINGS
- 2 pounds chicken wings
- 1½ tablespoons kosher salt
- Pepper
- One 18-ounce bottle spicy wing or barbeque sauce
- Optional: hot pepper sauce

DRESSING
- ½ cup mayonnaise
- ½ cup crumbled blue cheese (Roquefort is best)
- 2 tablespoons water

CELERY
- 5 stalks celery, rinsed and trimmed
- 2 cups water
- 2 teaspoons kosher salt

Buffalo Chicken Wings

Coat the wings with spicy sauce, marinate, roast, and serve. That's it! Use any sauce you prefer, but think in terms of how spicy, tart, and sugary you like it. The blue cheese dressing helps offset the spiciness of the wings. Try this recipe with chicken fillets or strips if you're not fond of bones.

① Using the chef's knife, chop each wing into 3 pieces, discarding the wing tips. In the large bowl, toss the wings with the salt, pepper, and ¾ of the wing or barbecue sauce (save remainder for serving, if desired). Cover with plastic wrap. Marinate the wings in refrigerator for at least 2 hours before cooking.

② While the wings are marinating, make the dressing and prep the celery. In the small bowl, stir together the mayonnaise, blue cheese, and water. Mix until smooth and creamy. Cover with plastic wrap and refrigerate until ready to use.

③ Cut each celery stalk in half lengthwise (½ inch wide), and into even 4-inch lengths. Place in the medium bowl with the water and salt. Cover with plastic wrap and refrigerate until ready to use.

④ Preheat the oven to 375°F. Spread out the wing pieces in the roasting pan, spoon on any extra marinade from the bowl, and bake for 35 to 40 minutes, or until wings look golden brown and crisp. If they don't seem golden brown or crisp, turn on broiler for final 3 minutes (watching all the time). Keep warm in a 200°F oven until you are ready to serve.

⑤ To serve, place a small dish of blue cheese dressing in the middle of a platter. Surround with the wings. Drain and dry the celery sticks and serve on the side.

STEP 1 (A)

STEP 1 (B)

STEP 4

① ② ③
LEVEL

SERVES 6
PREP TIME 10 minutes
MARINATING TIME
20 minutes to 2 hours
COOK TIME 20 minutes

Gear

- Cutting board
- Chef's knife
- Medium bowl
- 6 to 12 skewers (wooden or metal; if using wooden skewers, soak them in water for 30 minutes prior to using)
- Baking sheet

Ingredients

- One 10-ounce jar satay sauce or spicy peanut sauce
- 4 boneless, skinless chicken breast halves, cut into 1½-inch cubes
- Salt and pepper
- Cayenne pepper
- ½ cup peanuts, finely chopped
- ½ cup chopped fresh cilantro leaves
- 4 scallions, trimmed and finely chopped (about ½ cup)

Satay Chicken Skewers

This is one of the fastest and tastiest snacks you can make. Served with rice, it makes an awesome main meal.

① Pour ⅔ of the satay or spicy peanut sauce into the medium bowl and add the chicken. Cover with plastic wrap and refrigerate for at least 20 minutes; 2 hours is preferable for optimum flavor. While the chicken is marinating, preheat the oven to 375°F.

② Twenty-five minutes before serving time, remove the chicken from the refrigerator and divide it into 6 portions. Slide pieces onto skewers (depending on size of skewer, this may mean 1 or 2 skewers per person) and place on baking sheet. Discard remaining marinade (raw chicken juices in it make it unsafe). Dust the skewered chicken with salt, pepper, and cayenne.

③ Bake for 20 minutes. For the final 2 minutes, turn on the broiler and broil the skewers close to the heat, until the edges look crisp but not burned.

④ To serve, place the skewers on a serving platter and sprinkle with the peanuts, cilantro, and scallions. Pour the remaining satay sauce (not marinade) into a bowl on the side for dipping.

Satay Chicken Bites   For diced bites instead of skewers, simply pan-fry (page xxiv) the chicken for 10 minutes, then transfer to the baking sheet and cook in a 375°F oven for 10 minutes. Serve warm.

PREP

STEP 2

Easy Main Dishes

Okay, you've assembled a few fresh, simple salads, and made your friends happy with some terrific snacks. Now let's take things up a step and make some hearty meals.

The theory behind this chapter is simple: If you can make a Hamburger Deluxe (page 60), you can also cook a delicious Rustic Meatloaf (page 62); if you can make the Basic Basics Spaghetti with Meat Sauce (page 42), then a pot of Quick Chili (page 64) will be a snap.

These basic recipes provide the building blocks and skills you need, and your confidence level will grow by leaps and bounds. You'll just have to get used to saying: "Why don't you come over to my place for dinner? I'll cook."

IN THIS CHAPTER

In this chapter, you'll find recipes for:
○ Pasta with Basic Basics Tomato Sauce
○ Spaghetti with Meat Sauce
○ Seasonal Pasta
○ Rigatoni with Red Pepper Sauce
○ Macaroni and Cheese
○ Baked Fusilli with Chicken, Mushrooms, and Pesto
○ Vegetable Stir-Fry with Black Bean Sauce
○ Sesame Noodles with Teriyaki Chicken
○ Pan-Fried Chicken Breasts
○ Fajitas with Chicken, Beef, or Shrimp
○ Steak, Four Ways
○ Pork Chops
○ Meatballs
○ Hamburger Deluxe
○ Rustic Meatloaf
○ Quick Chili
○ Jumbo Shrimp with Lemon, Garlic, and Tarragon
○ Sole with Capers and Lemon
○ Fish Tacos

And you'll develop the skills and know-how to:
○ Turn basic tomato sauce into something exotic
○ Make homemade versions of bread crumbs, white sauce, and teriyaki sauce
○ Warm tortillas
○ Cook a hamburger more than one way
○ Cook fish without it breaking apart

LEVEL

**MAKES 4 CUPS SAUCE;
SERVES 4**

PREP TIME 10 minutes

COOK TIME 30 minutes

Gear

- Cutting board
- Chef's knife
- Paring knife
- 3-quart saucepan with lid
- Wooden spoon
- 8-quart stockpot
- Colander

Ingredients

- 1 medium red onion, peeled and finely diced
- 1 clove garlic, peeled, crushed, and minced
- ½ cup olive oil
- ¼ cup tomato paste
- ½ cup red or white wine
- One 28-ounce can or two 14.5-ounce cans diced tomatoes, not drained
- 1 vegetable bouillon cube
- Salt and pepper
- ½ bunch fresh basil (about 20 large leaves), washed and coarsely chopped
- 1 pound of your favorite pasta
- Freshly grated Parmesan cheese

How Do I . . . ?

The longer you cook the sauce, the better it tastes. If it gets too thick, just add liquid (wine, water, and/or stock) to maintain the desired consistency.

Pasta with Basic Basics Tomato Sauce

This is my go-to tomato sauce—the perfect base for pasta sauces, lasagna, or chili, or by itself with a bowl of your favorite pasta. Once you master this basic sauce, you can rework the recipe to make it your own—add more or less of any given ingredient or consider adding other ingredients, like finely chopped mushrooms, chile peppers, or fresh herbs.

1. In the saucepan set over medium heat, sweat (page xxiv) the onion and garlic in 2 tablespoons of the oil for 5 minutes, until the onions are just translucent.

2. Add the tomato paste, stir with the wooden spoon, and simmer (page xxiii) for 1 minute. Stir in the wine and cook for 4 minutes to allow the wine to reduce (page xxv).

STEP 2

3. Stir in the diced tomatoes with their liquid and the bouillon cube; simmer over low heat for 15 to 20 minutes. Add salt and pepper to season. Stir in ¼ cup olive oil and the basil.

4. While sauce is simmering, prepare the pasta: Fill the stockpot ¾ full with water and bring to a boil. Add 1 tablespoon salt and 1 tablespoon olive oil. Cook pasta according to package directions, drain in the colander, and toss with the remaining olive oil.

5. To serve, divide the pasta among four plates and spoon the sauce evenly over the pasta. Top with freshly grated Parmesan cheese.

SERVES 4 (ABOUT 5 CUPS)
PREP TIME 15 minutes
COOK TIME 25 minutes

Gear

- Cutting board
- Chef's knife
- Fry pan
- Slotted spoon
- Medium bowl (for draining)
- Wooden spoon
- 3-quart saucepan
- Ladle (for serving)
- 8-quart stockpot
- Colander

Ingredients

SAUCE
- 1 tablespoon vegetable oil
- 1½ pounds ground or diced beef
- ½ pound bacon, diced, or 1 tablespoon olive oil
- ½ medium onion, peeled and diced
- 2 cloves garlic, peeled, crushed, and minced
- 1 packet brown gravy mixed with ½ cup hot water (yields about ¾ cup)
- ½ pound mushrooms, sliced
- 1½ cups Basic Basics Tomato Sauce (page 41)
- 1 teaspoon kosher salt
- 1 teaspoon pepper
- ½ teaspoon cayenne pepper
- 1 teaspoon sugar

SPAGHETTI
- 1 tablespoon salt
- 2 tablespoons olive oil
- 1-pound package spaghetti
- Freshly grated Parmesan cheese

Spaghetti with Meat Sauce

A good meat sauce requires two key ingredients: quality meat and a terrific tomato base. With the Basic Basics Tomato Sauce and a few additions you have a dish that will instantly become a staple in your repertoire.

(1) Place the fry pan over medium-high heat. When hot*, add the vegetable oil, then brown the beef, stirring to break apart (5 to 7 minutes). Drain off fat from the beef using a slotted spoon or a colander in the sink.

(2) In the 3-quart saucepan, fry the bacon (if using) over medium-high heat until crisp. Without draining, add the onions and garlic and sweat (page xxiv) for 5 minutes until onions are just translucent, not browned. If not using bacon, sweat onions and garlic in olive oil.

(3) Add the drained beef, gravy, mushrooms, tomato sauce, salt, pepper, cayenne, and sugar. Simmer (page xxiii) for 20 minutes, until sauce appears reddish-brown.

(4) While the sauce is cooking, prepare the spaghetti. Fill the stockpot ¾ full with water and bring to a boil. Add the salt and 1 tablespoon olive oil. Cook the spaghetti according to package directions, drain in the colander, and toss with the remaining olive oil.

(5) To serve, either return pasta to stockpot and mix in sauce, or transfer pasta to individual plates and spoon sauce on top. Top with freshly grated Parmesan cheese.

*Is your pan hot enough? Test it with a drop of water. If it sizzles, you're ready to cook.

STEP 1

STEP 3 (A)

STEP 3 (B)

Gear

- Cutting board
- Chef's knife
- 8-quart stockpot
- Colander
- Slotted spoon
- Medium bowl
- Fry pan
- Wooden spoon
- Tongs
- Microplane grater

Ingredients

- Kosher salt
- ¼ cup plus 2 tablespoons olive oil
- 1 pound of your favorite pasta
- Ice water (for blanching)
- 2 cloves garlic, peeled, crushed, and minced
- 1 shallot, peeled and minced
- ½ cup white wine
- 1 cup vegetable stock (canned or boxed)
- Optional: 1 cup heavy cream
- ½ cup freshly grated Parmesan cheese, plus additional for serving
- 2 tablespoons butter plus 1 teaspoon (for serving)
- Pepper

VEGETABLES (SEE CHART)

- Vegetables of choice
- Fresh herb of choice, chopped (leaves only, stems discarded)
- Spice of choice

Seasonal Pasta

This recipe gives you the tools to serve a vegetarian pasta dish based on fresh seasonal ingredients. The combination of blanched and raw vegetables adds a variety of flavors and textures. Mix and match the ingredients to your liking, and choose any pasta you wish.

SEASONAL VEGGIE CHART

Use the following measurement guidelines for ingredients to add to your pasta:

	BLANCHED ½ cup per person	RAW ⅓ cup per person	HERBS/SPICES 2 tablespoons fresh herbs and ¼ teaspoon spice
Spring	Asparagus, pieces	Chopped hothouse tomatoes	Parsley; smoked paprika
Summer	Corn kernels, cut off the cob	Chopped heirloom tomatoes	Basil; celery salt
Fall	Butternut squash, peeled and cubed	Halved cherry or grape tomatoes	Sage; Ground Coriander
Winter	Broccoli florets	Sliced mushrooms	Thyme; cayenne

① Fill the stockpot ¾ full with water and bring to a boil. Add 1 tablespoon salt and 1 tablespoon olive oil. Cook pasta according to package directions, and drain in the colander. Set aside while you prepare the sauce.

② Refill the stockpot half full with water. Add 1 tablespoon salt, and bring to a boil. Blanch (page xxiii) the vegetables in boiling water, then refresh in ice water.

continues

STEP 1

STEP 3

STEP 4

③ Place the fry pan over medium-high heat. When hot*, add 2 tablespoons olive oil and sweat (page xxiv) garlic and shallots until just translucent, not browned. Stir in ¼ cup of the wine, ½ cup of the vegetable stock, and ½ cup of cream, if using. Turn up heat to high and cook for 3 minutes, but avoid reducing (page xxv) all of the liquid. Add the blanched vegetables and cook for 2 minutes. Stir in remainder of cream, if using, and continue to cook until sauce is reduced by about half.

④ Add 2 tablespoons of the Parmesan to sauce to thicken. Add in drained pasta. Toss and stir with tongs until the pasta is well coated. Add the remaining white wine and stock. Cook down, stirring occasionally, until the sauce is slightly thickened. Add the spices (see chart) and salt and pepper to taste.

⑤ Toss in the raw vegetables, 2 tablespoons butter, then the fresh herbs. Stir for 1 minute, then remove from the heat. Add ¼ cup Parmesan, and toss to coat evenly.

⑥ To serve, add in the additional teaspoon of butter, toss, then serve with tongs in pasta bowls, sprinkling additional Parmesan cheese on top. Have freshly ground pepper and grated Parmesan reserved on the side, and add if desired.

*Is your pan hot enough? Test it with a drop of water. If it sizzles, you're ready to cook.

SERVES 4
PREP TIME 15 minutes
COOK TIME 35 minutes

Gear

- 8-quart stockpot
- Cutting board
- Chef's knife
- Paring knife
- Microplane grater
- Colander
- Fry pan
- Blender
- Serving bowl

Ingredients

- Kosher salt
- 3 tablespoons olive oil
- 1 pound rigatoni
- 1 large red onion, peeled and diced
- 2 cloves garlic, peeled, crushed, and minced
- 3 red bell peppers, trimmed, seeded, ribs removed, diced
- ¼ cup white wine
- 1 teaspoon smoked paprika
- 1 vegetable bouillon cube
- 2 cups low-fat or nonfat plain yogurt
- 3 tablespoons low-fat cream cheese
- ⅓ cup freshly grated Parmesan cheese
- ¼ cup chopped fresh basil leaves
- Pepper

Rigatoni with Red Pepper Sauce

The secret to this deceptively light dish is low-fat yogurt substituted for cream. Use any pasta you want, though the sauce sticks best to larger noodles such as *rigatoni* or *pappardelle*. This sauce can serve as a base for other dishes; for example, serve with grilled fish, or even add to Basic Basics Tomato Sauce (page 41) for a rustic vegetarian spaghetti sauce.

(1) Fill the stockpot ¾ full with water and bring to a boil. Add 1 tablespoon salt and 1 tablespoon olive oil. Cook pasta according to package directions, then drain in the colander.

(2) Set the fry pan over medium heat. When hot*, add the remaining 2 tablespoons olive oil. Sweat (page xxiv) the onions, garlic, and peppers until onions are translucent, not brown, and peppers are soft.

continues

STEP 2

STEP 4

STEP 5

(3) Stir in the wine, 1 teaspoon salt, the paprika, and the bouillon cube. Bring to a boil, then simmer (page xxiii) for 10 minutes.

(4) Add the yogurt and cream cheese to the sauce, and allow to cook until just simmering, but not boiling. Take off the heat and cool for about 10 minutes, or long enough to safely transfer the sauce to the blender without risk of being burned by hot liquids. Blend until smooth and lump-free.

(5) Return pasta to stockpot and mix in sauce until pasta is well coated, or transfer pasta to individual plates and spoon sauce on top. Add freshly grated Parmesan, basil, and pepper, as preferred.

*Is your pan hot enough? Test it with a drop of water. If it sizzles, you're ready to cook.

Decadent Red Pepper Sauce For a richer sauce, substitute heavy cream for the yogurt, and butter for the cream cheese in Step 4. Allow the sauce to cook about 5 minutes, until just simmering and liquid level has reduced by ⅓ in the pot. Continue as directed above.

Gear

- 8-quart stockpot
- Medium saucepan
- Wooden spoon
- Box grater
- Whisk
- Colander
- Large bowl
- 24-ounce round ovenproof casserole dish or 9-inch square baking dish
- Baking sheet
- Small ladle

Ingredients

- Salt
- 1 tablespoon olive oil
- 1 pound macaroni
- 2 cups White Sauce (page 48)
- 1 cup grated medium-sharp cheddar cheese
- 1 teaspoon Dijon mustard
- Pepper
- ¼ cup heavy cream
- Optional: 4 tablespoons (½ stick) butter

(continues)

Macaroni and Cheese

Who says mac and cheese is just for kids? This is one of the first dishes I learned to cook and it's still one of my favorites. Make a grown-up version of your own by including a few simple add-ins, like fresh vegetables, bacon, or ground meat, or giving your cheese a flavor twist by using Roquefort, Brie, or Gorgonzola. The possibilities are endless.

① Fill the stockpot with water. Bring to a boil and add 1 tablespoon salt, the olive oil, and the pasta. Cook the pasta for 5 to 6 minutes or according to package directions, then drain in the colander. While the macaroni is cooking, preheat the broiler. Set macaroni aside while you prepare the white sauce.

② Make the homemade White Sauce (page 48). As you stir the sauce with the wooden spoon, slowly add ¾ of the cheddar cheese and the mustard. Season with salt and pepper as you continue to stir, then beat the sauce quickly with the whisk while slowly adding the cream. Mix thoroughly.

③ Pour macaroni into the large bowl. Add the cheese sauce on top, and stir in the butter, if desired, with the wooden spoon. Mix well (being careful not to break up the pasta) until it is silky and smooth. Add salt and pepper to taste.

④ Transfer the mixture to the casserole or baking dish. Top with the remaining cheddar, the Parmesan, and the Bread Crumbs. Sprinkle with salt, pepper, and cayenne to season.

⑤ Place dish directly under the broiler. Cook until bread crumbs are golden brown, 3 to 4 minutes. *Do not* leave the dish unattended while under the broiler. Remove dish and place on a heat-resistant surface. Serve immediately.

continues

STEP 2 (A)

STEP 2 (B)

STEP 4

Ingredients (cont'd)

TOPPING
- ¼ cup freshly grated Parmesan cheese
- ½ cup Bread Crumbs (below right) or store-bought
- Cayenne pepper

Change It Up

For a richer sauce, add ¼ cup heavy cream to finish.

MAKE YOUR OWN . . .

White Sauce

MAKES 2½ CUPS

COOK TIME   10 minutes

GEAR
2 saucepans (1 medium, 1 small)
Whisk
Small ladle

INGREDIENTS
8 tablespoons (1 stick) butter
¼ cup all-purpose flour
2 cups milk (I prefer whole milk)
1 bay leaf
Salt and white pepper

STEP 2

Also known as *béchamel*, this sauce has a lot of uses throughout the book. It can be made ahead and stored in your refrigerator for up to 3 days.

1 In the medium saucepan set over low heat, melt 4 tablespoons of the butter. Stir constantly with the whisk while adding flour. Cook for 4 minutes, continuing to stir.

2 Using the small saucepan set over low heat, heat milk with the bay leaf and a pinch each of salt and pepper. When milk begins to steam, remove the bay leaf, then gradually add the milk to butter-flour mixture (called the *roux*) using the small ladle, mixing in about ¼ cup at a time. Whisk continuously, allowing sauce to thicken into a smooth paste before adding next ladle. Repeat this until you have used all the milk. If sauce is too thick and paste-like, add more milk.

3 Whisk in the remaining butter. The sauce should have a smooth but thick consistency. Taste and add more salt and pepper if necessary.

Bread Crumbs

MAKES ABOUT 2 CUPS

PREP TIME   3 minutes

GEAR
Food processor

INGREDIENTS
10 slices bread of choice, at least 1 day old (should be dry and crusty)

Coarsely chop crusty day-old bread. Leave on crusts if you want darker crumbs, or remove for white crumbs. Pulse in the food processor until you reach your desired crumb size. Make extra and freeze the crumbs for later use.

SERVES 4
PREP TIME 30 minutes
COOK TIME 25 minutes

Gear

- 8-quart stockpot
- Cutting board
- Chef's knife
- Box grater
- Medium saucepan
- Whisk
- Fry pan
- Wooden spoon
- 2 bowls (1 small, 1 large)
- 24-ounce round ovenproof casserole dish or 9-inch square baking dish
- Baking sheet

Ingredients

PASTA
- Salt
- 1 tablespoon olive oil, plus 1 tablespoon for cooking chicken
- ½ pound dried fusilli pasta (about 2½ cups)
- 2 cups White Sauce (opposite)
- 1 cup heavy cream
- 2 tablespoons Pesto (page 187, or store-bought)
- 2 large boneless, skinless chicken breast halves, cut into ½-inch cubes
- 1½ cups sliced white mushrooms
- ½ cup sliced scallions
- Pepper

TOPPING
- ½ cup grated cheddar cheese
- ¼ cup freshly grated Parmesan cheese
- ½ cup Bread Crumbs (opposite) or store-bought

Baked Fusilli with Chicken, Mushrooms, and Pesto

Here's a hearty twist to basic macaroni and cheese that's easy to assemble and even easier to cook. If you have a large casserole dish (or Dutch oven), consider doubling the ingredients for a casual dinner party or just for wonderful leftovers.

① Preheat the oven to 375°F. Fill the stockpot with water. Bring to a boil and add 1 tablespoon salt and 1 tablespoon olive oil. Cook the pasta according to package directions, drain in the colander in the sink, and set aside.

② Place the medium saucepan over medium heat with the white sauce in it, whisk the cream into the white sauce, remove from the heat, and stir in the pesto until well mixed. Set aside.

③ In the fry pan set over medium-high heat, sauté (page xxiv) the chicken until golden brown, 4 to 5 minutes per side. Stir in the mushrooms and scallions, combine well, and continue to cook for another 3 to 5 minutes, until golden brown.

④ In the large bowl, toss together the pasta, chicken mixture, and sauce. Season with salt and pepper. Combine the grated cheeses with the bread crumbs in the small bowl.

⑤ Pour the pasta mixture into the baking dish and top with the cheese and bread crumb mixture. Bake for 15 minutes, until top turns golden brown. Remove from the oven, place on a heat-resistant surface, and allow to cool for 5 minutes before serving.

STEP 2

STEP 3

STEP 5

LEVEL

SERVES 4
PREP TIME 15 minutes
COOK TIME 15 minutes

Gear

- Cutting board
- Chef's knife
- Paring knife
- 8-quart stockpot
- Slotted spoon
- Medium bowl
- Colander
- Large nonstick fry pan or wok

Ingredients

- 1 pound rice noodles, udon, or ramen
- Florets from 1 head of broccoli, cut into bite-size pieces
- Ice water (for blanching)
- 2 tablespoons vegetable oil
- 1 medium red bell pepper, seeded, ribs removed, and cut into thin strips
- 1 medium yellow bell pepper, seeded, ribs removed, and cut into thin strips
- 1 red onion, peeled and thinly sliced
- 2 large carrots, peeled and thinly sliced on an angle
- 2 cups trimmed and sliced small white mushroom caps
- 1 medium yellow squash or zucchini, ends removed, cut into evenly sized 2-inch strips, ¼ inch thick
- ¼ pound snow peas, ends removed, shredded lengthwise
- ½ cup bean sprouts
- One 8-ounce jar black bean sauce
- 2 tablespoons chopped fresh cilantro
- Salt and pepper

Vegetable Stir-Fry with Black Bean Sauce

When it's you against the takeout menu, you have the clear edge with this quick and nutritious recipe. Lower in salt and fat than your typical Chinese takeout, fresh ingredients will really make the difference here. Add in sautéed chicken or beef strips or even cooked, peeled shrimp for extra heartiness. Be attentive to your vegetables while cooking—they should be crunchy, well seasoned, and tasty (but not overcooked or soggy).

1. Fill the stockpot ¾ full with water and bring to a boil. Cook noodles according to package directions and drain in the colander. While noodles are cooking, prepare the vegetables.

2. Blanch (page xxiii) the broccoli and chill in ice water. Set aside to drain until ready to use.

3. Set the fry pan or wok over high heat and add the oil. Add the red and yellow peppers, onion, and carrots, and stir-fry for about 4 minutes, until golden brown.

4. Stir in the mushrooms, squash, snow peas, and bean sprouts and continue to cook over high heat for 1 to 2 minutes, until golden brown. Add the broccoli, then the black bean sauce, and mix until all ingredients are well combined. Reduce the heat to medium-high and cook for 2 minutes while stirring.

5. Remove from the heat and toss in the cilantro. Add salt and pepper to season and mix well. To serve, spoon the vegetables and sauce over the cooked noodles.

PREP

STEP 4

STEP 5

LEVEL

SERVES 4
PREP TIME 15 minutes
MARINATING TIME
20 minutes to 1 hour
COOK TIME 20 minutes

Gear

- Cutting board
- Chef's knife
- Paring knife
- Box grater
- 2 bowls (1 small, 1 large)
- 8-quart stockpot
- Colander
- Large nonstick fry pan or wok
- Medium spatula
- Tongs

Ingredients

CHICKEN

- 3 large boneless, skinless chicken breast halves (about 1 pound)
- ¾ cup Teriyaki Sauce (page 52) or store-bought
- 2 tablespoons sesame oil
- 1 large carrot, peeled and cut into strips
- 1 small red onion (or ½ large), peeled and grated into shards (sharp, 2-inch slices)
- ½ red bell pepper, trimmed, seeded, ribs removed, diced
- ½ green bell pepper, trimmed, seeded, ribs removed, diced
- ½ yellow bell pepper, trimmed, seeded, ribs removed, diced
- ¼ pound bean sprouts
- ¼ pound shiitake mushrooms, stems removed, trimmed, and quartered

(continues)

Sesame Noodles with Teriyaki Chicken

This easy-to-do take on stir-fry is a snap to cook, hard to mess up, and results in a delicious, satisfying meal (not to mention light and healthy). Try replacing the chicken with strips of beef or pork, or ready-to-cook shrimp. It's great for lunch the next day, so consider making extra.

1. Slice the chicken lengthwise into strips about ½ inch wide and 2 inches long. In the small bowl, marinate the strips in ½ of the teriyaki sauce, covered for 1 hour in the refrigerator.

2. While the chicken is marinating, fill the stockpot with water and bring to a boil. Add 1 tablespoon salt and the noodles, and cook for 3 to 4 minutes depending on thickness, following directions on package. Drain the noodles in the colander in the sink.

3. Transfer the noodles to the large bowl, toss with the sesame oil, sesame seeds, soy sauce, and 2 tablespoons of the chopped cilantro.

4. In the fry pan or wok set over medium-high heat, heat 2 tablespoons sesame oil and stir-fry the chicken strips, about 5 minutes (first drain off marinade and discard). Add the carrots, onions, peppers, and bean sprouts and stir-fry for 3 minutes. Add the mushrooms and sugar snaps. Continuing to stir, add in remaining teriyaki sauce, cook another 5 minutes. Set aside.

5. Toss the remainder of the cilantro with the chicken and vegetables and pour over the noodles. Mix well with tongs. Garnish with sliced scallions or fresh cilantro, if using, and serve immediately.

continues

PREP

STEP 1

STEP 5

Ingredients (cont'd)

- ¼ pound sugar snap peas, ends trimmed, sliced into strips
- Optional: 3 scallions, trimmed and sliced; fresh cilantro sprigs

NOODLES

- 1 teaspoon salt
- 2 tablespoons sesame oil
- 1 tablespoon soy sauce
- 2 tablespoons black sesame seeds or regular sesame seeds
- ¼ cup chopped fresh cilantro leaves
- 1 pound long, thin noodles (rice noodles, thin spaghetti, soba noodles—your choice)

MAKE YOUR OWN . . .

Teriyaki Sauce

GEAR

Microplane grater
Small saucepan
Blender

INGREDIENTS

1 cup soy sauce
3 tablespoons light brown sugar
3 cloves garlic, peeled, crushed, and minced
¼ cup sesame oil
2 tablespoons grated fresh ginger
2 tablespoons cornstarch dissolved
 in ¼ cup cold water

Juice of 1 small orange
⅓ cup honey
3 tablespoons black sesame seeds
Optional: chili oil

1 Combine the soy sauce, sugar, garlic, sesame oil, and ginger in the small saucepan over medium-high heat. When it comes to a boil, whisk in the dissolved cornstarch and return to a boil for approximately 45 seconds, until it thickens. (Don't worry if liquid appears too thick.) Remove from the heat. When cooled, transfer to the blender.

2 Add the orange juice and honey and pulse all together for 1 minute.

3 Add the sesame seeds. For added spice, mix in chili oil to taste.

SERVES 4
PREP TIME 10 minutes
COOK TIME 25 minutes

Gear

- Cutting board
- Chef's knife
- Nonstick fry pan
- Tongs
- Baking sheet
- Silicone mixing spatula
- Whisk
- Small ladle or serving spoon

Ingredients

- 1 tablespoon olive oil
- 4 large boneless, skinless chicken breast halves (about 1⅓ pounds)
- ½ pound white mushrooms, finely sliced
- ¼ cup white wine
- 1 cup heavy cream
- 1 cup White Sauce (page 48)
- Salt and pepper
- 2 tablespoons chopped fresh tarragon leaves

Pan-Fried Chicken Breasts

Chicken breasts are one of the most versatile ingredients in the kitchen, and knowing how to prepare them is an important basic skill every cook needs to know. Chicken breasts, no matter how they're prepared, are a great go-to dish for quick and simple meals.

1. Preheat the oven to 375°F. Place the fry pan over high heat and add the olive oil. Pan-fry (page xxiv) the chicken breasts until golden brown, about 2½ minutes on each side. Transfer the chicken to the baking sheet and bake in the oven for 20 minutes.

2. While the chicken is in the oven, lower the heat under the fry pan to medium-high. Add the mushrooms and sauté (page xxiv) for 3 to 4 minutes, until golden brown.

3. Add the white wine to the pan, use whisk to deglaze (pages xxiv–xxv), or mix it well with the cooking residue.

4. Stir in the cream and white sauce and bring mixture back to a boil, whisking continuously. Reduce the heat and simmer (page xxiii) for 5 minutes, until you have a mushroom-colored cream sauce. Add salt and pepper to season.

5. To serve, remove chicken breasts from oven and arrange on platter. Stir ¾ of the chopped tarragon into the sauce just before serving and ladle sauce over chicken. Garnish with the remaining of chopped tarragon.

STEP 3

STEP 5 (A)

STEP 5 (B)

LEVEL

SERVES 4
PREP TIME 20 minutes
COOK TIME 20 minutes

Gear

- Cutting board
- Chef's knife
- Paring knife
- Nonstick fry pan
- Wooden spoon
- Small bowl

Ingredients

FILLING

- 2 tablespoons olive oil
- For Chicken: 3 boneless, skinless chicken breast halves, cut into strips
- For Beef: 1 pound sirloin steak, trimmed and cut into thin strips
- For Shrimp: 1 pound medium shrimp, peeled and deveined
- 1 red bell pepper, trimmed, seeded, ribs removed, and cut into strips
- 1 yellow bell pepper, trimmed, seeded, ribs removed, and cut into strips
- 1 red onion, peeled and cut into matchsticks
- 6 medium white mushrooms, trimmed and sliced
- One 1.25-ounce packet fajita seasoning
- ½ cup hot water

FAJITAS

- 12 small flour tortillas
- Optional add-ins: ½ head iceberg lettuce, shredded; ½ cup sour cream; 1 cup Guacamole (page 35); Fresh Salsa (page 34); or grated cheddar and Jack cheese

Fajitas with Chicken, Beef, or Shrimp

Use fresh ingredients and these fajitas will be miles ahead of those at your local Mexican restaurant. At your next get-together, create a do-it-yourself fajita station by serving all the ingredients in separate small bowls.

1. Set the fry pan over medium-high heat for chicken or shrimp, or high heat for beef, and add the olive oil. When hot*, add the chicken, beef, or shrimp.

2. Using tongs, cook for about 3 minutes on each side for shrimp or 4 minutes on each side for chicken or beef, turning when underside is golden brown. Remove from pan and set aside. Add the red and yellow peppers, onions, and mushrooms. Turn up the heat to high and cook, stirring continuously, for 5 minutes.

3. In the small bowl, mix the fajita seasoning with the hot water and add to the fry pan. Stir well and cook for 5 minutes more. To serve, arrange flour tortillas on a platter or individual plates. Scoop topping onto center of each tortilla, and top with add-ins as preferred.

*Is your pan hot enough? Test it with a drop of water. If it sizzles, you're ready to cook.

CHICKEN

BEEF

SHRIMP

② ③

LEVEL

SERVES 4
PREP TIME 15 minutes
COOK TIME 10 to 15 minutes

Gear

- Cutting board
- Chef's knife
- Optional: boning knife
- Plastic wrap
- Rolling pin or meat mallet
- Regular (not nonstick) or cast-iron fry pan
- Optional: baking sheet

Ingredients

- Four 8- to 10-ounce boneless NY strip steaks (or cut of choice), cut 1-inch thick
- 1 tablespoon olive oil
- Salt and pepper

Kitchen FYI

• Don't season your steak too early, or the salt will start to extract juice from the meat; always season as it is going in the pan.

• For a really thick cut (2 inches or more), brown the sides as well.

Steak, Four Ways

Cooking steak is like driving a car: Once you learn to drive one, you can drive them all. The cut and the quality of the meat will affect the outcome, but the cooking principals are the same. And with these tips, you can make any good steak . . . *great!*

SIMPLE STEAK

① Leave steak out at room temperature. (Meat should be almost at room temperature just prior to cooking.) Trim fat from the steak by sliding the blade of a sharp knife between the fat and the meat. Gently slide blade away from the meat, remove fat, and discard.

② Coat the steak with a thin film of olive oil. Liberally season on both sides with salt and pepper. (Don't forget to wash your hands before and after!)

③ Place the fry pan over high heat. When hot*, cook the steak without moving it until browned on the bottom, about 5 minutes. Turn the steak over and lower the heat to medium. Cook for 3 minutes more or until done to your liking (see Four-Finger Firmness Guide, page xxvi). Remove from heat and let steak sit for 5 minutes so juices set, then serve.

Is your pan hot enough? Test it with a drop of water. If it sizzles, you're ready to cook.

continues

 STEP 1

 STEP 2

STEP 3

Ingredients

- Four 8- to 10-ounce boneless NY strip steaks (or cut of choice), cut 1 inch thick
- 1 tablespoon of olive oil
- Salt and pepper

FIRST-RATE MINUTE STEAK

A minute steak is a very thin cut of meat prepared in a short amount of time. It is usually made with beef round steak, but you can use almost any cut of meat, including filet mignon, NY strip, or rib eye; just make sure the meat is sliced *thin*.

STEP 1

1. Leave steak out at room temperature. Trim fat from the steak by sliding the blade of a sharp knife between the fat and the meat. Gently slide blade away from the meat, remove fat, and discard. Cover the meat with plastic wrap and pound with a rolling pin or meat mallet until about ½ inch thick or less. Season with salt and pepper.

2. Place the fry pan over high heat. When hot*, add 1 teaspoon vegetable oil and heat until oil is rippling (but not smoking). Gently add steak and fry for 1 minute on each side. Remove from heat and let steak sit for 5 minutes so juices set, then serve.

Ingredients

GARLIC BUTTER STEAK

- Four 8- to 10-ounce boneless NY strip steaks (or cut of choice), cut 1 inch thick
- 12 tablespoons (1½ sticks) salted butter
- 1½ teaspoons crushed garlic
- 1 tablespoon chopped flat-leaf parsley
- Salt and pepper

(continues)

GARLIC BUTTER STEAK

Dress up your steak by adding this flavorful sauce. Store leftover sauce covered in the refrigerator for up to 3 days.

1. Leave steak out at room temperature. Trim fat from the steak by sliding the blade of a sharp knife between the fat and the meat. Gently slide blade away from the meat, remove fat, and discard.

2. In a small bowl, mix together the butter, garlic, and parsley. Season with salt and pepper. Set aside while you cook the steak.

3. Coat the steak with a thin film of olive oil. Liberally season on both sides with salt and pepper.

4. Place the fry pan over high heat. When hot*, cook the steak without moving it until browned on the bottom, about 5 minutes. Turn steak over and lower the heat to medium. Cook for 3 minutes more or until done to your liking (see Four-Finger Firmness Guide, page xxvi). Remove from heat and let steak sit for 5 minutes so juices set. Allow 1 tablespoon garlic butter to melt on top of each steak.

Is your pan hot enough? Test it with a drop of water. If it sizzles, you're ready to cook.

Ingredients (cont'd)

STEAK WITH GREEN PEPPERCORN SAUCE

- Four 8- to 10-ounce center-cut filets mignons
- Kosher salt
- Olive oil to coat the steaks, plus 1 tablespoon for sauce
- ½ medium onion, peeled and finely diced
- 1 tablespoon cracked black pepper
- ¼ cup red wine
- ½ cup of store-bought brown gravy
- ½ cup heavy cream
- 2 tablespoons green peppercorns (drained if in brine)
- Pepper

STEAK WITH GREEN PEPPERCORN SAUCE

Green peppercorns are milder than black pepper, but stronger in flavor than pink, so they give steak a great kick.

STEP 2

(1) Preheat the oven to 375°F. Sprinkle the steaks with kosher salt and drizzle oil on both sides. In the fry pan set over high heat, fry steak until edges are well-seared (page xxiv), about 5 minutes on each side. When the steaks are brown on top, bottom, and sides, remove from the fry pan, place onto baking sheet, and transfer to oven to finish cooking according to the chart below for your preferred texture.

(2) While steak is cooking in the oven, make the sauce. Add 1 tablespoon olive oil and the diced onion to fry pan. Cook for 3 minutes, until onion is translucent and begins to brown. Add the black pepper and fry for 2 minutes, until you smell a peppery aroma. Add the red wine and stir to deglaze (pages xxiv–xxv). Add the gravy and cream and bring to a boil. Add the green peppercorns and season with salt and pepper.

(3) Remove the steaks from the oven and serve with sauce drizzled on top.

HOW DO YOU LIKE YOUR STEAK?

Use this chart to help determine how many minutes your steak should cook in the oven after searing.*

STEAK SIZE	TO COOK RARE	TO COOK MEDIUM-RARE	TO COOK MEDIUM-WELL	TO COOK WELL DONE
Filet mignon, 10 ounces	10 to 12 minutes	12 to 15 minutes	18 to 22 minutes	25 minutes

*Times apply to 375°F oven after searing/sealing in pan until brown on both sides.

SERVES 4
PREP TIME 10 minutes
COOK TIME 15 minutes

Gear

- Cutting board
- Chef's knife
- Fry pan
- Tongs
- Roasting pan or baking sheet
- Medium spatula

Ingredients

- 4 thick-cut pork chops
- Salt and pepper
- 1 tablespoon olive oil
- 1 teaspoon fresh thyme leaves, chopped
- 2 cups applesauce (jarred is fine)
- Optional: ½ cup homemade Chicken Stock (page 97), or store-bought, or ½ boullion cube dissolved in hot water)

How Do I . . . ?

To check doneness, look near the bone for best results. Make a small slice with the tip of your knife or use an instant-read thermometer (see page xxvii). When you make a cut, the juices of the meat should run clear.

Pork Chops

On a cold and damp evening, nothing warms you up like Irish pub chops and a pint of ale. Though they're just as good for a summer dinner (cook on the grill and serve with a fresh salad), pork chops and applesauce remind me of home, no matter when and where I have them.

① Preheat the oven to 375°F. Coat the pork chops with salt, pepper, and olive oil.

② Place the fry pan over medium heat. When hot*, sear (page xxiv) the chops without moving until they are golden brown on the bottom.

③ Turn the chops, sprinkle with thyme, and transfer to the roasting pan. Bake for 15 minutes. After 15 minutes, lower the oven heat to 225°F to keep chops warm until ready to serve.

④ To serve, transfer chops from the oven to a platter or individual plates. Add the chicken stock to the pan to deglaze (pages xxiv–xxv). Scrape the browned bits from the bottom of the pan into the stock and pour over the chops. Serve with applesauce on the side.

Broiled Pork Chops   These chops can also be cooked under the broiler, without the use of searing. Just keep an eye on them as they cook so they don't burn or dry out. Instead of using applesauce, simply peel and slice a couple of apples and place them under or around the chops in the roasting pan.

Is your pan hot enough? Test it with a drop of water. If it sizzles, you're ready to cook.

PREP

STEP 1

STEP 3

SERVES 4 (PLUS LEFTOVERS)
PREP TIME 20 minutes
COOK TIME 25 minutes

Gear

- Large bowl
- Cutting board
- Chef's knife
- Nonstick fry pan
- Tongs
- Optional: instant-read thermometer
- Large saucepan
- Slotted spoon

Ingredients

- 2 pounds ground beef or ground turkey, or use a mix of beef, veal, and pork
- 1 large onion, peeled and finely diced (about 1 cup)
- 3 cloves garlic, peeled, crushed, and minced (about 1½ tablespoons)
- 2 tablespoons chopped fresh flat-leaf parsley
- 1 egg
- ½ cup Bread Crumbs (page 40)
- 3 tablespoons ketchup
- 1 tablespoon Worcestershire sauce
- 1 teaspoon kosher salt
- Pepper
- 2 shakes of seasoning salt (such as Lawry's)
- 1 cup corn oil
- 2 cups Basic Basics Tomato Sauce (page 41)
- 1 pound of pasta, cooked (see page 41), tossed with 1 tablespoon butter instead of olive oil, and seasoned with salt and pepper; or 4 hoagie or hero rolls, toasted and lightly buttered

Meatballs

Meatballs can be made large to serve with tomato sauce over pasta, or small to toss in sauce and serve on a toasted hoagie roll. Serve extra-small ones on toothpicks as a hearty appetizer. The secret to simple meatballs is keeping your hands moist so that the meat doesn't stick.

1. Break up the ground beef with your hands in the large bowl. Gently mix in the onion, garlic, parsley, egg, and bread crumbs. Knead in the ketchup, Worcestershire sauce, salt, pepper, and seasoning salt until well incorporated into one big ball.

2. Use your hands to divide mixture and form individual evenly sized meatballs, making them as large or small as you prefer. Set aside.

3. Place the fry pan over medium-high heat. When hot*, add the oil. Using tongs, gently place the meatballs in the pan one at a time, as space allows, taking care not to splash hot oil.

4. Fry on each side for 3 to 4 minutes, until crisp and deep brown in color. Continue until all meatballs are browned, and set aside. Repeat with remaining meatballs in batches. Set meatballs aside while you prepare the sauce.

5. Place the large saucepan over medium-high heat and add the tomato sauce. Warm sauce until simmering (page xxiii). Using the slotted spoon, transfer the meatballs to the sauce and cook for 5 minutes. Remove meatballs using slotted spoon and serve with sauce over a bowl of your favorite pasta, or on a toasted bun for a meatball sandwich.

Is your pan hot enough? Test it with a drop of water. If it sizzles, you're ready to cook.

STEP 2

STEP 4

STEP 5

SERVES 4

PREP TIME 10 minutes, plus 30 to 40 minutes refrigeration

COOK TIME 10 minutes

Gear

- Cutting board
- Chef's knife
- Paring knife
- Medium bowl
- Disposable kitchen gloves (optional)
- Plate
- Wide spatula
- Large nonstick fry pan

Ingredients

- 2 pounds ground beef (ground chuck for meatier flavor or lean ground sirloin for a less fatty alternative)
- 5 tablespoons ketchup
- ½ large red onion, peeled and finely diced
- 2 cloves garlic, peeled, crushed, and minced
- 2 teaspoons Worcestershire sauce
- ¼ teaspoon kosher salt
- Pepper
- Optional: 3 tablespoons vegetable oil
- 4 burger buns
- 1 large beefsteak tomato, ends discarded, thinly sliced
- 4 large lettuce leaves

(continues)

Hamburger Deluxe

What makes a truly great burger is simple: juicy, well-seasoned meat, a fresh toasted bun, and any topping you prefer. You can use this same method when serving premade veggie burgers, or substitute ground turkey or lamb for the beef.

1. Place the ground beef, ketchup, onion, garlic, and Worcestershire sauce in the medium bowl. Combine with clean hands (or use gloves), using a scrunching motion so the meat will absorb the seasonings. Add the salt and pepper and mix well.

2. Divide mixture in four and mold into balls about the size of your fist. Press each into 4½-inch diameter patties with the palms of your hands. Place burgers on the plate, wrap with plastic, and store in the fridge for 30 to 40 minutes to set.

3. Place the fry pan over high heat. When hot*, add oil, if using, and, using the spatula, gently place the burgers in the pan. Cook for 2 minutes, then reduce heat to medium. Cook for 2 to 3 minutes more, or until underside is dark brown. Using spatula, gently flip burgers over and cook other side until dark brown, about 3 to 5 minutes. Test doneness (see Four-Finger Firmness Guide, page xxvi).

STEP 2

STEP 3

STEP 5

Ingredients (cont'd)

- Optional add-ins: 4 slices cheese (cheddar, or as you prefer); 1 large red onion, peeled, sliced ⅓ inch thick, brushed with olive oil, and grilled or sautéed; 8 large white mushrooms, sliced ⅓ inch thick, brushed with olive oil, and grilled or sautéed; 8 slices bacon, cooked crisp (see page 12); 1 avocado, pitted, peeled, and sliced; mayonnaise, ketchup, pickles, or other condiments as desired

Kitchen FYI

Only cooking for one or two? Wrap the extra uncooked burgers in wax paper, place in a resealable plastic bag, and freeze until ready to use. Always remember to mark the date on the plastic bag, so you know how long your food has been frozen.

④ While burgers are cooking, toast the buns: Preheat the broiler. Place the buns open faced on the rack (or use a toaster oven) and toast until golden brown. Watch carefully to keep from burning. Carefully remove the buns and set aside.

⑤ To serve, use the spatula to gently slide a burger on each bun. Add a slice of cheese, if desired; top with tomato slices, lettuce, and other add-ins as preferred.

Is your pan hot enough? Test it with a drop of water. If it sizzles, you're ready to cook.

BURGER COOKING ALTERNATIVES

On the Grill—Use the same method of cooking (4 to 5 minutes on each side, flipping only once) but pay careful attention to the varying heat given off by outdoor grills. Add 2 minutes to each side with a small grill with low heat, subtract 1 minute for each side for a hot gas or charcoal grill that's flaming.

Under the Broiler—Place the patties on a baking sheet (or slotted broiling pan), and place directly under a broiler (closer than 3 inches) until top is dark brown, about 5 minutes. Flip and cook for 3 more minutes. Turn off the broiler and place cheese on top to melt (if using) for a minute prior to serving.

SIDES FOR YOUR BURGER

Coleslaw (page 30)—A classic accompaniment to serve with any grilled fare.

Baked Potato (page 73) or **Twice-Baked Potato** (page 135) or **Roasted Potato Slices** (page 71)—Burgers and potatoes (whether baked or cut into fries) are the ultimate combination.

Corn on the Cob (page 138)—The fresher the better. Break in half, toss with melted butter, and sprinkle with a bit of kosher salt or grated Parmesan cheese.

SERVES 4 (PLUS LEFTOVERS)
PREP TIME 20 minutes
COOK TIME 1½ hours

Gear

- Cutting board
- Chef's knife
- Paring knife
- Vegetable peeler
- Food processor
- Optional: 1 medium bowl
- Large bowl
- Roasting pan or baking sheet
- Timer
- Instant-read thermometer
- Small saucepan
- Aluminum foil

Ingredients

MEATLOAF

- 2 carrots, peeled and diced
- 3 stalks celery, peeled (use a vegetable peeler to remove stringy exterior) and coarsely chopped
- 1 clove garlic, peeled, crushed, and minced
- 1 large yellow onion, peeled and coarsely chopped
- 6 large white mushrooms (about 4 ounces), trimmed and coarsely chopped
- 1 egg
- 2 pounds ground beef (chuck is heartier than sirloin; or use ½ pound each of ground pork and veal and 1 pound ground beef)
- 5 tablespoons ketchup
- 3 tablespoons Worcestershire sauce

(continues)

Rustic Meatloaf

This recipe is all about the prep: Preheat your oven; mix everything together, put it in the oven, and then just wait until the timer goes off. It's easy to adjust this recipe to make it your own—add stuff that you like or remove ingredients that you don't. This recipe is sure to become a classic in your cooking repertoire.

1. Preheat the oven to 350°F. In the food processor, pulse the carrots, celery, and garlic for 1 minute; add the onions and pulse for 30 seconds; add the mushrooms and pulse for 30 seconds. (If you are using a mini food processor, pulse one vegetable at a time, then combine all together in a medium bowl.) Process until you have a very small dice.

2. In the large bowl, beat the egg with a fork. Add the ground meat, veggies, ketchup, Worcestershire, mustard, salt, and pepper. Combine using your hands, adding the bread crumbs little by little. (Don't overwork the meat

STEP 2 (A)

STEP 2 (B)

STEP 2 (C)

Ingredients (cont'd)

- 2 tablespoons Dijon mustard
- 2 tablespoons kosher salt
- Pepper
- ½ cup Bread Crumbs (page 48)

GRAVY

- ½ cup store-bought brown gravy
- Salt and pepper

or it will be too dense and tough.) Mold the mixture into one large loaf (about the size of a loaf pan) and place it in the roasting pan. Sprinkle with a few drops of water. Add salt and pepper to season.

③ Bake the meatloaf for about 1½ hours or until an instant-read thermometer reads 180°F and top and sides are brown. (Or make a discreet cut in the middle to view the color—it should be brown, *not* pink, in the center.) If meat is still not cooked, turn up heat to 425°F and bake for 8 to 10 minutes more. Remove pan from oven, set aside on a heat-resistant surface, and let the meatloaf rest for 5 minutes under foil.

④ While meatloaf rests, make the gravy. Measure the pan juices for the gravy; if you don't have enough liquid as directed, whisk in enough water to create about ½ cup of juices. Incorporate any browned bits.

⑤ In the small saucepan, combine the brown gravy and the pan juices. Stir together over medium heat until thick. Taste and add salt and pepper to season.

⑥ To serve, slice the meatloaf into 1-inch-thick pieces; top with the gravy or serve it on the side.

SERVES 4
PREP TIME 12 minutes
COOK TIME 30 minutes

Gear

- Cutting board
- Chef's knife
- 3-quart saucepan
- Wooden spoon

Ingredients

- ½ teaspoon chili powder
- ½ teaspoon ground cumin
- ½ teaspoon ground coriander
- 2½ cups Meat Sauce (page 42)
- One 15- to 15.5-ounce can red kidney beans, drained
- Optional add-ins: 1 cup grated cheddar cheese; ½ medium white onion, peeled and finely chopped; 1 tomato, diced; ½ cup sour cream; ¼ cup chopped fresh cilantro or flat-leaf parsley (for garnish)

Quick Chili

This chili is a terrific use for extra meat sauce: It's fast and hearty—and a great way to get all your major food groups in a single dish. Like the meat sauce, it tastes even better the next day. Try serving it over Boiled Long-Grain White Rice (page 74) for added texture and flavor.

① In the saucepan set over low heat, toast the chili powder, cumin, and coriander for 1 to 2 minutes.

② Add the meat sauce and beans and increase the heat to medium-high. Stir well until simmering (page xxiii), then turn down to medium heat and cook for about 20 minutes, stirring continuously. If the chili thickens too much, stir in ¼ cup water.

③ To serve, spoon the chili into bowls and top with grated cheese, chopped onions, fresh tomato, and/or sour cream, as preferred. Garnish with cilantro or parsley, if you like.

STEP 2

STEP 3

STEP 3

SERVES 4
PREP TIME   10 minutes
MARINATING TIME
  20 minutes
  (for grilled version only)
COOK TIME   10 minutes

Gear

- Cutting board
- Chef's knife
- Microplane grater
- Juicer
- Large fry pan or outdoor grill
- Tongs
- Wooden or metal skewers
  (if grilling on wooden skewers,
  soak them in water for
  30 minutes prior to using)

Ingredients

- 16 jumbo shrimp, peeled and deveined
- 2 tablespoons olive oil
- 2 cloves garlic, peeled, crushed, and minced
- 8 tablespoons (1 stick) butter, diced
- Juice and grated peel of 1 lemon (about ¼ cup juice)
- 2 tablespoons chopped fresh tarragon
- Salt and pepper

Jumbo Shrimp with Lemon, Garlic, and Tarragon

This is a quick and easy dish that embodies the fresh flavors of summer. As an alternative to the pan-fried version found here, try grilling the shrimp instead, then toss them with the fresh lemon juice, minced garlic, and chopped fresh tarragon and olive oil.

① Slide shrimp onto skewers. Place the fry pan over high heat. When hot*, add the olive oil and place skewers one at a time in the pan, as space allows. Pan-fry (page xxiv) for 3 minutes or until shrimp turns slightly pink.

② Using tongs, gently turn over shrimp skewers. Add the garlic and cook for 3 more minutes or until shrimp turn white with pink edges.

③ Keeping shrimp in the pan, stir in the butter. When it starts to foam, add the lemon juice and grated peel. Stir in the tarragon. Using tongs, turn shrimp skewers over to coat with sauce. Remove skewers from heat. Add salt and pepper to season and serve immediately.

*Is your pan hot enough? Test it with a drop of water. If it sizzles, you're ready to cook.

HOW TO COOK TENDER SHRIMP

The best way to keep shrimp tender is to pan-fry until golden brown over consistent heat, toss with butter, then serve immediately. Avoid:

- Cooking for more than 3 minutes per side or shrimp will be overcooked and chewy.
- A grill or pan that is too cool, as slow cooking toughens the shrimp.
- Cooking ahead of time— shrimp gets tougher the longer it sits around.

PREP

STEP 1

STEP 2

SERVES 4
PREP TIME   10 minutes
COOK TIME   12 minutes

Gear

- Cutting board
- Chef's knife
- Baking sheet
- Small bowl
- Large nonstick fry pan
- Wide spatula
- Wooden spoon

Ingredients

- 8 tablespoons (1 stick) butter, plus extra for the baking sheet
- Four 6-ounce sole fillets
- ¼ cup all-purpose flour
- 1 tablespoon olive oil
- ½ small jar of capers, drained
- Juice of 1 lemon (about ⅓ cup)
- Kosher salt
- White pepper
- 1 tablespoon chopped fresh flat-leaf parsley

Sole with Capers and Lemon

If you are afraid to cook fish, here is a recipe that will change your mind. Fish is not as fragile as you might think. The most important tools you'll need are a nonstick pan and a wide spatula. With these tools, this simple recipe, and a little patience, you'll definitely succeed.

1. Preheat the oven to 375°F. Lightly butter a baking sheet. In the small bowl, combine the flour and a pinch each of salt and pepper. Toss until well-combined.

2. Fold each sole fillet in half lengthwise. Sprinkle the seasoned flour on the outside of each fillet until covered.

3. Place the fry pan over medium-high heat. When hot*, add the olive oil. Fry the fillets for 2 minutes on the floured side only until golden brown (do not flip). Using the wide spatula, carefully lift the fillets onto the baking sheet, browned side up, transfer baking sheet to the oven, and bake for 8 minutes.

4. While the fish is in the oven, make the sauce. Do not rinse fry pan. Add the butter to the pan and heat for about 2 minutes, until the butter foams, froths, and turns golden brown.

5. Stir in the capers, wait 30 seconds, and add ½ of the lemon juice. Taste (check for a pleasing acidity), then add more if needed. Season with salt, pepper, and some of the parsley, then remove pan from heat. Do not let the sauce sit or it will become too acidic and discolor the parsley.

STEP 2

STEP 3

STEP 4

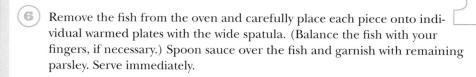

(6) Remove the fish from the oven and carefully place each piece onto individual warmed plates with the wide spatula. (Balance the fish with your fingers, if necessary.) Spoon sauce over the fish and garnish with remaining parsley. Serve immediately.

Is your pan hot enough? Test with a drop of water. If it sizzles, you're ready to cook. Fish will stick to a too-cold pan, so be sure you don't put the fish on too soon.

FISH FRYING RULES

You can use this recipe for almost any white, flaky fish like halibut, fluke, flounder, or tilapia, but you'll need to experiment with different types to gauge their "fall-apart" factor. The best way to avoid this is to pan-fry (page xxiv) your fish until golden, then finish cooking in the oven. Follow these three simple instructions to avoid having your fish break apart while cooking:

- **Support Your Fish:** Be sure to use a sturdy, wide spatula big enough to fit completely under the fish for extra support.
- **Start in the Pan:** Lightly cook your fish in the pan until golden, but do not cook it all the way through. This will keep the fish intact as you carefully transfer it to a baking sheet, ready for the oven.
- **Finish in the Oven:** Finish fish in a preheated oven. When done, gently transfer it to the plate, being careful not to break it apart.

LEVEL

SERVES 4
PREP TIME 20 minutes
COOK TIME 25 minutes
ASSEMBLY 10 minutes

Gear

- Chef's knife
- Cutting board
- Bowls (1 small, 1 medium)
- Small saucepan with lid
- Nonstick fry pan
- Silicone mixing spatula
- Ovenproof platter

Ingredients

FISH

- 1½ pounds white fish fillets (flounder, tilapia, cod, or halibut), skin and bones removed, cut into 1-inch cubes
- ½ teaspoon salt
- Pepper
- Pinch each of ground coriander, cayenne pepper, and smoked paprika
- 1 tablespoon all-purpose flour
- 1 tablespoon olive oil

BLACK BEANS

- ½ medium red onion, peeled and diced
- 1 clove garlic, peeled, crushed, and minced
- 1 tablespoon olive oil
- One 15- to 15.5-ounce can black beans, drained
- 1 tablespoon ketchup
- 1½ teaspoons light brown sugar
- Pinch of red pepper flakes
- 1 tablespoon white vermouth or beer

(continues)

Fish Tacos

The best thing about tacos is the versatility: You can add or subtract ingredients as you wish. I prefer to use soft tacos, so they wrap completely around the filling, but hard taco shells work just as well. Try filling your tacos with shrimp, scallops, or even leftover fillet of sole. With wholesome ingredients, this dish really can't go wrong. *¡Cerveza, por favor!*

① Preheat the oven to 250°F. Toss fish in the medium bowl with the salt, pepper, spices, and flour. Refrigerate until ready to cook.

② In the small saucepan over medium heat, sweat (page xxiv) the onions and garlic in the olive oil. Add the beans, ketchup, brown sugar, red pepper flakes, and white vermouth or beer. Turn down the heat and simmer (page xxiii) for 10 minutes.

③ Place the fry pan over medium-high heat. When hot*, add olive oil. Gently swish oil around pan for 2 to 3 minutes, or until a film-like base forms. Place fish in pan and fry, stirring gently with the spatula, for about 5 minutes or until golden brown.

④ Remove fish from the heat and place on an ovenproof platter. Leave platter uncovered and place it in the oven to keep warm until you're ready to assemble your tacos.

STEP 2

STEP 5

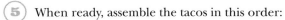

Ingredients (cont'd)

TORTILLAS AND FILLING

- 8 small soft flour or corn tortillas, warmed
- ½ cup sour cream
- ½ cup grated cheddar cheese
- ½ cup grated Monterey Jack cheese
- 1½ cups Fresh Salsa (page 34) or store-bought mango salsa
- ½ head lettuce (iceberg or green leaf), coarsely chopped
- 1 large ripe tomato, diced
- 1 ripe avocado, pitted, peeled, and diced
- ½ cup chopped fresh cilantro
- Optional add-ins: Boiled Long-Grain White Rice (page 74); hot sauce
- 2 limes, ends removed, each cut into 8 wedges

⑤ When ready, assemble the tacos in this order:

a. Lay out warm soft tortillas as space allows.

b. Spread a thin coat of sour cream on each tortilla. (If using hard taco shells, simply spoon in ingredients evenly.)

c. Divide the fish equally among the tortillas.

d. Add a spoonful of black beans and rice, if using.

e. Sprinkle each taco with cheddar and Jack cheeses.

f. Add 1 tablespoon of salsa to each taco.

g. Cover each taco with small handful of lettuce, 1 tablespoon of tomato, and 1 tablespoon of avocado.

h. Top each taco with a generous pinch of fresh cilantro.

i. Squeeze a lime wedge over each taco, fold in half, and serve with more lime on the side. Let each person add hot sauce as desired.

Is your pan hot enough? Test it with a drop of water. If it sizzles, you're ready to cook.

HEATING SOFT TORTILLAS

Here are two easy ways to heat your tortillas. Use either corn or flour tortillas.

1. **In the microwave:** Microwave tortillas for 30 to 45 seconds, remove, and cover with a damp paper towel or foil to keep warm.

2. **In the oven:** Wrap in foil and bake at 300°F for about 5 minutes, until warm to touch.

Simple Sides

Here are some easy sides that are intended to be cooked along with the main courses in this book (which are referenced, when appropriate.) These staples are meant to complement your main dishes and help you create a well-rounded (and well-balanced) meal. And they're tasty enough to enjoy on their own as snacks. Timing-wise, either integrate them into the full plan of your meal, or cook before you begin your main dishes and reheat before serving.

IN THIS CHAPTER

In this chapter, you'll find recipes for:
○ Roasted Potato Slices
○ Roasted Rosemary Potato Wedges
○ Baked Potatoes
○ Boiled Long-Grain White Rice
○ Couscous

And you'll develop the skills and know-how to:
○ Make a homemade version of potato chips
○ Get a perfectly baked potato

LEVEL

SERVES 4
PREP TIME 5 to 10 minutes
COOK TIME 25 minutes

Gear

- Cutting board
- Chef's knife
- Large bowl
- Baking sheet
- Medium spatula

Ingredients

- 4 large Yukon Gold potatoes, washed and dried well
- 1 tablespoon olive oil
- Leaves from 5 sprigs fresh flat-leaf parsley
- Salt and pepper
- Paprika

Roasted Potato Slices

These crispy potatoes make a great side dish for Hamburgers (page 60) or steak. And since there is no deep-frying involved, these are healthier than french fries or potato chips from a bag, and easier to make.

1. Preheat the oven to 425°F. Slice potatoes crosswise, ¼ inch thick (like a thick potato chip). Discard the ends. In the large bowl, lightly toss the pieces with the olive oil to coat.

2. On each slice of potato, place one parsley leaf in the center and flatten; flip each over onto the baking sheet, in one layer. The olive oil should hold the parsley in place. Lightly season the potato slices with salt, pepper, and a pinch of paprika.

3. Bake until golden and soft (test with a fork), about 25 minutes. While the potato slices are baking, chop the remaining parsley leaves.

4. Remove the potatoes from the baking sheet with the spatula and lightly garnish with a handful of chopped parsley leaves.

STEP 1  **STEP 2**  **STEP 4**

Simple Sides **71**

LEVEL ① ② ③

SERVES 4
PREP TIME 10 minutes
COOK TIME 50 minutes

Gear

- Chef's knife
- Cutting board
- Fry pan
- Medium spatula
- Baking sheet

Ingredients

- 6 large Yukon Gold potatoes, washed and dried well
- 2 tablespoons olive oil
- Salt and pepper
- 2 tablespoons chopped fresh rosemary leaves (stems discarded)
- Optional: 2 tablespoons (¼ stick) butter

Roasted Rosemary Potato Wedges

The fresh rosemary adds a fresh and vibrant taste to these everyday roasted wedges. These are great to serve with hamburgers or alongside a lunch omelet. They also make a wonderful (and healthy) snack.

① Preheat the oven to 400°F. Cut each potato in half lengthwise, then slice each half into 3 long wedges.

② Place the fry pan over medium-high heat. When hot*, add the olive oil. Fry the wedges until golden brown, turning them with the spatula, about 5 minutes on each side. Remove from heat and, using the spatula, transfer the wedges to the baking sheet. Season with salt, pepper, and chopped rosemary.

③ Bake wedges for 40 to 50 minutes or until golden brown and fully cooked through (test with a knife; if it slides easily in and out of the wedge, then it's done). If desired, add the butter to the baking sheet and swirl sheet around until the butter has melted and wedges are coated. Remove from heat and serve immediately.

*Is your pan hot enough? Test with a drop of water. If it sizzles, you're ready to cook.

STEP 1

STEP 2

STEP 3

SERVES 4

PREP TIME 5 minutes

COOK TIME 1¼ to 1½ hours

Gear

- Fork
- Aluminum foil
- Paring knife

Ingredients

- 4 equal-size Yukon Gold pota-toes, washed and dried well
- Salt and pepper
- 1 tablespoon (⅛ stick) butter
- Optional add-ins: 4 teaspoons sour cream (1 per potato); chopped fresh chives; ½ cup crumbled bacon; ¼ cup finely shredded cheddar cheese

Baked Potatoes

There's almost nothing simpler than baked potatoes—nor as satisfying. These make a perfect pair with Pork Chops (page 58) or Rustic Meatloaf (page 62), and are super-easy to make. When done, they're good to go with just a little butter, or filled with extra toppings like sour cream, chopped chives, and/or crumbled crisp Bacon (page 13).

1. Preheat the oven to 375°F. Prick each potato using a fork, to release steam while baking. Place each potato on a square piece of foil and add salt and pepper to season. Divide the butter in 4 pats and place one on each potato.

2. Close up the foil and prick foil with a fork, to release steam while baking. Place potatoes directly in the oven and bake for 1¼ to 1½ hours, or until tender. To check doneness, slide a knife into the potato; if it slides through easily, the potatoes are ready; if it is too hard, continue baking until soft.

3. Remove potatoes from the oven, unwrap, and remove from foil. Serve with optional add-ins, if using.

STEP 1

STEP 2

LEVEL

SERVES 4
PREP TIME 5 minutes
COOK TIME 15 minutes

Gear

- Medium saucepan
- Colander or fine-mesh sieve or strainer

Ingredients

- 1 cup rice
- 2 cups water
- 1 tablespoon (⅛ stick) butter
- 1 teaspoon kosher salt

Kitchen FYI

Always remember the ratio is two-to-one (2:1) water to rice, and then a little more water just to be sure.

Boiled Long-Grain White Rice

A staple in many cuisines, rice is the perfect accompaniment to almost any hearty dish. It comes in a number of varieties, from the subtly aromatic jasmine rice to rustic hearty brown or wild rice. Cooking times will vary, so be sure to follow package instructions carefully for the variety you choose.

STEP 2

1. Place the saucepan over medium-high heat. Combine the rice and water in the saucepan, cover, and bring to a boil. Simmer (page xxiii) for 12 to 15 minutes. To test doneness, bite a grain to check if it is cooked; the grains should be firm, but not crunchy.

2. Remove rice from heat. If serving immediately, drain in the colander or strain through a sieve, then return to the saucepan, and mix in butter and salt. If waiting to serve, keep the rice in the pot with the heat off and drain just before serving.

LEVEL

SERVES 4
PREP TIME 5 to 10 minutes
COOK TIME 10 minutes

Gear

- Medium bowl
- Paring knife
- Fry pan
- Large wooden spoon

Ingredients

- 1 cup instant couscous
- 2 tablespoons olive oil
- 2 cups homemade Chicken Stock (page 97) or vegetable stock (canned or boxed), heated in the microwave until boiling
- Salt and pepper
- Optional add-ins: ½ diced red onion; ½ cup diced bell peppers; 6 sliced mushrooms; ½ diced zucchini; 1 clove garlic, crushed; plus 1 tablespoon olive oil (for sautéing)

How Do I . . . ?

To reheat cooled couscous, cover the bowl with a damp paper towel and cook on high for 1 minute in the microwave. Serve immediately.

Couscous

Couscous is made from coarsely ground semolina wheat. Similar to rice, it is a staple in many cuisines, serving as a hearty base to meats and vegetables. For an extra kick, add finely minced vegetables, such as onion and red pepper, sautéed in a touch of olive oil.

(1) In the bowl, mix the couscous and oil with your hands until all the grains are coated.

(2) Pour boiling stock onto couscous, and season with salt and pepper. Cover with plastic wrap and let sit in a warm place for 10 minutes. Remove plastic wrap and toss with a fork to fluff.

(3) Add optional add-ins, if using. Place the small fry pan over medium heat. When hot*, add the olive oil and sauté (page xxiv) each ingredient individually until golden brown. Remove from heat, fold into the finished couscous with the wooden spoon, and serve.

Is your pan hot enough? Test it with a drop of water. If it sizzles, you're ready to cook.

STEP 1

STEP 3

Basic Basics Desserts

Dessert is your fail-safe flourish at the end of an evening. Whether you want a cool treat on a warm summer evening, or freshly baked brownies right from the oven, there's a dessert for almost any occasion.

While baking sometimes requires more precise steps, the key is to learn basic building-block techniques and tips that can help you turn out almost any sweet treat.

More importantly, dessert is meant to be fun. These simple, but delicious recipes are sure to be a hit, no matter when or how they are served.

IN THIS CHAPTER

In this chapter, you'll find recipes for:
O Chocolate Sauce
O Toffee Sauce
O Fresh Fruit with Whipped Cream
O Chocolate Chip Cookies
O Brownies

And you'll develop the skills and know-how to:
O Caramelize sugar
O Make your own homemade whipped cream
O Remove brownies from the pan without breaking

LEVEL

SERVES 4

COOK TIME 7 minutes

Gear

- Small saucepan
- Small whisk

Ingredients

- 1 cup heavy cream
- 1 cup bittersweet chocolate chips (or substitute semisweet)
- 1½ pints vanilla ice cream or sorbet (your choice of flavor)

Chocolate Sauce

Nothing brings on a smile faster than warm melted chocolate over ice cream. This is an easy and impressive sauce; once you make it, you'll never go back to the store-bought version. The higher the quality of chocolate you use, the richer this sauce will be.

1. Place the small saucepan over medium-high heat and bring the cream to a simmer (page xxiii). Reduce the heat slightly and whisk in the chocolate chips until thick and all the chocolate is melted.

2. Remove saucepan from heat and transfer sauce to a heat-resistant bowl. Drizzle over a bowl of ice cream or sorbet and serve immediately.

White Chocolate Sauce Substitute the same quantity of white chocolate chips for a white chocolate sauce. Serve over chocolate or mint chocolate chip ice cream or raspberry sorbet.

STEP 1

STEP 2

LEVEL

SERVES 4

COOK TIME 14 minutes

Gear

- Medium saucepan
- Wooden spoon
- Whisk

Ingredients

- 1 cup sugar
- 8 tablespoons (1 stick) butter
- 1½ cups heavy cream

Kitchen FYI

As sugar melts over high heat, it caramelizes, developing a sticky brown texture with a nutty flavor.

Toffee Sauce

Toffee sauce takes a few minutes longer to cook than chocolate sauce, and it requires a bit more stirring. But it's worth the effort! This sauce pairs wonderfully with vanilla or even chocolate ice cream. Be sure to read the Safety First sidebar before you begin

1. Place the saucepan over high heat. Combine the sugar and butter, *stirring constantly* with the wooden spoon until the sugar and butter are a tan-golden color and the sugar caramelizes, 6 to 8 minutes.

2. Pour in the cream. Using the whisk, mix cream and sugar together in steady, easy movements for about 3 minutes. (The intensity of the heat may cause the sauce to curdle or split, but it won't affect the taste; continue to whisk.)

3. Remove sauce from heat and allow it to cool slightly. Drizzle over a bowl of ice cream and serve while sauce is still warm.

SAFETY FIRST

Read This Before Making Toffee Sauce

While stirring butter and sugar, wrap a dish towel around your stirring hand to protect it from getting hit by "spitting" caramel. It's especially important to have your whisking hand protected when adding cream, as it tends to erupt in the pot.

The first time I made this sauce, I got caramel on my finger, so I put it straight into my mouth and sizzled both my finger *and* my tongue. Lesson learned! I had no fingerprint and a blistered tongue. *Proceed with caution.*

STEP 2

STEP 3

LEVEL

SERVES 4

PREP TIME 15 minutes

Gear

- Cutting board
- Paring knife
- Medium stainless-steel bowl
- Hand-held mixer or whisk

Ingredients

- 1 cup heavy cream
- 1 cup per person fruit in season, cleaned, peeled, and chopped as appropriate

Kitchen FYI

Soft peaks form when cream is whipped vigorously until it turns opaque and starts to hold a shape on its own. Be sure not to whip too much, or cream will start to curdle and turn to butter.

Fresh Fruit with Whipped Cream

Fresh fruit needs little more to accompany it than a dollop of cold, freshly whipped cream. Use fruit that is in season for the best taste and texture. Try serving a bowl of Chocolate Sauce (page 77) along with the whipped cream, or substitute vanilla-flavored mascarpone for the whipped cream, for additional dipping options.

1. Chill an empty stainless-steel bowl in fridge. While the bowl is cooling, prepare the fruit and set aside until ready to use.

2. Pour the cream into the chilled bowl. Using the hand-held mixer or whisk, whip until soft peaks form. Spoon whipped cream over fruit, or serve in a separate bowl.

STEP 2 (A)

STEP 2 (B)

LEVEL

MAKES 36 COOKIES
PREP TIME 10 minutes
COOK TIME 12 to 15 minutes per batch

Gear

- Large bowl
- Electric mixer
- Silicone mixing spatula
- Baking sheet
- Medium spatula
- Wire cooling rack

Ingredients

- 1 cup vegetable oil
- 1 cup light brown sugar
- 1 cup white sugar
- 2 eggs
- 2 cups all-purpose flour
- 1 teaspoon baking soda
- 1 teaspoon salt
- 1 teaspoon vanilla extract
- One 12-ounce bag chocolate chips
- Nonstick cooking spray
- Optional, for serving: vanilla ice cream

Kitchen FYI

• Fresh cookie batter will keep for 4 to 5 days refrigerated in an airtight container.

• Spray baking sheets and dishes with cooking spray over the sink to avoid getting greasy spray on your floor. You don't want any accidents in the kitchen!

Chocolate Chip Cookies

These cookies are a true classic. They won't last long in your house; they never do in mine! Have cold milk ready for dunking, or place a scoop of ice cream between two cookies for a tasty sandwich.

1. Preheat the oven to 350°F. In the large bowl, use an electric mixer to blend oil, brown sugar, white sugar, and eggs until well combined. Add the flour, baking soda, salt, vanilla, and chocolate chips, continue blending to combine. Set aside.

2. Spray the baking sheet with cooking spray. To lay out cookies, use 1 heaping tablespoon of mixture and roll into a ball with your hands. Place on baking sheet and repeat with additional dough as space allows. Place balls 2 inches apart, or about 6 balls per pan.

3. Bake for 12 to 15 minutes, until golden brown. Remove from oven and using the spatula, carefully transfer cookies from baking sheet to the wire rack to cool.

4. Repeat with remaining dough in batches. Be sure to allow baking sheet to cool completely before baking another batch. Or use more than one baking sheet at a time.

STEP 2

MAKES 16 BROWNIES
PREP TIME 10 minutes
COOK TIME 35 minutes

Gear

- 2 stainless-steel bowls (1 small, 1 medium)
- Medium saucepan
- Whisk
- Silicone mixing spatula
- Strainer, flour sifter, or fine mesh sieve
- 9-inch cake pan, square glass baking dish, or nonstick square baking pan
- Wire cooling rack

Ingredients

- 3 eggs
- 1 cup light brown sugar
- 1 teaspoon vanilla extract
- 1⅓ cups semisweet chocolate chips
- 8 tablespoons (1 stick) salted butter, cut into pieces
- 2 tablespoons cocoa powder
- 1 cup all-purpose flour
- Nonstick cooking spray
- Vanilla ice cream or whipped cream, for serving

Brownies

Chocolate brownies, right from the oven, are simply divine. For a nutty alternative, add some pecans or chopped walnuts to the batter just before baking.

1. Preheat the oven to 350°F. In the medium bowl, whisk together the eggs, brown sugar, and vanilla.

2. Place the chocolate chips in the small stainless bowl on top of the medium saucepan of simmering water (page xxiii). As the chips begin to melt, whisk in the butter and cocoa until smooth. Remove from the heat.

3. With the spatula, gently fold mixture in a circular motion, scooping the sides of the bowl into the center, until the chocolate and egg mixture are well combined. Add the flour, shaking it through the strainer or sieve and folding it in with the spatula until well combined and smooth.

4. Spray the pan or baking dish with nonstick cooking spray and pour in the batter. Bake for 35 minutes or until a toothpick inserted in the center of the brownies comes out clean. (Otherwise bake for 3 to 4 minutes more, then test again.) Remove baking dish from oven and set aside on the wire rack. Allow brownies to cool for 5 minutes.

5. To remove brownies from the pan, run a butter knife around the inside edge to release the sides. Gently turn pan upside down, using pot holders or oven mitts, until brownies rest on wire rack. Place a plate over the brownies. Grip the plate and the wire rack together and carefully flip upside down. Remove wire rack and cut brownies. Serve with vanilla ice cream or fresh whipped cream.

STEP 3

STEP 4

STEP 5

MENUS

Invite your friends or family over and show off your new cooking skills! Here are three **easy** menu suggestions for you to start with. Of course, feel free to substitute dishes or create your own inventive menu combinations.

I've included a **basic** plan of work with every menu. This is a suggested game plan of how you're going to organize, cook, and serve your meal on the big day. The process is pretty simple: Do what you can ahead of time, so when it's time to finish the meal, things should progress smoothly. Just remember that **organization** is the key to pulling off a successful meal. Here are a few quick tips to get you started:

- **Plan ahead** Get your food shopping done the day before, or even two days before your big get-together. Got all your gear? Be sure you have everything you need, from the utensils to the bowls to the serving dishes, so you're not scrambling to find them (or realize you don't have them!) at the last minute.

- **Basics first** Set up your entertaining space the night before or early in the morning. You shouldn't be worrying about cleaning or setting the table while you're busy in the kitchen.

- **Start early** Be sure to leave enough time to prepare each of your dishes. Most should be done cooking by the time your guests arrive.

Weeknight Dinner

Outta-the-Bag Salad (page 25) • Rustic Meatloaf (page 62) or Rigatoni with Red Pepper Sauce (page 45) • Ice Cream with Chocolate Sauce (page 77)

Here's an easy menu that can be pulled together with minimum fuss for maximum satisfaction. And don't forget to make enough for leftovers.

Outta-the-Bag Salad (page 25)

Prep

Begin at least 2½ hours before mealtime or do the day before (as directed)

○ Gather all needed gear and ingredients (try to integrate shopping with your regular weekly grocery store trip).

○ Do all vegetable prep work for meatloaf or for red pepper sauce.

○ For meatloaf: Assemble the meatloaf and put in the oven to bake. Once meatloaf is done, cover the pan with foil and refrigerate (after it cools). For rigatoni: Make and blend rigatoni sauce. Transfer from blender to a storage container, cover, and refrigerate.

○ Assemble salad in a large bowl, without the dressing. Cover with damp paper towels and refrigerate.

○ Make the chocolate sauce. If not using right away, let the sauce cool, then transfer to a storage container and refrigerate.

Rustic Meatloaf (page 62)

Okay, You're On!

○ Preheat the oven to 350°F. Cover meatloaf with foil, heat either whole or in slices. Make the gravy. If serving rigatoni, boil pasta, heat sauce in a small saucepan. Prepare Parmesan for grating.

○ Set table. Get drinks or wine ready.

○ When it's warm and steamy, take the meatloaf out of oven and transfer to a platter along with the gravy (or serve on the side, as preferred). If serving rigatoni, toss sauce with pasta, serve with cheese for topping.

○ Serve the salad along with main course.

○ When ready for dessert, heat the chocolate sauce in the microwave, or if still in the saucepan, then whisk for about 2 minutes over medium heat until melted and smooth. Scoop out ice cream, top with sauce.

Rigatoni with Red Pepper Sauce (page 45)

Ice Cream with Chocolate Sauce (page 77)

**Baked Frittata
(page 10)**

**Bacon (page 12) or
Sausage (page 14)**

**Fresh Fruit with
Whipped Cream (page 79)**

Sunday Brunch

*Baked Frittata (page 10) • Bacon (page 12) or Sausage (page 14) • Fresh Fruit
with Whipped Cream (page 79) • Coffee and Tea*

There's nothing like starting a Sunday morning with a hearty meal of
eggs, fresh fruit, and a mug of hot coffee. The frittata recipe is easy to pull off,
even when the caffeine has yet to kick in. For something special, prepare an easy-
to-make drink like Mimosas (Champagne and orange juice) or Bellinis (Champagne and peach juice)—either one makes the perfect brunch cocktail.

Prep

Begin early in the morning or the night before

○ Gather all needed gear and ingredients.
○ Prep, cut, or grate all fillings needed for frittata. Store in airtight storage
   containers.
○ Cut up and prep all fresh fruit. Separate out any juices and keep in another
   container, to combine with fruit the next day. (If using apples or pears, don't
   prepare until ready to serve.) Cover and refrigerate until ready to serve.
○ Whip the cream, cover, and refrigerate.
○ Prepare the bacon or sausage on trays, ready to cook, then refrigerate be-
   tween pieces of parchment paper. (This must be done in the morning).
○ Set table. Organize coffee and tea.

Okay, You're On!

○ Begin 45 minutes before your guests arrive. Set up cooking space, have all
   sides and ingredients prepped and ready to go.
○ Brew fresh coffee.
○ Get drinks ready, if serving. Lay out champagne glasses for Mimosas, fill part-
   way with juice, then top with Champagne.
○ Lay out the fresh fruit (add back the juices) with whipped cream on the side.
○ Cook frittata; hold in a warm (200°F) oven until ready to cut and serve.
○ Heat up the bacon or sausage in the oven, and serve hot along with frittata.

Game Day Munchies

Nachos with Guacamole and Salsa (page 34) • *Potato Skins with Bacon and Cheese (page 36) or Fajitas with Chicken, Beef, or Shrimp (page 54)* • *Chocolate Chip Cookies (page 80)*

Nachos with Guacamole and Salsa (page 34)

These easy bites are just the thing to keep your attention where it should be—on the game. Prep these in the morning (or the day before), stick 'em in the oven, and you're good to go.

Prep

Begin early in the day or the day before

- ○ Gather all needed gear and do all food shopping.
- ○ Set up the serving area; make sure the bar is stocked and fridge is full of beer and ice.
- ○ Prep and assemble the potato skins on a baking sheet; cover and refrigerate until ready to finish cooking.
- ○ Prep all filling ingredients for fajitas; cover and refrigerate.
- ○ Prep all topping ingredients for nachos; cover and refrigerate.
- ○ Make the salsa. Pour into plastic storage container and refrigerate. Guacamole should not be prepared the day before.
- ○ Make chocolate chip cookie dough; cover and refrigerate.

Potato Skins with Bacon and Cheese (page 36)

Okay, You're On!

- ○ Begin 45 minutes before serving. Assemble all ingredients near your cooking space.
- ○ Divide cookie dough onto a baking sheet. (Or use two sheets, depending upon number of guests.) Bake cookies, then set aside to cool.
- ○ Get drinks or beers ready.
- ○ Make the guacamole. Assemble the nachos, ready for the broiler. Just before guests arrive, pop them in to cook. Watch them carefully so they don't burn. Serve immediately.
- ○ Place the prepared potato skins into the oven. When done cooking, arrange on a platter and put out for guests, or cook the fajitas. Assemble and serve, either on individual plates or on a big platter.

Fajitas with Chicken, Beef, or Shrimp (page 54)

Chocolate Chip Cookies (page 80)

RAISING

Take your cooking to the next level. This section offers recipes that start with the basic methods and building blocks you learned in the previous section, but feel a little more sophisticated and, in some cases, are a bit more involved in prep or to cook.

There are **dynamite starters,** like Goat Cheese Crostini with Caramelized Red Onions (page 90), and comforting soups and stews, such as Butternut Squash and Ginger Soup (page 100). All-around great **classics** like Baked Lasagna (page 114) and Traditional Pot Roast (page 125)

THE

may seem complicated, but instead are demystified with **straightforward** instructions and helpful tips. Simple salads are brought to new heights, with recipes like Niçoise Salad with Fresh Tuna (page 108). Of course, you can't forget about the sweet side of things with recipes for **satisfying desserts** like Banana Cream and Toffee Pie (page 148). Three new menu suggestions provide clear, easy-to-follow plans of work to help you prepare for your first dinner party or a romantic dinner with that special someone.

BAR

Savory Starters

Start your next party off with delicious small bites to set the mood for the evening. Or, think of these tasty crowd pleasers as a great way to compliment your main dishes.

A step up from the simple snacks you learned to make in Level 1, the starters included here are sure to put a smile on the faces of your guests. While these dishes are a bit more sophisticated, they're still simple to pull together. Many of them, like Crab Cakes with Smoked Paprika Aïoli (page 94), can also make a great light dinner; just serve them alongside a salad or hearty soup.

> ## IN THIS CHAPTER
>
> In this chapter, you'll find recipes for:
> - Antipasto Platter
> - Goat Cheese Crostini with Caramelized Red Onions
> - Stuffed Mushrooms
> - Crab Cakes with Smoked Paprika Aïoli
>
> And you'll develop the skills and know-how to:
> - Arrange an elegant appetizer spread
> - Mix and match ingredients based on seasonality
> - Make your own fresh basil oil
> - Dredge meat and vegetables in flour and bread crumbs for frying

SERVES 8
PREP TIME 10 minutes
COOK TIME 3 minutes
ASSEMBLY TIME 7 minutes

Gear
- Vegetable peeler
- Chef's knife
- Cutting board
- Serving platter
- Basket and cloth napkin
- 4 small bowls

PREP

PREP

Antipasto Platter

This traditional first course in an Italian meal is made up of cured meats, various cheeses, vegetables, bread, and condiments for dipping. The wide variety of flavors makes this dish perfect for a big party or a casual dinner.

Arrange the meats, cheeses, and vegetables on a platter. Place bread in a basket lined with a cloth napkin. Fill small bowls with condiments.

INGREDIENTS   *Choose 2 or 3 from each group*

CURED MEATS
- ◯ Salami
- ◯ Prosciutto
- ◯ Bresaola
- ◯ Chorizo

CHEESES
- ◯ Aged Parmesan or other hard cheeses, shaved or chopped into chunks
- ◯ Taleggio or other semisoft cheeses
- ◯ Gorgonzola or other blue cheeses
- ◯ Gouda or other sharp aged cheeses
- ◯ Buffalo mozzarella or other fresh milk cheeses

FRESH VEGETABLES AND HERBS
- ◯ Medium ripe tomatoes, sliced ¼ inch thick
- ◯ Eggplant slices, grilled or roasted with olive oil and lightly salted

PRESERVED VEGETABLES
- ◯ Roasted bell peppers
- ◯ Extra-large capers
- ◯ Mixed cured olives
- ◯ Artichoke hearts
- ◯ Sun-dried tomatoes

BREADS
- ◯ Semolina
- ◯ Country loaf
- ◯ Bread sticks

CONDIMENTS
- ◯ Olive oil
- ◯ Aged balsamic vinegar
- ◯ Country Dijon mustard

LEVEL

SERVES 8
PREP TIME 25 minutes
COOK TIME 15 minutes

Gear

- Cutting board
- Chef's knife
- Paring knife
- Food processor or blender
- Fry pan
- Wooden spoon
- Whisk
- Baking sheet

Ingredients

- 1 cup coarsely chopped fresh basil leaves (20 to 30)
- 5 tablespoons olive oil
- Salt and pepper
- 1 large red onion, peeled and cut into ¼-inch slices
- ½ cup balsamic vinegar
- 2 tablespoons light brown sugar or granulated sugar
- 1 tablespoon (⅛ stick) butter
- 1 baguette (preferably all-natural), sliced ½-inch thick at 45-degree angle
- 1 large tomato or handful of cherry tomatoes, cut into ½-inch dice
- 8-ounce log soft goat cheese or two 4-ounce logs, cut into ½-inch chunks

Goat Cheese Crostini with Caramelized Red Onions

This is one of my favorite appetizers to serve. These mini toasts with savory toppings can serve as a foundation for many different appetizers; you are limited only by your imagination. As a time-saver, you can make the toasts and toppings separately early in the day, then assemble and bake just prior to serving.

(1) Preheat the oven to 400°F.

(2) Make basil oil: Combine fresh basil and 2 tablespoons of the olive oil in a food processor until creamy. Add salt and pepper to season. Refrigerate in small, covered container until ready to use.

STEP 1

STEP 6 (A)

STEP 6 (B)

(3) Place the fry pan over medium-high heat. When hot*, add 2 tablespoons olive oil. Carefully add onion slices and sauté (page xxiv), stirring with the wooden spoon, for 6 to 8 minutes, or until golden brown. Reduce the heat to medium; cook for 8 to 10 minutes more, until onions are soft and well cooked.

(4) Stir in the balsamic vinegar and sugar, and cook for 10 minutes more, until syrupy. Whisk in the butter until melted and remove from the heat.

(5) Make the toasts: Place bread slices on the baking sheet and drizzle the remaining 1 tablespoon of olive oil on the slices until lightly coated. Bake for 5 minutes, until golden brown and crisp around the edges. Remove baking sheet from oven, place it on a heat-resistant surface, and turn on the broiler.

(6) Top each piece of toast with a spoonful of cooked onions, then add the diced tomatoes. Place 2 or 3 goat cheese chunks on top of each assembled toast. Place under broiler until cheese is slightly melted, about 2 minutes, watching carefully to avoid burning.

(7) To serve, remove the basil oil from the refrigerator and allow it to return to room temperature. Arrange the warm appetizers on a plate or serving platter. Use a teaspoon to drizzle basil oil around and on top of the crostini.

*Is your pan hot enough? Test it with a drop of water. If it sizzles, you're ready to cook.

LEVEL

SERVES 4
PREP TIME 25 minutes
COOK TIME 15 minutes

Gear

- Cutting board
- Chef's knife
- Fry pan
- Tongs
- Baking sheet
- 2 bowls (1 small, 1 medium)
- Silicone mixing spatula
- Spreader knife or teaspoon

Ingredients

- 3 tablespoons olive oil, plus extra to drizzle
- 16 medium white mushrooms, cleaned, stems removed and discarded

STUFFING
- One-half 8-ounce package cream cheese
- 2 medium scallions, ends trimmed, finely chopped
- Three ¼-inch-thick slices uncooked cured ham, such as Parma or San Daniele prosciutto, finely diced
- 2 tablespoons Bread Crumbs
- Salt and pepper

TOPPING
- 4 tablespoons (½ stick) butter, softened (see page 14)
- 1 tablespoon mashed garlic (see page xx)
- 1 tablespoon chopped fresh flat-leaf parsley
- ½ cup Bread Crumbs (page 48)
- Salt and pepper
- Freshly chopped chives, for garnish

Stuffed Mushrooms

The cream cheese filling gives these mushrooms an unexpected twist of texture. These are easy to make and even easier to serve. For a meatless alternative, omit the ham altogether.

1. Preheat the oven to 375°F.

2. Place the fry pan over high heat. When hot*, add 3 tablespoons olive oil. Using tongs, gently place mushrooms in pan and cook, open side up, for 4 minutes or until underside is golden brown. Turn the mushrooms over, being careful not to splash the hot oil, and cook for an additional 2 minutes.

3. Remove pan from heat and set on a heat-resistant surface. Using tongs, remove mushroom caps from the oil and place them, open end up, on the baking sheet to cool. While mushroom caps are cooling, make the stuffing and topping.

4. Make the stuffing: In the medium bowl, combine cream cheese, scallions, ham, and bread crumbs until ingredients are well mixed. Taste, and add salt and pepper to season. Set aside.

STEP 2

STEP 6

(5) Make the topping: In the small bowl, combine the butter, garlic paste, parsley, and bread crumbs until ingredients are well mixed and spreadable. Taste, and add salt and pepper to season.

(6) Using a spreader or teaspoon, gently fill each mushroom cap with stuffing, distributing evenly. Scrape off excess so filling is even with the mushroom. When all are filled, add a generous teaspoon of topping on each cap, pressing down gently with your fingers to set in place.

(7) Place baking sheet in the oven and bake the caps for 5 to 7 minutes, or until warm and slightly toasted. Remove from oven and set on a heat-resistant surface. Using tongs, carefully transfer mushroom caps to plates or a serving platter. Drizzle olive oil across mushrooms, garnish with fresh chives, and serve warm.

*Is your pan hot enough? Test it with a drop of water. If it sizzles, you're ready to cook.

SERVES 4
PREP TIME 20 minutes
COOK TIME 15 minutes

Gear

- Cutting board
- Chef's knife
- Paring knife
- 3 bowls (1 large, 1 medium, 1 small)
- Silicone mixing spatula or wooden spoon
- 3 large rimmed plates
- Nonstick fry pan
- Wide spatula
- Baking sheet

Ingredients

CRAB CAKES

- 1 pound crabmeat (fresh or canned), picked over for shell and cartilage
- ¼ cup minced medium red bell pepper (about ½ pepper)
- ¼ cup minced medium yellow bell pepper (about ½ pepper)
- ¼ small red onion, peeled and minced
- 1 tablespoon minced fresh chives
- ¼ cup fresh white corn kernels or frozen kernels, thawed and drained
- 3 tablespoons mayonnaise
- 3 dashes of Tabasco sauce
- 1 teaspoon Dijon mustard
- Salt and pepper
- ½ cup all-purpose flour
- 1 large egg
- 4 tablespoons milk
- 1½ cups Bread Crumbs (page 48)

(continues)

Crab Cakes with Smoked Paprika Aïoli

For the taste of summer on the coast, this classic can't be beat. The key is to use the very best quality crabmeat you can find—preferably fresh jumbo lump meat. Pasteurized crab is fine, but fresh is always best, resulting in a light and fluffy crab cake. You can also substitute crumbled saltines for the bread crumbs and dust the crab cake with Old Bay seasoning for an authentic Chesapeake flair.

① Preheat the oven to 375°F. In the large bowl, combine the crabmeat, red and yellow peppers, onion, chives, corn, mayonnaise, Tabasco, and mustard. Add salt and pepper to season. Using a silicone mixing spatula, gently fold ingredients together until well blended.

② Use your hands to form four individual, evenly sized crab cakes (about ¾ inch thick and 2½ inches wide), flattening them between the palms of your hands, and set aside.

③ Prepare three plates for dredging the crab cakes: Place the flour on the first plate; in a small bowl, lightly beat together the egg and milk, and pour mixture onto second plate; combine bread crumbs and cayenne on third plate. Carefully dip each crab cake in the flour. Set aside as you repeat with the remaining cakes.

④ Dip each crab cake first in the egg mixture, and then bread crumb mixture, until well coated. Set aside as you repeat with the remaining cakes. You should have an even, light crust on all sides of each crab cake.

STEP 2

STEP 4

STEP 5

Ingredients (cont'd)

- Pinch of cayenne (or Old Bay seasoning)
- ½ cup canola oil, for frying

AÏOLI

- ½ cup mayonnaise
- Juice of ½ lemon (about 1 tablespoon)
- 1 medium clove garlic, peeled, crushed, and minced
- ½ teaspoon smoked paprika
- Salt and pepper

How Do I . . . ?

To keep the crab cakes from falling apart when frying, follow the egg wash/flour–process closely to make sure the crab cake is coated thoroughly and evenly. And make sure your oil is hot before frying.

Kitchen FYI

Aïoli is a French term for garlic-flavored mayonnaise. It's packed with flavor, making it a great garnish for many meat and fish dishes.

5. Place the fry pan over medium-high heat. When hot*, add the oil and heat until rippling but not smoking. Using the wide spatula, carefully place each crab cake in the pan, as space allows. Fry for 3 to 4 minutes or until a light golden brown crust has developed. Slide spatula under cakes and gently turn them over, being careful not to splash the hot oil. Fry for 3 to 4 minutes more, or until golden brown.

6. Remove cakes and place them on the baking sheet carefully to keep the crab cakes intact. Place baking sheet in the oven and bake crab cakes for 6 minutes, or until heated through. Remove from oven and set aside on a heat-resistant surface.

7. While the crab cakes are in the oven, make the aïoli: In the medium bowl, combine the mayonnaise, lemon juice, garlic, paprika, and salt and pepper to taste. To serve, place a crab cake in the center of each plate and top with a dollop of aïoli, or place aïoli off to the side.

*Is your pan hot enough? Test it with a drop of water. If it sizzles, you're ready to cook.

Soups and Stews

There's nothing more comforting than a bowl of hot soup. Making delicious homemade soup doesn't have to be a challenge. The soups and stews in this section will not leave you slaving over a hot stove all day. They are designed to be prepared fast, with lightly cooked ingredients and fresh herbs for clean and bright flavors. (In other words, don't overcook your vegetables!)

A few tips to keep in mind: Green vegetables should be bright green and lively, not brown; fresh herbs should be added at the end of cooking so they retain their color, flavor, and fragrance; and colorful vegetables should retain their color and add to the overall look and taste of your soup or stew.

IN THIS CHAPTER

In this chapter, you'll find recipes for:
○ Chicken Stock
○ Chicken and Sweet Corn Noodle Soup
○ Tomato and Basil Soup
○ Butternut Squash and Ginger Soup
○ Hearty Beef Stew

And you'll develop the skills and know-how to:
○ Properly store homemade stock for later use
○ Skim fat from soup or broth
○ Cleanly break dry noodles into smaller pieces
○ Work with hot chile peppers
○ Adjust a soup's consistency
○ Properly strain liquids, separating out solids
○ Make your own croutons

LEVEL

MAKES 10 CUPS
PREP TIME   15 minutes
COOK TIME   2½ hours

Gear

- Cutting board
- Chef's knife
- Vegetable peeler
- Roasting pan
- 8-quart stockpot
- Tongs
- Large spoon
- Slotted spoon
- Fine-mesh sieve or strainer
- Large bowl or saucepan
- Quart-size plastic containers for storage

Ingredients

- 5 pounds chicken pieces (necks and backs only)
- 3 medium yellow onions, peeled and coarsely chopped
- 5 medium carrots, peeled and coarsely chopped
- 1 small bunch celery, coarsely chopped
- 3 medium leeks, washed, trimmed (dark green parts discarded), and coarsely chopped
- 6 medium cloves garlic, peeled and coarsely chopped
- 1 sprig of thyme
- 1 medium sprig of rosemary
- 2 bay leaves
- Salt and pepper

Chicken Stock

Homemade chicken stock should be a staple in your cooking repertoire, since it's so versatile. It's also a great way to use up leftover Whole Chicken Roasted with Herb Butter (page 120). Just omit step 1 below. Homemade stock takes some time to make, but it's well worth it; the result is a delicious stock that is much more flavorful than any store-bought version. I always make a large pot of stock and freeze it in individual-size containers for later use.

1. Preheat oven to 400°F. Place chicken pieces in the roasting pan and cook for 30 minutes, until golden brown. Remove from heat and set aside.

2. Place the stockpot over medium-high heat. Add onions, carrots, celery, leeks, garlic, thyme, rosemary, and bay leaves. Using tongs, transfer the chicken pieces from the roasting pan and cook for 10 to 15 minutes, stirring occasionally, until chicken and vegetables are all golden brown.

3. Add enough water to stockpot to cover the chicken by about 2 inches. Bring to a boil, then reduce the heat to low. Allow stock to simmer (page xxiii) for approximately 2½ hours. Check liquid level occasionally; if the liquid level reduces (page xxv), exposing chicken pieces, add just enough water to cover them. Add salt and pepper to season.

4. Remove stock from heat. Skim the surface of the stock with a spoon to remove fat and discard. Strain the stock through a fine-mesh strainer into a large bowl or saucepan. Discard large solids. Allow stock to cool.

5. To store, ladle the stock into individual containers, label, and freeze for later use. Use frozen stock within 6 months.

STEP 2
STEP 4 (A)
STEP 4 (B)

SERVES 4 TO 6
PREP TIME 5 minutes
COOK TIME 25 minutes

Gear

- Cutting board
- Chef's knife
- Microplane grater
- 8-quart stockpot
- Large spoon
- Large ladle

Ingredients

- 3 ounces Asian egg noodles, rice noodles, or udon noodles
- 1 tablespoon olive oil
- 2 whole boneless, skinless chicken breasts (about 1 pound)
- 3 cups homemade Chicken Stock (page 97) or store-bought, or 2 bouillon cubes dissolved in 3 cups hot water
- 1 tablespoon chopped fresh chile pepper (about 1 small pepper)
- 1 tablespoon grated fresh ginger
- ¾ cup sweet corn kernels, frozen, canned, or freshly cut off the cob
- 3 tablespoons soy sauce
- 3 tablespoons sesame oil
- ⅓ cup chopped fresh cilantro leaves

Kitchen FYI

When chopping chile peppers, be careful not to touch your eyes. This stuff burns! Wash your hands well after handling chiles.

Chicken and Sweet Corn Noodle Soup

This is one of my favorite soups; the ginger and cilantro in this dish give it a fresh and spicy taste. I use homemade chicken stock here, but you may also use bouillon cubes dissolved in hot water, if you prefer.

1. Break up the noodles: Wrap the noodles in a clean dish towel and crush with your palm or a rolling pin on a flat surface until noodles are broken up into approximately ¾-inch lengths, to fit on a soup spoon. Set aside.

2. Place the stockpot over medium-high heat. When hot*, add the olive oil and chicken breasts. Sear (page xxiv) until golden brown on each side, about 8 minutes total.

3. Stir in the chicken stock, chile, and ginger and reduce the heat to simmer (page xxiii) for 10 minutes.

4. Remove the chicken and set aside to cool for 10 minutes. Allow broth level to reduce (page xxv) by ⅓. Add the noodles, sweet corn, soy sauce, and sesame oil, and stir continuously, 4 to 5 minutes. Remove from heat and set aside.

5. Dice the cooled chicken into ¼-inch cubes and return (along with any juices) to the soup. Stir until soup and chicken are well mixed. To serve, ladle soup into bowls and garnish with chopped cilantro.

*Is your pan hot enough? Test it with a drop of water. If it sizzles, you're ready to cook.

STEP 1

STEP 2

STEP 3

③
LEVEL

SERVES 4
PREP TIME 15 minutes
COOK TIME 10 minutes

Gear

- Chef's knife
- Cutting board
- Medium saucepan
- Baking sheet
- Tongs
- Medium bowl
- Blender
- Large ladle

Ingredients

SOUP

- 2 tablespoons olive oil
- 1 medium red onion, peeled and diced
- 1 medium clove garlic, peeled and coarsely chopped
- 2 tablespoons tomato paste
- 1 cup vegetable stock (canned or boxed)
- 2 cups water
- 6 medium-size ripe unpeeled tomatoes (about 1¼ to 2 pounds), coarsely chopped
- ½ cup chopped fresh basil leaves, plus a few whole leaves for garnish
- Salt and pepper
- Optional: freshly grated Parmesan cheese, for serving

CROUTONS

- Four ¾-inch-thick slices of any soft, crusty bread, cubed
- 3 tablespoons olive oil
- Salt and pepper
- 2 tablespoons freshly grated Parmesan cheese

Tomato and Basil Soup

Whether you make this fresh soup with seasonal fresh farmers' market tomatoes or ripe hothouse varieties available all year long, the taste of summer really comes through. Use the ripest red tomatoes, and heat them just enough to bring out their full flavor. Serve this soup chilled for a light summer lunch.

① Preheat the oven to 375°F. Place the saucepan over medium heat. When hot*, add the olive oil and onions and sweat (see page xxiv) for 2 minutes; add the garlic and continue to sweat until the onions are soft and translucent, about 2 minutes. Add the tomato paste and cook, stirring, until onions are fully coated, about 3 minutes.

② Add the vegetable stock and water, and bring the mixture to a boil. Reduce the heat to a simmer (page xxiii). Stir in the tomatoes and cook for 5 minutes, but no longer. Remove the saucepan from the heat and set aside to cool for about 20 minutes.

③ While the soup is cooling, make the croutons: Spread the bread cubes on a baking sheet, drizzle with olive oil until just moistened, and add salt and pepper to season. Bake for 10 to 12 minutes, turning once with tongs, until golden brown. Remove from the oven, transfer croutons to the medium bowl, and toss with the Parmesan cheese. Set aside until ready to use.

④ Add the basil to the cooled soup and transfer the mixture to a blender in batches (see Safety First, page 101). Blend until smooth and silky. Taste and add salt and pepper to season.

⑤ To serve, reheat the soup briefly in a saucepan over medium heat. Ladle into bowls and garnish with a basil leaf and grated Parmesan, if using. Add Parmesan croutons just before serving, so they don't get soggy.

*Is your pan hot enough? Test it with a drop of water. If it sizzles, you're ready to cook.

STEP 1

STEP 3

STEP 4

LEVEL

SERVES 4
PREP TIME 20 minutes
COOK TIME 35 to 40 minutes

Gear

- Cutting board
- Chef's knife
- Vegetable peeler
- 8-quart stockpot or Dutch oven
- Baking sheet
- Tongs
- Blender or food processor
- Large ladle

Ingredients

SOUP

- 2 tablespoons olive oil
- 1 medium white onion, peeled and coarsely diced
- 1 teapoon chopped garlic
- 1 medium leek, white part only, chopped
- 1 medium carrot, peeled and coarsely diced
- 2 stalks celery, coarsely diced
- 1 tablespoon minced fresh ginger
- 1 butternut squash, halved lengthwise, peeled, seeded, and coarsely chopped
- 3 cups vegetable stock, homemade Chicken Stock (page 97) or store-bought, or 2 bouillon cubes dissolved in 3 cups hot water
- 2 teaspoons chopped fresh thyme leaves or 1 teaspoon dried
- 1 teaspoon ground allspice
- Salt and pepper
- ½ cup heavy cream

(continues)

Butternut Squash and Ginger Soup

I love to make this soup in the fall, when there is an abundance of squash in the market and a nip in the air. The rich and earthy undertones and spicy bite of this soup will warm you up in an instant.

1. Preheat the oven to 375°F.

2. Place the stockpot or Dutch oven over medium-high heat. When hot*, add the olive oil, onions, garlic, leeks, carrots, and celery, and sweat (page xxiv) for 6 to 8 minutes, until the onions are soft and translucent. Add the ginger and squash, and continue to cook for 3 to 5 minutes more.

PREP  **PREP**  **STEP 3**

2

Ingredients (cont'd)

- Optional add-ins: ¼ cup crumbled cooked Bacon (page 13); 4 tablespoons crème fraîche (1 dollop for each serving)

CROUTONS

- Three ¾-inch-thick slices of any soft, crusty bread, cubed
- 3 tablespoons olive oil
- Salt and pepper

③ Add stock to pot. Season with thyme, allspice, salt, and pepper. Bring to a boil, then lower to a simmer (page xxiii) for 20 minutes. Remove from heat and allow to cool for 20 minutes.

④ While the mixture is cooling, make the croutons: Spread the bread cubes on a baking sheet, drizzle with olive oil until just moistened, and add salt and pepper to season. Bake for 10 to 12 minutes, turning once with tongs, until golden brown. Remove from the oven and set aside to cool.

⑤ Once soup is cooled, transfer the mixture to a blender in batches (see Safety First, below), gradually add the heavy cream, and puree until smooth and silky.

⑥ To serve, reheat the soup briefly in a saucepan (do not boil) over medium heat. Ladle into bowls and garnish with bacon or a dollop of crème fraîche, if using. Add croutons just before serving.

Is your pan hot enough? Test it with a drop of water. If it sizzles, you're ready to cook.

SAFETY FIRST

Hot Soup Coming Through!

Before blending any soup, always allow it to cool so you don't get scalded by spills or splashes. Pour soup into blender until it's about half full. Begin blending at the lowest speed while holding the lid down tightly with a dish towel. Never fill a blender to the top; proceed in batches if necessary.

SERVES 4

PREP TIME 20 minutes

COOK TIME 2½ hours

Gear

- Cutting board
- Chef's knife
- Vegetable peeler
- Fry pan
- Slotted spoon
- 8-quart stockpot or Dutch oven

Ingredients

- 2 tablespoons vegetable oil
- 2 pounds stewing beef, cut into 1-inch cubes
- Salt and pepper
- 4 medium Yukon Gold potatoes, peeled and cut into 1-inch cubes (about 1½ cups)
- 1 medium celery root, peeled and cut into ½-inch cubes (about 1 cup)
- 1 large white onion, peeled and diced (about 1½ cups)
- 2 medium carrots, peeled, sliced on the bias into large pieces
- ½ cup red wine
- 2 tablespoons all-purpose flour
- 2 tablespoons tomato paste
- 4 cups homemade Chicken Stock (page 97) or store-bought, or 2 bouillon cubes dissolved in hot water
- 1 packet brown gravy mix, prepared to make 1 cup
- 1 sprig of thyme
- 2 bay leaves
- 1 loaf crusty bread, toasted, for serving

Hearty Beef Stew

Nothing is more comforting on a cold day like a bowl of hot stew. Stew is heartier than soup; it's prepared by stewing meat and/or vegetables in a thick broth to tenderize them and allow the natural flavors of the ingredients to blend together for extra richness. This is a great way to utilize your homemade Chicken Stock (page 97). Paired with slices of warm crusty bread, it makes the perfect winter meal.

1. Place the fry pan over medium-high heat. When hot*, add 1 tablespoon oil and the beef, as space allows (pieces should not touch), and add salt and pepper to season. Sear (page xxiv) until golden brown on each side, about 8 minutes total. Remove from heat and transfer beef to the stockpot or Dutch oven using a slotted spoon.

2. Without cleaning the fry pan, return it to medium-high heat, add the remaining 1 tablespoon oil, the potatoes, and celery root, and cook, stirring occasionally, for 6 to 8 minutes, until golden brown.

3. Transfer potatoes and celery root to the beef, then return the fry pan to medium-high heat. Add the onions and carrots and cook, stirring occasionally, for about 4 minutes, until golden brown. Deglaze (pages xxiv–xxv) the pan with the red wine. Reduce the heat to low and stir in the flour and tomato paste. Add salt and pepper to season, and cook, stirring, for about 2 minutes.

4. Add ½ the chicken stock to the fry pan. Cook over low heat for 5 minutes, then add the remaining stock. Turn up heat to medium-high and bring the mixture to a boil. Carefully transfer to the stockpot and add the brown gravy, thyme, and bay leaves. Add salt and pepper to season.

STEP 1

STEP 5

STEP 6

⑤ Place the stockpot over high heat and bring to a boil, stirring continuously. Reduce the heat to low and bring stew to a simmer (page xxiii) and cover with lid. Cook, stirring occasionally, for 2 to 2½ hours, until the beef is tender. To check, remove a piece of beef from the pot with a slotted spoon, allow to cool for 30 seconds, and gently squeeze it between your forefingers and thumb. It should fall apart in your fingers; if there is any resistance, continue to cook stew for an additional 30 minutes.

⑥ Remove stockpot from heat. Scoop out thyme and bay leaves with a spoon and discard. Add additional salt and pepper to season, if needed. To serve, ladle the stew into shallow bowls. Serve with slices of warm crusty bread.

Is your pan hot enough? Test it with a drop of water. If it sizzles, you're ready to cook.

Hearty Lamb Stew   To make a delicious lamb stew, replace the beef with 2 pounds of lamb cut into 1-inch cubes, and replace the thyme with rosemary. Add 3 cloves of garlic, finely chopped, in Step 2.

SOUP PRIMER

Mix It and Finish It

You can finish your soup any number of ways, depending on the flavors, the texture, and how heavy you want the soup to be.

Blend It—Place the soup in a food processor or blender to combine the ingredients and puree.

Smooth It Out—Pour soup through a sieve or strainer to remove lumps. Place sieve over a pot or bowl, pour in soup, and press on solids with a ladle in a circular motion until all liquid passes through sieve.

Add Cream or Butter—Thicken soup with cream or butter, which also adds a silky texture.

Add Solids—Add ingredients such as chopped fresh vegetables or grilled chicken or fish during the cooking process or when serving.

Serve It

To heat a soup that has been stored in the refrigerator, pour soup into a saucepan or stockpot while cold. Place over medium-high heat and bring it to a boil while stirring. Remove from heat and serve.

Elegant Salads

In Level 1, you learned how to make simple, versatile salads. Now build on those skills to make these more elegant, refined salads that will work alongside a variety of main courses or become fantastic—and healthy—main dishes on their own.

The basic structure of a salad is lettuce with dressing and added toppings, but it's the way you make your dressing and choose your toppings that can make a difference. These recipes will elevate your simple salads to new heights with creative ideas and new twists on the classics. Each recipe also includes homemade dressings so simple and delicious that you'll never use the bottled stuff again.

IN THIS CHAPTER

In this chapter, you'll find recipes for:
○ Classic Caesar Salad
○ Arugula with Crisp Salami and Taleggio Croûtes
○ Niçoise Salad with Fresh Tuna

And you'll develop the skills and know-how to:
○ Emulsify a liquid
○ Make two kinds of Caesar salad dressing
○ Add hearty toppings to your salad for easy lunch or dinner options
○ Blanch vegetables

LEVEL

SERVES 4

PREP TIME 20 minutes

ASSEMBLY TIME 10 minutes

Gear

- Optional: salad spinner
- Cutting board
- Chef's knife
- Food processor or blender
- Microplane grater
- Large bowl
- Large spoon

Ingredients

SALAD

- 2 heads romaine lettuce, washed, dried, and coarsely chopped
- Caesar Dressing
- ½ cup freshly shaved Parmesan cheese
- Optional: 4 to 5 ounces sliced Pan-Fried or grilled Chicken Breasts (page 53); 1½ cups Parmesan Croutons (page 99)

Kitchen FYI

Be careful not to "split" or break the emulsion (when the ingredients don't combine smoothly or separate). Do not:

1 Use yolks and oil that are too cold (should be room temperature).

2 Use yolks that are not fresh. Check the expiration date prior to use.

3 Add olive oil too quickly.

Classic Caesar Salad

There are two options for Caesar dressing, one traditional and a quick-and-easy alternative without raw egg. Add chicken and croutons to turn this side salad into lunch or a light dinner.

1   Using clean hands, toss leaves in a large bowl while adding dressing with a spoon. Toss until leaves are evenly coated.

2   Add ⅓ of the Parmesan to the lettuce and mix. Add in chicken and croutons, if using. Sprinkle remaining Parmesan on top and serve.

TRADITIONAL CAESAR DRESSING

MAKES 1 CUP

PREP TIME 5 minutes

2 egg yolks*	1½ tablespoons fresh lemon juice
Optional: 6 anchovy fillets, chopped	⅔ cup olive oil
3 cloves garlic, peeled, crushed, and minced	4 tablespoons freshly grated Parmesan cheese
1 teaspoon Dijon mustard	Salt and pepper to season
2 teaspoons Worcestershire sauce	* See warning on page 5 about using raw eggs.

1   Place the egg yolks, anchovies, if using, garlic, and mustard in the food processor, and pulse until mixture becomes a paste. Blend in the Worcestershire sauce and lemon juice.

2   Add oil in a slow, steady stream while the machine is on. Process until emulsified (below left) or well mixed. Add Parmesan and salt and pepper to season.

QUICK AND EASY CAESAR DRESSING

MAKES 1 CUP

PREP TIME   5 minutes

3 medium cloves garlic, peeled and minced
1 teaspoon Dijon mustard
1 tablespoon fresh lemon juice
2 teaspoons Worcestershire sauce

½ cup mayonnaise
3 tablespoons olive oil
2 tablespoons freshly grated Parmesan cheese
Salt and pepper

Pulse the garlic in the food processor until smooth. Add the mustard, lemon juice, and Worcestershire sauce and pulse for 1 minute. Add the mayonnaise and pulse for 1 minute, while adding the olive oil in a slow, steady stream. Fold in the Parmesan and add salt and pepper to season.

SALAD RULES

- Make sure the lettuce is well drained and dried, or it will dilute your dressing.
- Toss salad at the last possible minute, as the acid in the dressing reacts with the lettuce and will make it soggy and limp after a few minutes.
- Any add-ins or toppings should be evenly arranged on top of the salad. If tossing salad, finish by arranging some garnish (fresh herbs used, or vegetable cuts from the salad) on top for a colorful presentation.

LEVEL

SERVES 2
PREP TIME 7 minutes
COOK TIME 12 minutes

Gear

- Cutting board
- Bread knife
- Chef's knife
- Baking sheet
- Optional: salad spinner
- Tongs
- 2 bowls (1 small, 1 large)
- Whisk
- Nonstick fry pan

Ingredients

SALAD

- Six ½-inch-thick slices French or Italian baguette, cut on an angle (about ½ of a large loaf)
- Olive oil, to drizzle
- 6 slices Taleggio cheese, the size of the baguette slices
- ⅓ pound thinly sliced Genoa salami
- One 5-ounce package baby arugula, washed and well dried

DRESSING

- ¼ cup balsamic vinegar (aged, if possible)
- 1 teaspoon Dijon mustard
- 1 teaspoon sugar
- ¾ cup extra-virgin olive oil

Arugula with Crisp Salami and Taleggio Croûtes

Croûtes are simply mini toasts with a savory topping, and they are delicious when paired with this salad. There are plenty of other ingredients you can substitute while still keeping the same great balance of flavor. Vegetarians can substitute toasted walnuts for the salami; if you can't find Taleggio (a semisoft Italian cheese) at your local store, try camembert or Brie instead.

1. Preheat the oven to 375°F. Make the croûtes: Place baguette slices on a baking sheet and drizzle with olive oil. Bake for 5 minutes, until golden brown. Remove from oven (keep oven on) and place on a heat-resistant surface. Place 1 slice of Taleggio on top of each croûte and set aside while preparing the dressing and salad.

2. Make the dressing: Using a whisk, combine vinegar, mustard, and sugar in a small bowl, then whisk in oil slowly. Set aside until ready to use.

3. Place the nonstick fry pan over medium-high heat. When hot*, add salami and fry for 5 to 6 minutes, tossing regularly, until crisp. Remove from heat and set aside.

4. Heat the croûtes by returning them to the oven. Bake until cheese begins to bubble, about 2 minutes. Remove from heat and set aside.

5. In a large bowl, toss the arugula with ¼ cup of the dressing until evenly coated. Drizzle remaining dressing on each plate in a continuous circle, about 1 inch from the plate rim. Gently make a ball of the arugula in the palm of your hand and place in center of the plate. Place 3 croûtes on each plate and add warm salami on top.

*Is your pan hot enough? Test it with a drop of water. If it sizzles, you're ready to cook.

STEP 1

STEP 3

STEP 5

LEVEL

SERVES 4
PREP TIME 15 minutes
COOK TIME 20 to 40 minutes
ASSEMBLY TIME 10 minutes

Gear

- Cutting board
- Chef's knife
- 8-quart stockpot
- Slotted spoon
- Vegetable peeler
- 2 saucepans (1 medium, 1 small)
- Medium fry pan
- Tongs or wide spatula
- Blender or food processor

Ingredients

- 6 equal-sized unpeeled baby potatoes (russet or Yukon Gold), scrubbed and dried
- 4 eggs
- ½ pound French green beans (also called haricots verts), ends removed so that beans are equal in length
- Ice water (for blanching)
- ½ teaspoon corn oil
- Four 6-ounce tuna steaks
- 1 head Boston or Bibb lettuce, washed and dried (leaves kept whole)
- 2 medium-size ripe tomatoes, each cut into eighths
- 20 pitted black olives, sliced
- Salt and pepper
- ½ cup French Dressing (opposite page) or Balsamic Dressing (page 28)

Niçoise Salad with Fresh Tuna

Inspired by the coastal flavors of Nice, France, *niçoise* (nee-SWAHZ) salad is at home wherever fresh market produce is found. I usually like to make it after a trip to the farmers' market, so I know that my ingredients are as fresh as possible. Instead of fresh tuna, try substituting swordfish, mahi mahi, or salmon steaks.

1. Place the stockpot filled with water over medium-high heat, add a pinch of salt, and bring to a boil. Add potatoes and boil for 15 to 20 minutes, until soft. Remove from heat. Using a slotted spoon, remove the potatoes from the stockpot, allow to cool, peel off skin, and cut each into 6 wedges. Set aside.

2. Cook the eggs in a small saucepan according to the recipe instructions for Hard-Boiled Eggs (page 6). Remove eggs from the heat and allow to cool. Peel off shell and slice each into 6 slices. Set aside.

3. Place a medium saucepan filled with water over medium-high heat. When boiling, add the green beans and blanch (page xxiii) for 4 to 5 minutes, until al dente (cooked but still crisp). Using a slotted spoon, remove the beans and immediately plunge them in a bowl of ice water. Drain the beans in a colander and set aside.

4. Place the fry pan over high heat. When the pan is very hot*, coat the pan with a thin film of corn oil. Place the tuna steaks in the pan, as space allows. Sear (page xxiv) until underside is browned, about 2 minutes for medium-rare. Gently turn over using a wide spatula and sear for 1 to 2 minutes more, until browned. For extra-thick pieces of tuna, gently sear the sides as well, holding it upright with the tongs. Remove from the pan and set aside.

STEP 1

STEP 4

STEP 5

(5) Arrange 3 or 4 whole lettuce leaves on each plate to resemble the open leaves of a flower. Place 4 small tomato pieces around the leaves, add egg slices, and sprinkle with sliced olives. Place 6 potato slices in the center and top with a bundle of beans. Add salt and pepper to season. Liberally spoon dressing over each salad, then gently place seared tuna steak on top. Serve remainder of dressing on the side.

Is your pan hot enough? Test it with a drop of water. If it sizzles, you're ready to cook.

HOMEMADE FRENCH DRESSING

MAKES 1 CUP

PREP TIME 5 minutes

1 tablespoon Dijon mustard
2 egg yolks*
¼ cup white wine vinegar

¾ cup olive oil
Optional: 1 teaspoon sugar
Salt and pepper

Place the mustard, egg yolks, and vinegar in a blender. Cover and combine on low speed while adding oil in a very slow, steady stream to make an emulsion (see page 105). Taste; add 1 teaspoon of sugar, if needed. Add salt and pepper to season. Transfer to an airtight storage container and refrigerate until ready to use.

* See warning on page 5 about using raw eggs (or leave eggs out if preferred).

Marvelous Main Dishes

The variety of entrées in this section will build upon the skills you mastered in Level 1, but with an added level of sophistication and flair.

Learn how to bump up your repertoire to include hearty pastas, a savory roast, and delicate fish and seafood. You'll develop the skills to make your own multistep cream sauce and master the steps to putting together a delicious risotto. The delicious sauces and sides will elevate your meat and seafood dishes to new heights. You'll learn tons more along the way, and have a great time doing it!

IN THIS CHAPTER

In this chapter, you'll find recipes for:
- Linguine with Clams
- Tortellini with Peas, Basil, and Italian Sausage
- Baked Lasagna
- Eggplant Parmesan
- Asparagus, Pecorino, and Pea Risotto
- Whole Chicken Roasted with Herb Butter
- Crispy Chicken Cutlets with Mushrooms
- Chicken Cacciatore
- Traditional Pot Roast
- Veal Milanese
- Medallions of Pork
- Salmon Steaks with Champagne Butter
- Coconut Shrimp with Pineapple Salsa
- Chilean Sea Bass with Leeks

And you'll develop the skills and know-how to:
- Clean and cook shellfish safely
- Chiffonade basil leaves
- Make a perfect risotto in a few simple steps
- Braise meat for extra flavor and tenderness
- Pound chicken and veal into thin cutlets
- Roast a whole chicken

LEVEL 2

SERVES 4

PREP TIME 15 minutes

COOK TIME 20 minutes

Gear

- Cutting board
- Chef's knife
- Large bowl
- Scrubbing brush
- 8-quart stockpot
- Colander
- Large fry pan with lid
- Wooden spoon
- Tongs

Ingredients

- 3 dozen littleneck clams or cockles in the shell
- 1 tablespoon salt for pasta water
- ¾ pound dried linguine
- 3 tablespoons olive oil
- 1 large clove garlic, peeled and chopped
- 1 medium shallot, peeled and minced
- ½ cup white wine
- 3 tablespoons (⅜ stick) butter, diced
- ½ cup plus 1 tablespoon freshly grated Parmesan cheese
- 1½ tablespoons chopped fresh flat-leaf parsley
- Salt and pepper
- Pinch of red pepper flakes

Kitchen FYI

To eat the clams, pull out the meat, discard the shells in an empty bowl, and mix well with the pasta and sauce.

Linguine with Clams

The beauty of this dish is the combination of simple flavors: light and salty clams combined with a sharp bite from the Parmesan, some heat from the red pepper flakes, and freshness from the parsley. I always serve crusty bread with pasta, to soak up any leftover sauce.

1. Pick through clams, discarding any that are chipped, broken, or do not remain tightly closed. Place clams in a large bowl of water and soak for 20 minutes. Pull clams from water and scrub clean under running water with a brush to remove debris. Set aside until ready to use.

2. Fill the stockpot ¾ full with water and bring to a boil over medium-high heat. Add 1 tablespoon salt and the pasta, and cook according to instructions on the package, until pasta is al dente. Drain in a colander in the sink, and toss with 1 tablespoon olive oil. While pasta is cooking, start the clam sauce.

3. Place a large fry pan over medium-high heat. When hot*, add 2 tablespoons olive oil, the garlic, and shallots, and sweat (page xxiv) until soft and translucent, about 2 minutes. Add white wine and deglaze (pages xxiv–xxv) the pan, stirring with a wooden spoon.

4. Add the clams to the pan; cover. Steam the clams until ¾ of them open, 2 to 4 minutes. Remove lid and stir in the butter and 1 tablespoon of the Parmesan until sauce thickens. Allow sauce level to reduce (page xxv) by ⅓ (but still covering the clams).

5. When all clams have opened, reduce the heat to medium. Discard any unopened clams. Add ½ cup of Parmesan, parsley, salt and pepper to season, and red pepper flakes. Transfer the pasta to the pan, and toss all together, using tongs. To serve, divide pasta and clams into bowls using tongs, and garnish with remainder of Parmesan.

Is your pan hot enough? Test it with a drop of water. If it sizzles, you're ready to cook.

STEP 1

STEP 5

SERVES 8 TO 10
PREP TIME 35 minutes
COOK TIME 15 minutes

Gear

- Cutting board
- Chef's knife
- 2 saucepans (1 medium, 1 small)
- Fine-mesh sieve or strainer
- 8-quart stockpot
- Colander
- Large fry pan
- Plate
- Slotted spoon
- Whisk
- Wooden spoon
- Large spoon

Ingredients

- Kosher salt
- 1½ cups frozen peas
- 3 packages cheese tortellini (about 27 ounces total)
- 2 tablespoons olive oil
- 1 cup White Sauce (page 48)
- 1½ pounds (4 large links) Italian sausage (hot or mild), cut into 1-inch-wide pieces, casings intact
- 1 medium white onion, peeled and finely diced
- 3 cloves garlic, peeled, crushed, and minced
- ½ cup white wine
- 2 chicken bouillon cubes dissolved in hot water
- Pepper
- 1½ cups heavy cream
- ⅔ cup freshly grated Parmesan cheese
- 20 basil leaves, rolled and finely chopped just before using (page xix)

Tortellini with Peas, Basil, and Italian Sausage

This hearty dish is easy to prepare for large groups and always a favorite of my friends and guests. If your grocery store butcher doesn't offer Italian sausage, try substituting with packaged sausage (not the smaller breakfast links), the spicier, the better.

① Fill a medium saucepan ¾ full with water and bring to a boil over high heat. Add 1 teaspoon salt and the peas and blanch (page xxiii) for about 3 minutes, until al dente (cooked but still crisp). Pour into a strainer over the sink and immediately plunge peas into a bowl of ice water. Drain in a colander and set aside.

② Fill a stockpot ¾ full with water and bring to a boil over high heat. Add 1 tablespoon salt and the pasta, and cook according to instructions on the package, until pasta is al dente. Drain in a colander in the sink and toss with 1 tablespoon olive oil.

③ While pasta is cooking, prepare the White Sauce per the recipe instructions on page 48. Set aside until ready to use.

④ Place a large fry pan over medium-high heat. When hot*, add the sausage pieces and fry until golden brown and crisp, approximately 3 minutes each side. Remove from heat and transfer to a plate using a slotted spoon. Return fry pan to heat.

⑤ Reduce the heat to medium and add 1 tablespoon olive oil and the onions. Sweat (page xxiv) for 4 minutes, until the onions are soft and translucent.

PREP

STEP 7

STEP 8

(6) Add the garlic, white wine, and bouillon cubes, and salt and pepper to season. Simmer (page xxiii) for 4 minutes, until liquid level reduces (page xxv) by ⅓. Add the white sauce and heavy cream, and whisk until creamy.

(7) Place stockpot over medium heat and pour in the sauce. Add sausage and stir occasionally with a wooden spoon until well combined. Stir in peas, mix, then fold in tortellini.

(8) Sprinkle ½ the grated Parmesan into the pasta to thicken. Taste, and add salt and pepper to season. Fold in the basil, mix well, then remove from heat. To serve, transfer pasta and sauce into a large bowl or individual plates with a large spoon. Garnish with basil leaves and Parmesan.

*Is your pan hot enough? Test it with a drop of water. If it sizzles, you're ready to cook.

Ravioli with Peas and Pancetta Replace the tortellini with 2 packages fresh ravioli. Fry ½ cup chopped pancetta in a fry pan until golden brown on both sides, then add to pasta in Step 7.

SERVES 4
PREP TIME 30 minutes
COOK TIME 55 minutes

Gear

- 8-quart stockpot
- Cutting board
- Chef's knife
- Box grater or Microplane grater
- Colander
- Pastry brush
- 12- by 18-inch baking dish (also called a lasagna dish)
- Narrow spatula (for serving)

Ingredients

- 1 tablespoon salt
- 8-ounces lasagna noodles
- 2 tablespoons olive oil
- 3 cups Meat Sauce (page 42)
- 1 cup ricotta cheese (whole or part-skim)
- 1 tablespoon chopped fresh oregano leaves
- 3 tablespoons freshly grated Parmesan cheese
- 1 cup White Sauce (page 48)
- 1 cup grated mozzarella cheese

Kitchen FYI

Save time by assembling your lasagna earlier in the day. Simply cover the baking dish with plastic wrap and store it in the refrigerator until you're ready to bake.

Baked Lasagna

This is the perfect dish to utilize leftover Meat Sauce (page 42). Pair this lasagna with a side of Arugula and Parmesan with Balsamic Dressing (page 28) for a delicious Italian feast.

1. Preheat the oven to 375°F.

2. Fill a stockpot ¾ full with water and bring to a boil over high heat. Add the salt and the pasta, and cook according to package directions. Drain in a colander in the sink and toss with 1 tablespoon olive oil.

3. Brush the bottom and sides of a baking dish with about 1 tablespoon olive oil. Layer lasagna noodles across the bottom of the dish. Spread 1 cup of the meat sauce evenly over the lasagna.

4. Add a second layer of lasagna noodles. Spread the ricotta evenly over the lasagna. Sprinkle ½ of the chopped oregano and ½ of the Parmesan across the top. Pour ½ of the white sauce over and spread evenly.

STEP 3

STEP 4

STEP 5

5. Add a third layer of lasagna noodles and the remainder of the meat sauce. Top with a final layer of lasagna sheets and cover with remaining white sauce. Sprinkle evenly with the mozzarella and the remainder of the oregano and Parmesan. Drizzle 1 tablespoon olive oil across the top.

6. Place the assembled lasagna in the oven uncovered and bake for 40 to 45 minutes. Remove from oven and set aside to rest for 10 minutes before slicing. To serve, cut into even slices and gently lift out each piece with a spatula, using your fingers to steady if needed.

Beef and Cheddar Bake   Traditional lasagna isn't the only way to utilize that leftover meat sauce. It's easy to turn your classic lasagna recipe into something more unique, like this Beef and Cheddar Bake. Simply replace the mozzarella with 1 cup shredded cheddar cheese.

LEVEL

SERVES 4
PREP TIME 30 minutes
COOK TIME 25 minutes

Gear

- Cutting board
- Chef's knife
- Vegetable peeler
- Microplane grater
- 3 dinner plates
- Small bowl
- Whisk or fork
- Nonstick fry pan
- Tongs or wide spatula
- Baking sheet
- Baking dish

Ingredients

- 1 cup all-purpose flour
- 2 eggs
- ¼ cup whole milk
- 2 cups Bread Crumbs (page 48)
- 1 cup freshly grated Parmesan cheese
- Salt and pepper
- Pinch of cayenne pepper
- 2 large eggplants, peeled, trimmed, and sliced into ½-inch-thick disks
- ¼ cup plus 1 tablespoon olive oil
- 2 cups Basic Basics Tomato Sauce (page 41)
- 1-pound ball of fresh mozzarella, sliced into ½-inch-thick disks
- 20 whole basil leaves, plus 10 whole leaves finely chopped (page xix)

Eggplant Parmesan

Fresh, quality ingredients make this homemade version far superior to the eggplant Parmesan served in most restaurants. Follow these same steps for delicious Chicken Parmesan.

① Preheat the oven to 400°F.

② Prepare three plates for dredging the eggplant slices: Place the flour on the first plate; in a small bowl, lightly beat together the eggs and milk and add to second plate; combine bread crumbs and ¼ cup Parmesan on third plate, and add salt, pepper, and cayenne to season.

③ Carefully dip each eggplant slice first in the flour, then the egg mixture, then in the bread crumb mixture, until well coated. Set aside as you repeat with the remaining slices.

STEP 2

STEP 3

STEP 4

(4) Place the fry pan over medium-high heat. When hot*, add ¼ cup of the olive oil and the eggplant slices as space allows. Fry the eggplant, 3 to 4 minutes on each side, until golden brown. Using a spatula, transfer eggplant slices to a baking sheet (without stacking) until ready to use. Repeat with remaining batches if necessary.

(5) To assemble, pour ⅓ of the tomato sauce in bottom of a baking dish. Cover with a layer of eggplant slices. Add another layer of tomato sauce and remaining eggplant. Top with remainder of tomato sauce and the mozzarella. Garnish with whole basil leaves and drizzle with 1 tablespoon olive oil.

(6) Bake for 5 to 6 minutes, until mozzarella is fully melted. Remove from oven and set aside to rest for 10 minutes before serving. To serve, gently lift out each piece with a spatula, using your fingers to steady if needed. Garnish with remaining grated Parmesan and basil chiffonade.

*Is your pan hot enough? Test it with a drop of water. If it sizzles, you're ready to cook.

Chicken Parmesan   Make Chicken Parmesan easily by following the same steps for Eggplant Parmesan. Simply replace the eggplant with 4 chicken breast cutlets (about 5-ounces each) pounded to ½-inch thickness with a meat mallet or directly from the butcher.

LEVEL 2

SERVES 4
PREP TIME 20 minutes
COOK TIME 40 minutes

Gear

- Cutting board
- Chef's knife
- Microplane grater
- 8-quart stockpot
- Wooden spoon
- Fine-mesh sieve or strainer
- Medium bowl
- Slotted spoon
- Colander
- Medium saucepan
- Small ladle
- Silicone mixing spatula

Ingredients

RISOTTO

- 6 tablespoons (¾ stick) butter
- 1 medium yellow onion, peeled and finely diced (1 cup)
- 1 medium leek, trimmed and finely chopped (1 cup)
- 2 stalks celery, chopped
- 1 bay leaf
- 1 bunch asparagus, trimmed, 1-inch tips removed and reserved, the rest sliced into ¼-inch-thick rounds
- 2 cups frozen peas
- 4 cups homemade Chicken Stock (page 97) or store-bought, or vegetable stock (canned or boxed)
- 2 teaspoons olive oil
- 2 shallots, peeled and minced
- 1⅓ cups Arborio rice (do not substitute other kinds of rice)

(continues)

Asparagus, Pecorino, and Pea Risotto

Risotto has a reputation for being really difficult to prepare, but I disagree. It requires time and patience, but once you master the basics, you'll find that it's really accessible and worth the effort. The most important step: constant stirring. The result is a creamy and luxurious dish that just may surprise you (or your guests).

1. Place the medium stockpot over medium-high heat. When hot*, add 2 tablespoons of butter, the onions, leeks, and celery and sweat (page xxiv) for 5 minutes, until onions are soft and translucent. Add the bay leaf, chopped asparagus stalks, and 1 cup of the peas.

2. Stir in the chicken stock and cook for 20 minutes. Strain mixture through the fine-mesh strainer into the bowl, pressing on the solids. Discard the solids and return the liquid to the saucepan and bring to a boil.

3. Blanch (page xxiii) the asparagus tips and the remaining 1 cup of peas for 2 minutes each in the stock, until al dente (cooked but still crisp). Using the slotted spoon, remove asparagus and peas and immediately plunge them in a bowl of ice water. Drain in the colander and set aside. Reduce the heat under the saucepan to a simmer (page xxiii) and keep hot to make the risotto.

4. Place the medium saucepan over medium-high heat. When hot*, add the olive oil and shallots and sauté (page xxiv) for 1 to 2 minutes, until soft and translucent.

STEP 1

STEP 5

STEP 6

Ingredients (cont'd)

TO FINISH

- ¼ cup white wine
- ¼ cup heavy cream
- 1 tablespoon minced fresh chervil
- 1 tablespoon minced fresh tarragon
- 1 tablespoon minced fresh chives
- ¼ cup finely diced pecorino cheese
- 3 tablespoons freshly grated Parmesan cheese

Kitchen FYI

Risotto's key characteristic is its rich, creamy texture. If the rice is too stiff, add more stock and stir just before you serve. Just be warned: The risotto *cannot* sit on the stove; it will begin to absorb the stock after about 30 seconds, and will overcook if left over heat. Be sure to serve immediately after additional stock is added and well mixed.

⑤ Reduce the heat to medium and add the rice. Cook, stirring constantly, for 1 minute. Add the stock to the pot one ladle at a time while stirring with the silicone mixing spatula until the liquid is absorbed. Add more stock and continue stirring. Repeat until all stock is absorbed and rice is translucent, but creamy, about 15 to 20 minutes.

⑥ Stir in the wine, cream, the remaining 4 tablespoons of butter, ½ cups of blanched peas, blanched asparagus, chopped herbs, and ½ the pecorino. Continue to stir until smooth, then add the remaining pecorino. Remove from heat and spoon into shallow bowls or onto plates, and garnish with the Parmesan and remaining ½ cup of peas.

Is your pan hot enough? Test it with a drop of water. If it sizzles, you're ready to cook.

SERVES 4 PLUS LEFTOVERS
PREP TIME 15 minutes
COOK TIME 2 hours

Gear

- Cutting board
- Chef's knife
- Paring knife
- Vegetable peeler
- 2 bowls (1 small, 1 medium)
- Nonstick fry pan
- Roasting pan
- Baster or large spoon
- Tongs
- Instant-read thermometer
- Baking sheet
- Medium saucepan
- Whisk
- Fine-mesh strainer
- Optional: gravy separator; gravy bowl or boat; gravy ladle

Ingredients

- 1 tablespoon chopped fresh thyme (reserve stems)
- 1 tablespoon chopped fresh rosemary (reserve stems)
- 1 tablespoon chopped fresh flat-leaf parsley (reserve stems)
- 6 tablespoons (¾ stick) butter, softened (see page 14)
- 4- to 5-pound whole roasting chicken
- Salt and pepper
- Pinch of cayenne pepper
- 1 tablespoon olive oil
- 1 onion, peeled and coarsely chopped

(continues)

Whole Chicken Roasted with Herb Butter

There are countless flavor combinations to add to chicken, but this is my personal favorite: plain and simple, roasted with herb butter for a savory, tender finish.

1. Preheat the oven to 375°F. In the small bowl, mix the chopped herbs into the softened butter until fully blended.

2. Place chicken on the cutting board. With your fingers, lift the skin from the chicken breast and push 3 tablespoons of herb butter between the skin and the meat. Rub remaining herb butter on the outside of the chicken, covering the skin and legs. Add salt, pepper, and cayenne to season. Set aside until ready to use.

3. Place the fry pan over medium-high heat. When hot*, add the olive oil and potatoes and sauté (page xxiv) until golden brown, about 10 minutes. Remove from heat and set aside.

4. Place the onions, celery, carrots, and reserved herb stems in the center of the roasting pan. Using your hands, place the chicken on top of the vegetables breasts up.

5. Place chicken in the oven and roast for 1 hour. Every 20 minutes, remove the chicken from the oven using oven mitts, place it on a heat-resistant surface, and baste it with the pan juices using the baster or spoon. Using tongs, turn the potatoes. Return chicken to the oven.

STEP 2

STEP 4

STEP 5

Ingredients (cont'd)

- 3 stalks celery, coarsely chopped
- 2 carrots, peeled and coarsely chopped into ½-inch-thick rounds

SAUCE
- 1 teaspoon tomato paste
- 1 tablespoon all-purpose flour
- ½ cup red wine
- 1 chicken bouillon cube
- 2 tablespoons (¼ stick) butter
- 2 cups homemade Chicken Stock (see page 97) or store-bought

How Do I . . . ?

To remove the fat from the pan juices, for a healthier alternative to the sauce, use a gravy separator or baster before transferring deglazed juices into the saucepan.

6. Roast for 45 minutes more, without basting or turning, until chicken is golden brown. Test doneness by making a discreet slice between the leg and the breast (juice should run clear, not red), or use an instant-read thermometer Test doneness by making a discrete slice between the leg and the breast (juice should run clear, not red). Using an instant-read thermometer (see Temperature Guide for an Instant-Read Thermometer, page xxvi) check that the internal temperature near the breast is 165 degrees..

7. Remove the chicken from the oven and place the roasting pan on a heat-resistant surface. Carefully transfer the chicken to the cutting board and allow to rest for 15 minutes. Using tongs, transfer the potatoes to the baking sheet and return them to the oven to keep crisp.

8. While the chicken is resting, place the roasting pan on the stove over medium heat. Stir in the tomato paste and flour and cook for 3 minutes. Deglaze (pages xxiv–xxv) the pan with the wine and add the bouillon cube. Bring to a gentle simmer (page xxiii) and stir the browned bits into the liquid. Remove from heat.

9. Carefully pour the juices and solids into the medium saucepan over medium-high heat, and allow the mixture to simmer for 3 minutes. Add the chicken stock, mix well, and allow to simmer for an additional 6 minutes. Strain the sauce through a fine-mesh strainer into a bowl, pressing on the onions, celery, carrots, and herb stems. Return the liquid to the saucepan. Whisk in the butter.

10. To serve, carve the chicken (see turkey carving instructions and photos, page 180) and carefully transfer slices onto plates. Drizzle sauce on top, and serve remaining sauce in a bowl or gravy boat.

ˣIs your pan hot enough? Test it with a drop of water. If it sizzles, you're ready to cook.

STEP 8

STEP 9

LEVEL

SERVES 4
PREP TIME 15 minutes
COOK TIME 12 minutes

Gear
- Cutting board
- Chef's knife
- Meat mallet or rolling pin
- 3 dinner plates
- Nonstick fry pan
- Wide spatula or tongs
- Wire cooling rack

Ingredients
- ½ cup all-purpose flour
- 2 eggs
- 1½ cups Bread Crumbs (page 48)
- Salt and pepper
- 2 large (20-ounce) boneless, skinless chicken breast fillets, halved horizontally, pounded flat to four ¼- to ⅓-inch-thick cutlets (opposite page)
- ½ cup olive oil or corn oil plus 2 tablespoons
- 6 tablespoons (¾ stick) butter, softened (see page 14)
- 1½ cups white, crimini, or shiitake mushrooms, trimmed and sliced
- 1 recipe Butter Mashed Potatoes (page 196)

Crispy Chicken Cutlets with Mushrooms

Simple chicken cutlets are elevated to new heights by adding flavorful mushrooms. Serve with Buttery Mashed Potatoes (page 196) for a truly classic combination.

1. Prepare three plates for dredging the chicken: Place the flour on the first plate; in a small bowl, lightly beat the eggs and add to second plate; combine bread crumbs, salt, and pepper on third plate.

2. Carefully dip each chicken breast first in the flour, then the egg mixture, then in the bread crumb mixture, until completely coated. Set aside as you repeat with the remaining chicken. You should have an even, light crust on all sides of each chicken breast.

STEP 2

STEP 3

③ Place the nonstick fry pan over medium-high heat. When hot*, add ¼ cup of the olive or corn oil and the chicken breasts as space allows. Sauté (page xxiv) the chicken, about 4 minutes on each side, until golden brown. Using the spatula, carefully transfer the chicken to the wire rack (over paper towels to catch drippings) or to a plate lined with paper towels until ready to use. Repeat with remaining batches if necessary, adding remaining ¼ cup of oil.

④ Discard the oil from the fry pan and return to medium-high heat. When hot*, add the 2 tablespoons of olive or corn oil and the mushrooms. Sauté for 3 to 4 minutes, until mushrooms are golden brown. Remove from heat and set aside.

⑤ To serve, spoon mashed potatoes onto each plate and top with chicken breast. Add mushrooms to top and drizzle with butter.

*Is your pan hot enough? Test it with a drop of water. If it sizzles, you're ready to cook.

Chicken with Capers and Lemon   Add 3 tablespoons of drained capers and the juice of 1 lemon in Step 4 (omitting the mushrooms) and mix well. Spoon mixture on top of the chicken, and garnish with 1 tablespoon chopped flat-leaf parsley.

HOW TO POUND A CHICKEN CUTLET

Here's the easy method . . .
Ask the butcher to do it for you when you purchase the meat.

Or the do-it-yourself method . . .
Place the chicken cutlet between two sheets of plastic wrap, or inside a resealable plastic bag, and lay it on a flat surface. Use a meat mallet, rolling pin, or a small, heavy fry pan to pound the wrapped fillet so that it spreads outward in all directions. You want an evenly flattened cutlet, between ¼ and ⅓ inch thick, depending on the type of meat and what your recipe calls for. This method can also be used for veal, pork, or turkey cutlets.

SERVES 4

PREP TIME 15 minutes

COOK TIME 2 hours

Gear

- Cutting board
- Optional: cleaver
- Chef's knife
- Paring knife
- Dutch oven
- Plate
- Wooden spoon
- Tongs

Ingredients

- 1 tablespoon olive oil
- 1 chicken (4 to 5 pounds), cut into 8 pieces (by butcher, if possible)
- 1 large red onion, peeled and sliced ½ inch thick
- ½ each red, yellow, and orange bell peppers, trimmed, seeded, and cut into ½-inch-wide strips
- 1 cup Basic Basics Tomato Sauce (page 41)
- One 28-ounce can chopped or diced tomatoes
- 1 chicken bouillon cube
- Salt and pepper
- 1 cup white mushrooms, trimmed and quartered
- 2 teaspoons chopped fresh oregano or 1 teaspoon dried
- ¼ cup chopped fresh basil leaves

Chicken Cacciatore

This hearty tomato-based chicken stew is a true Italian classic. It requires a few hours to cook, but not a lot of attention. Serve it over buttered linguine or Boiled Long-Grain White Rice (page 74) with a side of Roasted Brussels Sprouts with Almonds (page 140) or Green Bean Parcels (page 199).

① Preheat the oven to 375°F. Place the Dutch oven over high heat. When hot*, add the oil and chicken pieces and fry until golden brown, about 5 minutes on each side. Remove the chicken from the pot and set aside on the plate until ready to use.

② Add the onions and peppers to the pot and fry for 5 minutes, stirring constantly. Add the tomato sauce, chopped tomatoes (along with any juice), and bouillon cube. Add salt and pepper to season and bring mixture to a simmer (page xxiii), stirring constantly.

③ Mix in the mushrooms and oregano. Using tongs, add the chicken (along with any juices) to the mixture and gently stir until well combined and chicken is completely covered in sauce.

④ Transfer the pot to the oven and cook, uncovered, for 1¾ hours. Remove from oven, place on a heat-resistant surface, and stir in the basil. Set aside to cool for 3 to 5 minutes before serving.

Is your pan hot enough? Test it with a drop of water. If it sizzles, you're ready to cook.

STEP 1

STEP 3

STEP 4

③
LEVEL

SERVES 4 PLUS LEFTOVERS
PREP TIME 25 minutes
COOK TIME 3 hours,
20 minutes

Gear

- Cutting board
- Chef's knife
- Vegetable peeler
- Dutch oven with lid
- Tongs
- Large spoon or small ladle for skimming

Ingredients

- 2 tablespoons vegetable oil
- 3 pounds beef pot roast, such as brisket or eye of round
- Salt and pepper
- 2 carrots, peeled and coarsely chopped
- 2 medium yellow onions, peeled and coarsely chopped
- 4 stalks celery, coarsely chopped
- 2 large sprigs of fresh thyme
- 1 bay leaf
- 1 cup red wine
- 2 cups store-bought gravy
- 1 cup water

Kitchen FYI

If the pan juice gets too thick while the meat is cooking, thin it out with water; if the pan is drying out, add ½ cup of water, then return pot to the oven.

Traditional Pot Roast

Braising the meat truly enhances the flavor and keeps it moist and tender. You can use different cuts of meat, though the best ones will have lots of marbled fat for added flavor. Serve this roast with Buttery Mashed Potatoes (page 196) or Green Bean Parcels (page 199), or simply some dinner rolls or biscuits, warmed in the oven and lightly buttered.

① Preheat the oven to 350°F. Place Dutch oven over high heat. When hot*, add the oil, beef, and season with salt and pepper. Using tongs to hold it in place, sear (page xxiv) the meat on all sides, about 5 minute per side, until brown.

② Push the meat to one side of the pan and add the carrots, onions, celery, thyme, and bay leaf; using tongs, move the beef on top of the vegetables. Pour the wine, brown gravy, and water around the vegetables and beef.

③ Bring to a boil, then cover and transfer the Dutch oven to the oven. Cook for 2 hours, until gravy has thickened and the meat has browned. Taste, and add salt and pepper to season. Return pot to oven and cook for 1 hour more.

④ Remove pot from oven and place on a heat-resistant surface. Test the beef's doneness by pressing down gently; it should be soft and tender. If meat is still tough, return it to the oven and continue to cook, checking every 10 minutes, until desired texture is achieved. Using tongs, carefully transfer the beef to a large platter or cutting board. Skim off grease from the sauce using the spoon or small ladle.

⑤ Turn the meat on its side so the muscle fibers are parallel to the cutting board. Carefully slice the meat against the grain, or in the opposite direction of the muscle fibers. To serve, place meat slices on a plate and drizzle gravy across the top.

*Is your pan hot onough? Test it with a drop of water. It it sizzles, you're ready to cook.

STEP 1

STEP 2

STEP 5

LEVEL 2

SERVES 4

PREP TIME 20 minutes

COOK TIME 15 minutes

Gear

- Cutting board
- Chef's knife
- Meat mallet or rolling pin
- Microplane grater
- Optional: salad spinner
- 3 dinner plates
- Nonstick fry pan
- Tongs or metal spatula
- Wire cooling rack
- Vegetable peeler for Parmesan

Ingredients

- ½ cup all-purpose flour
- 1 egg
- 1 tablespoon milk
- 1½ cups Bread Crumbs (page 48)
- Salt and pepper
- Cayenne pepper
- Four 5-ounce boneless veal cutlets, pounded flat to ¼- to ⅓-inch thick
- ½ cup olive oil
- 1 lemon, ½ zested and juiced, ½ cut into 4 wedges for garnish
- 5 tablespoons butter
- 2 tablespoons chopped fresh flat-leaf parsley
- 1 bunch fresh arugula, trimmed, well washed, and tossed in olive oil

Veal Milanese

Like Crispy Chicken Cutlets (page 122), this recipe consists of thin cuts of meat that are breaded, then fried. I like my Milanese clean and simple—crispy, well-seasoned veal cutlets with a side of fresh arugula.

① Prepare three plates for dredging the veal: Place the flour on the first plate; in a small bowl, lightly beat the egg and milk and add to second plate; combine bread crumbs, salt, pepper, and cayenne on third plate.

② Carefully dip each cutlet first in the flour, then the egg mixture, then in the bread crumb mixture, until well coated. Set aside as you repeat with the remaining cutlets. You should have an even, light crust on all sides of each cutlet.

PREP

STEP 2

STEP 3

(3) Place the nonstick fry pan over medium-high heat. When hot*, add ¼ cup of the olive oil and the cutlets as space allows. Fry the cutlets for 2 to 3 minutes on each side, until golden brown. Using the spatula, carefully transfer the cutlets to the wire rack (over paper towels to catch drippings) or to a plate lined with paper towels until ready to use. Repeat with the remaining cutlets and remaining ¼ cup olive oil, if necessary.

(4) Remove the fry pan from heat and add the lemon zest, juice, and butter to the hot pan. Mix or swirl together with the pan juices. Add the parsley and mix until well combined. To serve, place one cutlet on each plate and carefully drizzle pan sauce across the top. Garnish with a handful of arugula tossed in olive oil and lemon wedges.

*Is your pan hot enough? Test it with a drop of water. If it sizzles, you're ready to cook.

Chicken Milanese   Replace the veal cutlets with 2 large (10-ounce) boneless, skinless chicken breast fillets, halved horizontally and pounded flat into ¼- to ⅛-inch thick cutlets.

LEVEL

SERVES 4
PREP TIME   10 minutes
COOK TIME   10 minutes

Gear

- Cutting board
- Chef's knife
- 2 plates
- Small bowl
- Fry pan
- Wide spatula
- Wooden spoon
- Whisk

Ingredients

- 1 tablespoon all-purpose flour, for dusting
- ¼ cup plus 1 tablespoon olive oil
- 1 tablespoon Dijon mustard
- 1½ pounds pork tenderloin, sliced into ¾-inch-thick medallions
- Salt and pepper
- ½ medium yellow onion, peeled and minced
- 1 clove garlic, peeled and minced
- 10 white mushrooms, trimmed and sliced ¾ inch thick
- ¾ cup Madeira, dry marsala, sherry, or white wine
- 1½ cups heavy cream
- ½ cup homemade Chicken Stock (page 97) or store-bought, or ½ bouillon cube dissolved in ½ cup hot water
- 2 teaspoons chopped fresh sage or flat-leaf parsley, plus extra (whole) for garnish
- Optional: 2 tablespoons (¼ stick) butter; cayenne pepper

Medallions of Pork

The rich flavors of pork combine well here with the light, creamy sauce. This simple dish can be easily doubled for eight people. For an even healthier alternative, omit the butter altogether.

1. Prepare two plates and one bowl for seasoning and dredging the pork: Place the flour on the first plate; in the small bowl, mix 1 tablespoon of the olive oil and the mustard; leave the second plate for finished medallions.

2. Season medallions with salt and pepper. Coat each medallion first with the oil and mustard mixture, then dip in the flour until well coated. Set aside as you repeat with the remaining pork. You should have an even, light flour coating on all sides of each medallion.

3. Place the fry pan over medium-high heat. When hot*, add ⅔ of the remaining oil and the medallions as space allows. Sauté (page xxiv) the medallions until underside is golden brown, about 5 minutes.

4. Gently turn medallions over, careful not to splash the oil, and cook for 1 minute more. Using the spatula, carefully transfer the medallions to a plate until ready to use. Test doneness by making a discreet slice in the middle of a medallion; center should be slightly pink.

5. Return pan to medium-high heat and add the remaining olive oil, the onions, and garlic. Sweat (page xxiv) for 4 minutes, until onions are soft and translucent.

STEP 6

STEP 9

(6) Add the mushrooms and sauté for 2 minutes. Add ⅓ cup of the wine and mix well, stirring in remaining browned bits at the bottom of the pan.

(7) Add the cream and chicken stock and simmer (page xxiii) until liquid level reduces (page xxv) by ⅓ in the pan, about 3 minutes. Stir in any remaining juice from the plate of pork, then whisk in the remaining wine.

(8) Add the herbs and butter, if using, and whisk until sauce is thick but still pliable, about 1 minute. Taste and add salt, pepper, and cayenne to season, if using.

(9) Transfer the medallions back to the pan and stir until the meat is warmed and coated with sauce. Cook for 3 to 4 minutes, then remove from heat. To serve, evenly distribute medallions on plates, and spoon mushrooms across the top and around the plate rim. Drizzle sauce over the medallions and garnish with whole herb leaves.

*Is your pan hot enough? Test it with a drop of water. If it sizzles, you're ready to cook.

②

LEVEL

SERVES 4

PREP TIME 20 minutes

COOK TIME 20 minutes

Gear

- Cutting board
- Chef's knife
- Vegetable peeler
- Small saucepan
- Strainer
- Colander
- Nonstick fry pan
- Wide spatula
- Baking sheet
- Wooden spoon
- Small bowl
- Whisk

Ingredients

- 1 medium carrot, peeled and finely diced (about ¼ cup)
- 1 small leek, white part only, washed, trimmed, and finely diced (about ¼ cup)
- 2 tablespoons olive oil
- 4 salmon steaks (6 to 7 ounces each)
- Salt and pepper
- 1 tablespoon vegetable oil
- 1 shallot, peeled and minced
- ⅓ cup Champagne, sparkling wine, or white wine
- 2 lemon slices, seeds removed
- ⅓ cup heavy cream
- 8 tablespoons (1 stick) cold unsalted butter, cut into small cubes
- 1 teaspoon finely chopped fresh tarragon leaves
- 1 teaspoon finely chopped fresh chives

Salmon Steaks with Champagne Butter

This refreshing dish is an elegant yet simple twist on a French bistro classic. Salmon steaks are not as delicate as other types of fish but they still need to be handled with care since they become more fragile when they cook. Finishing with champagne or wine butter gives this dish quite a romantic undertone.

(1) Preheat the oven to 300°F.

(2) Place the small saucepan over medium-high heat and add 2 cups of salted water. When boiling, add carrots and blanch (page xxiii) for 1 to 2 minutes until al dente (cooked but still crisp). Using the strainer, drain the carrots, then immediately plunge them in a bowl of ice water. Drain the carrots in the colander and set aside. Repeat process for the leeks and set aside.

(3) Place the fry pan over medium-high heat. When hot*, add the olive oil and salmon steaks and salt and pepper to season. Pan-fry (page xxiv) until underside is golden brown, about 3 minutes. Using the wide spatula, gently turn steaks over and fry for 3 minutes more, until golden brown.

(4) Transfer steaks to the baking sheet and place in the oven. Cook for 8 minutes more, until golden brown and firm to the touch, then remove from oven and set aside.

PREP

STEP 3 (A)

STEP 3 (B)

(5) While the salmon is cooking, make the sauce: Place the saucepan over medium-high heat. When hot*, add the vegetable oil and shallots and sweat (page xxiv) until shallots are soft, 2 to 3 minutes.

(6) Stir in ⅔ of the Champagne and the lemon slices, and reduce the heat to medium. Cook for 3 minutes more. Stir in the cream and continue cooking until the sauce is thick enough to coat the back of the wooden spoon. Reduce the heat to low, then whisk in the butter until dissolved.

(7) Strain the sauce into the small bowl, then return to the saucepan to continue cooking on low heat. Stir in the carrots, leeks, and herbs, then whisk in remaining Champagne. Remove from heat and set aside.

(8) To serve, place a salmon steak in the center of each plate and drizzle 2–3 tablespoon of sauce around and over each piece.

*Is your pan hot enough? Test it with a drop of water. If it sizzles, you're ready to cook.

Gear

- Cutting board
- Chef's knife
- Medium bowl
- 3 dinner plates
- Cast-iron fry pan
- Tongs
- Instant-read thermometer

Ingredients

SALSA

- ½ cup finely diced tomatoes (about 3 medium tomatoes)
- ½ cup finely diced fresh pineapple (about ⅛ of a whole pineapple)
- ¼ medium red onion, peeled and finely diced
- 1 tablespoon ketchup
- 1 tablespoon Thai sweet chili sauce or ½ tablespoon regular chili sauce plus ½ tablespoon olive oil plus ½ teaspoon sugar
- 2 tablespoons toasted sesame oil
- 1 tablespoon chopped fresh cilantro leaves
- Salt and pepper

SHRIMP

- ½ cup all-purpose flour
- 2 eggs
- 1 cup Bread Crumbs (page 48)
- ½ cup dried grated coconut
- 1½ pounds large shrimp, peeled (tails intact) and deveined
- ⅓ cup corn oil, for frying
- Salt and pepper

Coconut Shrimp with Pineapple Salsa

This flavorful dish is as easy as it is versatile; serve the shrimp on toothpicks for small bites that can be passed around, or with a side of Coconut Sticky Rice (page 141) as an appetizer.

1. Make the salsa: In the medium bowl, combine the tomatoes, pineapple, onion, ketchup, sweet chili sauce, sesame oil, and cilantro. Stir together, taste, and add salt and pepper to season. Cover and refrigerate until needed.

2. Prepare three plates for dredging the shrimp: Place flour on the first plate; in a small bowl, lightly beat the eggs and add to second plate; combine bread crumbs and coconut on third plate.

3. Carefully dip each shrimp first in the flour, then the egg, then the bread crumb and coconut mixture, until well coated. Set aside as you repeat with the remaining shrimp. You should have an even, light crust on all sides of the shrimp.

4. Place the fry pan over high heat. Add the corn oil and heat to 365°F (check using an instant-read thermometer). Reduce the heat to medium-high and adjust until the oil temperature remains steady. (Oil should be hot but not smoking.)

5. Use tongs to place shrimp, one by one, in the oil, as space allows. Fry until underside is golden brown, 1 to 2 minutes. Using tongs, gently turn over each shrimp, careful not to splash the oil, and fry for 1 to 2 minutes more, until edges of shrimp are pink and underside is golden brown. Transfer to a plate lined with paper towels. Add salt and pepper to season, and serve immediately with lemon wedges.

STEP 1

STEP 5 (A)

STEP 5 (B)

SERVES 4

PREP TIME 12 minutes

COOK TIME 20 minutes

Gear

- Cutting board
- Chef's knife
- Microplane grater
- 2 bowls (1 small, 1 large)
- Spreader
- Baking sheet
- Small saucepan
- Slotted spoon
- Colander
- Wooden spoon
- Metal spatula

Ingredients

CRUST

- 3 tablespoons (⅜ stick) butter
- 1 cup Bread Crumbs (page 48) or panko
- 1 tablespoon chopped fresh basil
- 1 tablespoon chopped fresh chives
- Grated zest of 1 lemon
- Grated zest of 1 lime
- Four 6-ounce fillets Chilean sea bass

LEEKS

- 2 medium leeks, well washed, sliced horizontally (white parts and ½ of green parts)
- Ice water
- 1 cup heavy cream
- ¼ cup white wine
- 2 tablespoons (¼ stick) butter
- Salt and pepper

Chilean Sea Bass with Leeks

The subtle fresh sea bass and the creamy leeks complement each other well in this dish. If Chilean sea bass isn't available, then buy whatever fish looks the most fresh that day. Red snapper, halibut, fluke, and cod all work well with this recipe.

1. Preheat the oven to 375°F. In the small bowl, add the butter and melt in the microwave, about 20 seconds on high. Combine the bread crumbs with the melted butter and mix in the herbs and lemon and lime zests.

2. Coat the top of the fish fillets with the crust and smooth down with fingers. Transfer the fillets to the buttered baking sheet, place in the oven, and bake for 12 to 15 minutes, until golden on top. Remove from oven and set aside.

3. While the fish is cooking, prepare the leeks: Place the small saucepan over medium-high heat and fill ¾ full with salted water. When boiling, add leeks and blanch (page xxiii) for 4 to 5 minutes, until al dente (cooked but still crisp). Using the slotted spoon, remove the leeks and immediately plunge them in a bowl of ice water. Drain the leeks in the colander and set aside.

4. Place the saucepan back over medium heat. When hot*, add the cream, wine, and butter and cook, stirring constantly, for 7 to 10 minutes, until sauce is thick and creamy. Taste and add salt and pepper to season.

5. Add in leeks and continue cooking for 2 to 3 minutes over medium heat, slowly stirring, until sauce is thick enough to coat the back of the wooden spoon. To serve, distribute leeks evenly on plates and place fish directly on top. Drizzle remaining sauce on top.

*Is your pan hot enough? Test it with a drop of water. If it sizzles, you're ready to cook

STEP 2

STEP 3

STEP 5

More Sides

Now that you've mastered some basics from Level 1, step it up and try these hearty side dishes. They're flavorful, nutritious, and simple to make.

Some of the recipes also offer multiple ways to cook your sides; try grilling vegetables in summer, or roast them when you want to stay indoors. Sides should complement the flavors and textures of your main dishes. And keep seasonality in mind: the fresher your vegetables, the more delicious your dish will be.

IN THIS CHAPTER

In this chapter, you'll find recipes for:
- Twice-Baked Potatoes
- Medley of Vegetables, Roasted or Grilled
- Corn on the Cob
- Pan-Roasted Carrots
- Roasted Brussels Sprouts with Almonds
- Coconut Sticky Rice

And you'll develop the skills and know-how to:
- Prepare a variety of vegetables to serve alongside your main dishes in just a few simple steps

SERVES 4

PREP TIME 10 minutes

COOK TIME 1¼ to 1½ hours

Gear

- Cutting board
- Chef's knife
- Box grater
- 2 bowls (1 large, 1 small)
- Baking sheet

Ingredients

POTATOES

- 4 Baked Potatoes (page 73), cooled
- 2 tablespoons cream cheese
- 2 tablespoons (¼ stick) butter
- 2 tablespoons chopped fresh chives
- Salt and pepper

TOPPING

- 2 tablespoons grated cheddar cheese
- 2 tablespoons grated Gruyère cheese

Twice-Baked Potatoes

Twice-baked potatoes use the skin of the potato to create a shell, which is then filled with a blend of the potato's fluffy inside, savory cheeses, and butter. Then it's baked a second time. Serve these alongside a juicy Traditional Pot Roast (page 125), Roast Turkey (page 178), or Boneless Leg of Lamb (page 184).

(1) Preheat the oven to 400°F.

(2) Prepare baked potatoes according to the recipe instructions (page 73). Set aside to cool for 10 minutes.

(3) Cut the baked potatoes in half lengthwise. Scoop out potato flesh into the large bowl and mix with cream cheese, butter, chopped chives, salt, and pepper.

(4) Fill each potato half with the potato and cheese filling and place on the baking sheet. Combine the cheeses in the small bowl and sprinkle on top of potato halves.

(5) Place potatoes in the oven and bake for 10 minutes, until cheese begins to melt. Turn on the broiler and cook potatoes for 1 minute more, or until cheese is golden brown. Remove from oven and serve immediately.

STEP 2

STEP 3

STEP 4

LEVEL

SERVES 4
PREP TIME   10 minutes
COOK TIME   10 to 20 minutes

Gear

- Cutting board
- Chef's knife
- Paring knife
- Blender
- Large bowl
- Fry pan
- Tongs
- 2 baking sheets

Ingredients

- 3 medium cloves garlic, peeled
- 2 tablespoons fresh thyme leaves
- ½ cup plus 2 tablespoons olive oil
- 1 red bell pepper quartered, trimmed, seeded, and cut into 2 wedges (8 pieces per pepper)
- 1 yellow bell pepper, quartered, trimmed, seeded, and cut into 2 wedges (8 pieces per pepper)
- 1 orange bell pepper, quartered, trimmed, seeded, and cut into 2 wedges (8 pieces per pepper)

(continues)

Medley of Vegetables, Roasted or Grilled

I love this as a summer side with a piece of simply grilled fish or chicken. It also makes the perfect light partner to Veal Milanese (page 126) or Jumbo Shrimp with Lemon, Garlic, and Tarragon (page 65). You should be able to find the ingredients year around.

(1) Preheat the oven to 375°F if roasting vegetables, or preheat grill or broiler on medium. Make the garlic oil: Add the garlic, thyme leaves, and ½ cup olive oil to blender. Puree until smooth.

(2) In the large bowl, add the vegetables and the garlic oil and toss well. Add salt and pepper to season.

(3) Place the fry pan over medium-high heat. When hot*, add the remaining 2 tablespoons of olive oil and the peppers. Sauté (page xxiv) for 2 to 3 minutes, until golden brown. Remove from heat and set aside on the baking sheet. Repeat with remaining batches of vegetables. Due to variable cooking times (see chart), eggplant, zucchini, and peppers should be placed on one baking sheet, mushrooms and asparagus on another.

(4) Finish cooking vegetables according to the Cooking Chart (opposite page). **To roast:** Place baking sheets in oven and cook according to chart. **To grill:** Place vegetables directly on grill rack. Cook until vegetables are soft to the touch and easily cut with a knife. Using tongs, turn once for even browning. Remove from heat and serve.

Is your pan hot enough? Test it with a drop of water. If it sizzles, you're ready to cook.

PREP

STEP 3

STEP 4

Ingredients (cont'd)

- 1 medium zucchini, trimmed, sliced on an angle ¾ inch thick
- 1 medium eggplant, top and ends trimmed, sliced on an angle into ½-inch rounds
- ½ bunch asparagus, bottom third removed, tips cut on an angle
- 3 large portobello mushrooms, trimmed and thickly sliced lengthwise
- Salt and pepper

Vegetable Cooking Chart

Portobello Mushrooms	5 to 6 minutes
Asparagus	6 minutes
Eggplant	8 to 10 minutes
Zucchini	8 to 10 minutes
Peppers	20 minutes

COOKING GREEN VEGETABLES

Follow these simple guidelines to help you get the most from your green veggies:

- Use 5 times the volume of water as vegetables. For example, boil 2 cups of peas in 10 cups of water.
- Never leave cooking vegetables unattended; they cook fairly rapidly. There is only a 30-second difference between bright, nutritious green vegetables and soft, discolored, tasteless ones.
- Vegetable cook times can be monitored visually (this will come with experience). But here's a basic timing list:
  - Broccoli: 4 to 5 minutes
  - Asparagus: 4 to 5 minutes
  - French green beans (also called haricots verts): 6 minutes
  - Sugar snap peas: 3 minutes
  - Snow peas: 30 to 45 seconds

SERVES 4
PREP TIME 5 minutes
COOK TIME 5 minutes

Gear

- 8-quart stockpot
- Colander

Ingredients

- 1 tablespoon salt, plus more to season
- 1 tablespoon pepper, plus more to season
- ¼ cup sugar
- 4 ears of corn, shucked (husk and silk removed)
- 2 tablespoons (¼ stick) butter

Corn on the Cob

I like to serve this corn with savory seafood dishes or as a casual side to anything grilled outdoors. For a great snack, roll warm, buttered corn on the cob in grated Parmesan cheese and dust with cayenne pepper.

① Fill stockpot ⅔ full of water and add the salt, pepper, and sugar. Place over medium-high heat and bring to a boil. Add the corn and cook for 4 to 5 minutes.

② Remove from heat and drain in the colander. Return corn to stockpot and toss with the butter and additional salt and pepper. Serve immediately.

PREP

STEP 1

Grilled Corn on the Cob, Two Ways:

Outdoor Grill: Preheat grill on high and place buttered, seasoned corn directly on the grate. Grill, turning continuously with tongs, until golden brown on all sides, about 3 minutes per side.

Broiler: Place buttered, seasoned corn on top of the baking sheet. Place directly beneath the broiler and cook, turning continuously with tongs, until golden brown on all sides.

BROILER

③
LEVEL

SERVES 4
PREP TIME   5 minutes
COOK TIME   10 to 15 minutes

Gear

- Cutting board
- Vegetable peeler
- Chef's knife
- Medium saucepan
- Colander

Ingredients

- 1 to 1½ pounds carrots, washed, peeled, and cut on an angle into ⅓-inch-thick slices
- 1 teaspoon sugar
- 1 tablespoon (⅛ stick) butter
- Salt and pepper
- ½ tablespoon olive oil

Change It Up

For a savory/sweet holiday side dish, add 1 tablespoon of maple syrup and a pinch of cinnamon to the carrots in step 2.

Pan-Roasted Carrots

This easy-to-prepare classic pairs well with any meat or fish dish. Pan-roasting the carrots really enhances their naturally sweet flavor. For a flavor twist, add a few dashes of soy sauce to the pan when cooking. Or add a few fresh sprigs of rosemary during the last few minutes of cooking time.

1. Place the medium saucepan over high heat and fill with water. Bring to a boil and add the carrots, sugar, butter, salt, and pepper. Cook for 6 to 8 minutes, until carrots are tender.

2. Drain carrots in the colander and return to the saucepan. Add the olive oil and sauté (page xxiv) carrots over high heat until golden brown, about 5 minutes. Remove from heat and serve immediately.

PREP  **STEP 1**  **STEP 2**

LEVEL

Gear

- Cutting board
- Paring knife
- Medium saucepan
- Slotted spoon
- Medium bowl
- Colander
- Fry pan
- Small roasting pan

Ingredients

- 1½ pounds Brussels sprouts, trimmed (remove ends of stems)
- 3 tablespoons olive oil
- 2 tablespoons (¼ stick) butter
- ¼ cup sliced almonds
- Salt and pepper

Roasted Brussels Sprouts with Almonds

Brussels sprouts are bitter by nature, but caramelizing them neutralizes the flavor. The sliced almonds give this dish an added element of flavor and texture, making it the perfect side to Whole Chicken Roasted with Herb Butter (page 120) or Medallions of Pork (page 128), or Roast Turkey with Stuffing (page 178).

1. Fill the medium saucepan ¾ full with salted water and place over medium-high heat. When boiling, add the sprouts and blanch (page xxiii) for 7 to 8 minutes, until tender (or a knife slides through easily).

2. Using the slotted spoon, remove the sprouts and immediately plunge them in a bowl of ice water. Drain the sprouts in the colander, then place on the cutting board. Slice the sprouts in half through the stem.

3. Preheat the oven 375°F. Place the fry pan over medium-high heat. When hot*, add the olive oil, and the sprouts, and add salt and pepper to season. Sauté (page xxiv) the sprouts until golden brown on all sides, 6 to 8 minutes. Stir in the butter and almonds.

4. Transfer sprouts to the small roasting pan and place in the oven. Cook for 4–5 minutes or until almonds are golden brown. Remove from oven and serve immediately.

Is your pan hot enough? Test it with a drop of water. If it sizzles, you're ready to cook.

PREP

STEP 3

SERVES 4
PREP TIME 5 to 10 minutes
COOK TIME 15 minutes

Gear

- Cutting board
- Chef's knife
- Paring knife
- Medium saucepan

Ingredients

- 1 cup basmati rice
- 1¼ cups water
- 1 cup unsweetened coconut milk
- Salt and pepper
- 3 medium scallions, trimmed and chopped
- 1 tablespoon chopped fresh cilantro leaves
- 1 tablespoon Thai sweet chili sauce

Coconut Sticky Rice

The coconut milk gives this short-grained rice added creaminess and a delicately fragrant flavor. It's particularly delicious with Chicken with Thai Green Curry (page 175), or Vegetable Stir-Fry (page 50).

1. Place the medium saucepan over high heat. Add the rice, water, and salt and pepper to season. Cover with a lid, and bring to a boil.

2. Reduce until simmering (page xxiii), and cook for 8 minutes or until water is almost completely evaporated. Add the coconut milk. Continue to cook, covered, until all liquid is absorbed, about 5 minutes.

3. Use a fork to fold in the scallions, cilantro, and sweet chili sauce. Remove from heat and serve warm.

STEP 2

STEP 3

Delicious Desserts

Now that you've mastered the basics, like cookies and brownies, you're ready to try more challenging desserts like flourless chocolate cake, bread pudding, and even a creamy pie. These decadent treats are sure to impress your guests and make the perfect end to a delicious meal.

The key to baking is timing and precision. Be sure to measure your ingredients carefully, don't overmix batters or creams, and keep an eye on your desserts while they're in the oven. Many of the desserts in this section require very little cooking or baking time, making it a snap to get a tasty, sophisticated dessert out on the table.

IN THIS CHAPTER

In this chapter, you'll find recipes for:
- Chocolate Pots
- Chocolate Truffle Cake
- Bread Pudding
- Banana Cream and Toffee Pie

And you'll develop the skills and know-how to:
- Use a springform pan to keep your cake intact
- Give a simple chocolate pot added flavor twists in just one step
- Use fresh vanilla beans
- Easily cut clean slices of cake and pie

SERVES 4

PREP TIME 5 minutes

COOK TIME 20 minutes

SETTING TIME 4 hours

Gear

- Cutting board
- Chef's knife
- Small saucepan
- Glass or stainless-steel bowl
- Whisk
- 4 ramekins (5 ounces)

Ingredients

- 1 cup heavy cream
- ¾ cup semisweet chocolate chips or chocolate bar (at least 60% cacao), coarsely chopped
- 2 egg yolks
- 2 tablespoons Bailey's Irish Cream liqueur
- 4 tablespoons (½ stick) butter
- Whipped Cream (page 79), for serving
- Fresh seasonal fruit, for serving

Kitchen FYI

Don't heat the cream beyond the just-boiling point. If mixture is too hot, the eggs will begin to scramble when mixed in with the cream, liqueur, and butter.

Change It Up

Substitute other liqueurs for flavor twists on this simple dessert. Tia Maria lends a coffee flavor; Cointreau will give it an orange taste; and if you like raspberry, use framboise.

Chocolate Pots

This smooth, silky dessert is the perfect way to end a special meal. The liqueur and fresh cream really give it an elegant and flavorful twist. I like to garnish this dessert with fresh fruit or berries.

1. Place the small saucepan over medium-high heat. Add the cream and bring just to a boil. Remove from the heat.

2. Place the chocolate in the glass or stainless-steel bowl and slowly whisk in hot cream. Gradually whisk in the egg yolks*, liqueur, and butter, one at a time until all ingredients are combined and mixture is thick and smooth.

3. Pour mixture into ramekins, distributing evenly, and allow to set in refrigerator, uncovered, for 4 hours, until thick and set. Remove the pots from the refrigerator 30 minutes prior to serving, and let come to room temperature. Serve with a dollop of whipped cream and garnish with fresh raspberries or other seasonal fruit.

*See warning on page 5 about using raw eggs.

STEP 2

STEP 3

LEVEL

SERVES 8
PREP TIME 15 minutes
COOK TIME 20 minutes
SETTING TIME 30 minutes

Gear

- 2 stainless-steel bowls (1 medium, 1 large)
- Medium saucepan
- Whisk
- Electric mixer
- 9-inch round springform cake pan
- Silicone mixing spatula
- Wire cooling rack

Ingredients

- 1 pound bittersweet chocolate (chips or chopped, at least 60% cacao)
- 2 sticks (½ pound) butter
- 6 large eggs
- ½ cup sugar
- Nonstick cooking spray
- Whipped Cream (page 79), for serving

Chocolate Truffle Cake

This luscious, flourless cake is quick to prepare and results in a thick, decadent chocolate treat. Be sure to combine ingredients well, but don't overmix or the batter will get tough.

1. Position a rack in the middle of the oven and preheat the oven to 400°F.

2. Place the chocolate and butter in the medium stainless-steel bowl over the saucepan of simmering (page xxiii) water. (Bowl should rest on top of the saucepan without tipping over.) Whisk together until melted, well combined, and creamy. Remove bowl and saucepan from heat and set aside.

STEP 2 (A)

STEP 2 (B)

STEP 4

(3) In the large bowl, use the electric mixer to beat the eggs and sugar together on medium speed until mixture is pale yellow and fluffy, 2 to 3 minutes. Pour the melted chocolate into the egg mixture and whisk gently until just incorporated.

(4) Spray springform cake pan with nonstick cooking spray. Pour the batter into the pan; using the silicone mixing spatula, scrape the batter from the sides and bottom of the bowl.

(5) Place pan on the middle rack in the oven and bake for 15 minutes. Remove from oven, and set aside on the wire rack to cool for 30 minutes. When cake is cool and firm, unclip the side of the pan and remove. Cut into even slices and serve with whipped cream.

LEVEL

Gear

- Cutting board
- Bread knife
- Paring knife
- Small bowl
- 8-inch loaf pan
- Spreader
- 2 saucepans (1 medium, 1 small)
- 2 medium bowls
- Whisk
- Microplane grater
- Roasting pan
- Wire cooling rack

Ingredients

- 2 tablespoons butter
- 1 cup heavy cream
- 1 cup whole milk
- 1 vanilla bean, split and scraped, or 1 teaspoon vanilla extract
- ½ cinnamon stick
- 4 egg yolks
- ½ cup granulated sugar
- 1 pound stale brioche, challah bread, or croissants, cubed
- ¼ cup raisins
- Whole nutmeg (to grate)
- 2½ tablespoon light brown sugar
- ¾ cup Toffee Sauce (page 78)

Bread Pudding

Don't throw out your day-old bread; it's perfect for giving this delicious pudding added texture. The combination of the warm bread, the extra-rich custard, and the luscious toffee sauce will make this traditional British dessert absolutely irresistible.

(1) Preheat the oven to 325°F. In the small bowl, add 1 tablespoon of butter and melt in the microwave, about 15 seconds on high. Grease the loaf pan with melted butter and set aside.

(2) Place the medium saucepan over medium-high heat. Add the cream, milk, vanilla bean pod and seeds, and cinnamon stick, and bring the mixture to a boil. Remove from heat.

(3) In a medium bowl, whisk together the egg yolks and granulated sugar until well combined. Then, slowly pour the hot cream mixture into the egg yolk mixture, whisking constantly as you pour. Set aside.

(4) In a medium bowl, add the bread cubes and the raisins. Toss until well combined.

STEP 4

STEP 5

(5) Place one layer of the bread mixture in the loaf pan and pour the egg-cream mixture over the layer until completely covered. Repeat until the pan is full of bread and custard. Grate about ¼ teaspoon of nutmeg on top and sprinkle with the brown sugar.

(6) Place the loaf pan inside the roasting pan and pour in hot water halfway up the side of the loaf pan (to ensure even cooking of the custard). Bake for 45 minutes, until bread is puffed, crusty, and golden brown.

(7) Remove from oven and set aside on the wire rack to cool for 10 minutes. Meanwhile, heat the toffee sauce in a small saucepan until warm. Serve pudding in slices and drizzle toffee sauce over the top.

USING VANILLA BEANS

Fresh vanilla beans give any dessert a delicious vanilla flavor. They are delicate, but simple to prepare. Just follow these easy steps:

1 Using a small paring knife, slice the bean in half lengthwise.

2 Scrape the seeds from both sides of the bean pod onto a cutting board or other clean surface, using the edge of your knife.

3 Add the seeds to your dish while cooking as directed in the recipe.

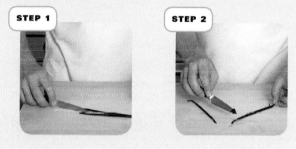

STEP 1   **STEP 2**

SERVES 8 TO 10

PREP TIME 20 minutes

COOK TIME 6 hours

Gear

- 8-quart stockpot
- Tongs
- Food processor
- 9-inch springform cake pan or 9-inch store-bought graham cracker crust
- Can opener
- Silicone mixing spatula
- Paring knife
- Medium bowl
- Hand-held mixer or whisk
- Microplane grater

Ingredients

FILLING AND TOPPING

- Three 14-ounce cans sweetened condensed milk
- 5 medium-size ripe bananas
- 1½ cups heavy cream
- 1 drop vanilla extract

CRUST

- 1½ cups (1 box) finely crushed graham crackers (22 to 23 squares)
- 3 tablespoons sugar
- 6 tablespoons (¾ stick) butter, melted
- Optional: store-bought graham cracker crust

GARNISH

- Block of semisweet chocolate

Banana Cream and Toffee Pie

Perhaps better known by its nickname, Banoffee Pie (Banana + Toffee = Banoffee), this classic treat was invented in England in the 1970s. Its crunchy cookie crust and smooth toffee and banana cream filling has delighted dessert lovers ever since.

1. Place the stockpot with 2½ quarts of water over high heat and bring to a boil. Reduce to a simmer (page xxiii) and place the unopened cans of condensed milk in the water. Cook for 4½ hours. Check the pot every 30 minutes and add water to keep level consistent (water should always cover the cans completely).

2. Remove from heat and allow the unopened cans to sit in the hot water for 1 hour. Using tongs, carefully remove them from the stockpot and transfer them to the refrigerator to cool for 30 minutes more.

STEP 4

STEP 5

STEP 5

3. While the cans are cooling, prepare the crust. Using the food processor, pulse together the cracker crumbs, sugar, and melted butter until well combined.

4. Pour the mixture into the springform pan. Using your fingers, firmly press the mixture evenly over the bottom and up the sides of the pan, forming the crust. Refrigerate for 20 minutes to set completely.

5. Open the cooled cans and pour the toffee mixture into the pan, spreading evenly on the crust with the spatula. Peel and slice the bananas and layer the slices across the top of the toffee filling. Set pie aside to set completely, about 1 hour.

6. Pour heavy cream and vanilla extract into the chilled medium bowl. Using a hand-held mixer or whisk, whip until stiff peaks form (see Kitchen FYI). Spoon whipped cream over bananas and grate semisweet chocolate across the top. Refrigerate the pie for at least 15 minutes before serving.

MENUS

Now that you're getting comfortable in the kitchen, get ready to show off your new skills and take your entertaining to a whole new level. Drawing upon the techniques you learned in Levels 1 and 2, these menu suggestions will get you ready to host your own dinner party or even make a romantic meal for **someone special.** Whatever combination of dishes you choose, you'll be sure to **dazzle and delight.**

The main key to success is planning ahead. In Level 1, you learned to proficiently pull together simple meals for casual occasions. As you add more complicated dishes to your repertoire and host more guests, you'll need to be **extra focused** on planning ahead and staying organized.

The best way to stay organized is with a **Plan of Work,** which is a really simple way to think about how much time it will take to shop for ingredients, set up your kitchen, prep the ingredients, cook, and then serve the meal. Keep these helpful hints in mind as you go:

- **Take it step-by-step** Read the whole recipe through to determine what can be done in advance and what needs to be accomplished day of, or "in the moment."

- **Set aside enough time** Don't underestimate how much time it will take to accomplish what you need to do to get ready. Some dishes cannot be prepared the night before, like fish or pasta, so you'll need to set aside enough time on the day of your party.

- **Start early** Do as much of your prep work in advance as you can, or even the day before, so you won't be stressed when your spouse/date/friends/co-workers walk through the door.

Weekend Cooking

Butternut Squash and Ginger Soup (page 100) • Crispy Chicken Cutlets with Mushrooms (page 122) or Baked Lasagna (page 114) • Bread Pudding (page 146)

Staying in on a cold, rainy day? There's nothing more comforting than making a delicious home-cooked meal. This hearty menu is guaranteed to warm things up. Make extras to last the entire weekend, or for an amazing lunch to take to the office on Monday.

Butternut Squash and Ginger Soup (page 100)

Prep

Begin early in the day (or the night before)—allow 4 hours, plus shopping time

- ○ Gather all gear and do all shopping.
- ○ Cut the soup croutons, store in a resealable plastic bag, and refrigerate.
- ○ Make the soup, put in an airtight container, and refrigerate.
- ○ Bread the chicken cutlets, put in an airtight container in between sheets of wax paper, and refrigerate; or prep and assemble the lasagna, cover with foil, and refrigerate (uncooked).
- ○ Prep and bake the pudding. Cover with plastic wrap and refrigerate.
- ○ Make toffee sauce, and refrigerate in a tightly closed container.

Crispy Chicken Cutlets with Mushrooms (page 122)

Okay, You're On!

- ○ Begin 2 hours before serving. Start with the chicken or lasagna (add 1½ hours if making lasagna). Preheat the oven. Fry the chicken cutlets. Place the chicken cutlets on a baking sheet and put in the oven to keep warm; or remove the foil from the lasagna, and put in the oven to cook. Make the mushroom topping for the chicken.
- ○ While the main course is cooking, set the table and get drinks or wine ready.
- ○ Heat the soup in a saucepan; place croutons under the broiler. Serve.
- ○ Take the main course out of the oven and allow to cool.
- ○ While main course is cooling, remove the plastic wrap from the pudding and reheat in 225°F oven.
- ○ When ready for dessert, reheat the toffee sauce and serve over the warm and steamy pudding.

Baked Lasagna (page 114)

Bread Pudding (page 146)

Romantic Meal for Two

Crab Cakes with Smoked Paprika Aïoli (page 94)

Asparagus, Pecorino, and Pea Risotto (page 118)

Veal Milanese (page 126)

Chocolate Pots (page 143)

Crab Cakes with Smoked Paprika Aïoli (page 94) • Asparagus, Pecorino, and Pea Risotto (page 118) or Veal Milanese (page 126) • Chocolate Pots (page 143)

Nothing says "I'm into you" like making a special meal and serving it with style (and maybe a little Champagne). No matter what, your efforts will be appreciated.

Keep in mind that most of the recipes in this book are made to serve four people, so you'll need to either cut the ingredient amounts in half or make the full recipe and store the leftovers for another day.

Prep

Begin the day before (or morning of)—allow 3 hours, plus shopping time

- ○ Gather all gear and do all shopping.
- ○ Set the table, prep living space, etc.
- ○ Chill Champagne or white wines.
- ○ Make the chocolate pots. Refrigerate to set for at least 4 hours.
- ○ Make the stock for the risotto, or prepare all dry ingredients for veal dish; prep any vegetables to be used. Cover and refrigerate as needed.
- ○ Assemble the crab cakes, wrap tightly, and refrigerate.
- ○ Make the aïoli and salad dressing for crab cakes, cover, and refrigerate.
- ○ Whip the cream, cover, and refrigerate.

Okay, You're On!

- ○ Begin 2 hours before serving the starter course. Lay out all ingredients so you are ready to cook.
- ○ Chop any fresh herbs, grate Parmesan, or bread veal, as needed.
- ○ Prepare the side salad for the crab cakes.
- ○ Cook the crab cakes; when in oven, dress the salad. Serve.
- ○ Cook the main dish (add an additional 30 minutes for the risotto). Serve.
- ○ When ready, pull out dessert, top with whipped cream and fresh berries, and serve.

Casual Dinner for Four (or Eight)

Stuffed Mushrooms (page 92) • *Classic Caesar Salad (page 105)* •
Eggplant Parmesan (page 116) • *Banana Cream and Toffee Pie (page 148)*

**Stuffed Mushrooms
(page 92)**

It's no more challenging to cook for a larger group than it is to cook
for two. Just remember to stay organized and plan accordingly. The dishes in
this menu can be easily doubled for a bigger party, or followed exactly for four.

Prep

Begin the day before (or early morning of)—allow 7 hours, plus shopping time

○ Gather all gear and do all shopping.
○ Make the toffee for the pie—this takes 4½ hours so begin this first, then work
  on other tasks while the milk cans are boiling and cooling.
○ Gather tableware and set the table.
○ Refrigerate any Champagne or white wine.
○ Prep and assemble the mushrooms (don't cook yet), cover, and refrigerate.
○ Make salad dressing, cover, and refrigerate.
○ Prep any vegetables; cover tightly and refrigerate.
○ Get the coffee maker or tea ready.

**Classic Caesar Salad
(page 105)**

Okay, You're On!

○ Begin 2½ hours before your guests arrive. Wash and spin dry the lettuce,
  cover with a damp paper towel, and refrigerate.
○ Sauté the eggplant and assemble, ready for the oven.
○ Assemble the salad, but don't dress it until ready to serve.
○ Cook mushrooms and set out for arriving guests.
○ Dress the salad and serve.
○ Bake the eggplant in the oven and serve.
○ Heat bread (if serving) in oven, set out.
○ When ready, slice and set out pie along with dessert plates, forks, and napkins.

**Eggplant Parmesan
(page 116)**

**Banana Cream and
Toffee Pie (page 148)**

NOW

Now that you feel more confident in the kitchen, you're ready to make the most of your new skills with the recipes in Level 3. What you've learned in Levels 1 and 2 will now be applied with more **attention to detail,** method refinement, and more control over timing.

The recipes in this section use unique, **exciting,** and slightly more challenging seasonal ingredients. Learn how to make delicious hors d'oeuvres like Blue Cheese Puffs with Avocado-Lemon Dip (page 160) or Shrimp Pot Stickers with Sweet Soy Sauce (page 164) for your next

YOU'RE

cocktail party. Having guests over for an elegant dinner party? Serve first courses like Mussels in White Wine Sauce (page 171) and hearty main dishes like Boneless Leg of Lamb (page 184). No meal would be **complete** without accompanying sides; dress up your dishes with Vegetable Puree, Three Ways (page 193). **Sophisticated,** yet easy-to-make desserts like Cinnamon-Roasted Pears (page 201) are the perfect way to end any meal, no matter what the occasion.

COOKIN'!

Hors d'Oeuvres

In Level 1, you learned how to make some simple snacks. Level 2 taught you how to start out a meal with elegant appetizers. In Level 3, I apply these same concepts to hors d'oeuvres. What's the difference between hors d'oeuvres and appetizers? I think of an appetizer as a first course, something to be served on a plate, that sets the tone for the meal. Hors d'oeuvres, on the other hand, are a variety of bite-size morsels that get the taste buds going, are either passed on a tray or laid out on a platter, and can be picked up and enjoyed along with a cocktail or that first glass of wine.

IN THIS CHAPTER

In this chapter, you'll find recipes for:
○ Roasted Pepper, Brie, and Tomato Tartlets
○ Blue Cheese Puffs with Avocado-Lemon Dip
○ Beef Teriyaki with Ginger Dipping Sauce
○ Shrimp Pot Stickers with Sweet Soy Sauce
○ Assorted Cheeses with Pickled Asian Pear

And you'll develop the skills and know-how to:
○ Work with puff pastry
○ Make your own dipping sauce
○ Marinate meat for added flavor
○ Mix and match cheeses for an elegant spread

LEVEL

MAKES 30 PIECES
PREP TIME 10 minutes
COOK TIME 15 minutes

Gear

- Cutting board
- Chef's knife
- Paring knife
- 1-inch round pastry cutter or ring mold
- Nonstick fry pan
- Pastry brush
- Optional: small metal spatula
- 2 baking sheets
- Parchment paper

Ingredients

- 2 tablespoons all-purpose flour, for dusting
- 1 sheet (½ package) frozen puff pastry, thawed in the fridge according to package directions
- 1 teaspoon olive oil
- ½ medium red bell pepper, seeded, ribs removed, sliced into thin ¾-inch-long strips
- ½ medium green or yellow bell pepper, seeded, ribs removed, sliced into thin ¾-inch-long strips
- 1 tablespoon melted butter, for the baking sheet
- 15 ripe cherry tomatoes (at least 1-inch diameter), ends discarded, sliced into thin rounds
- 8 ounces Brie cheese, diced into ½-inch cubes, including the rind
- Salt and pepper
- ½ cup basil oil (see page 90)

Roasted Pepper, Brie, and Tomato Tartlets

Think of these as elegant mini pizzas. Be creative with different topping combinations: Try spicy tomatoes with cooked Italian sausage; spinach with crumbled Gorgonzola cheese; or sliced salami with Taleggio cheese.

1. Preheat the oven to 375°F.

2. Lay out the puff pastry sheet on a flat, dry, well-floured surface. Coat the rolling pin with flour and gently roll out one sheet of puff pastry until flat and smooth, then roll it out an additional 1 inch in each direction. Use a pastry cutter or ring mold to cut out at least 30 rounds. Set aside.

3. Place the fry pan over medium-high heat. When hot*, add the olive oil and pepper strips, and sauté (page xxiv) until soft and golden brown, 4 to 5 minutes. Remove from heat and set aside.

4. Lightly brush melted butter on the baking sheet to grease. Using your fingers or a small spatula, carefully transfer each puff onto the baking sheet, leaving enough space between so none are touching. Place one sheet of parchment paper on top of the pastry rounds. Then gently place the second baking sheet on top, flat side down.

continues

STEP 2

STEP 4

STEP 5

(5) Bake for 8 to 10 minutes, until rounds are puffy and golden brown. Remove the top baking sheet and the parchment paper. Place one cherry tomato slice and one Brie cube on each pastry round, then top with ½ teaspoon of the pepper strips. Add salt and pepper to season.

(6) Just prior to serving, return the baking sheet to the oven for 2 to 3 minutes, until the Brie has melted. Transfer the warm pastry rounds to a plate or platter and use a teaspoon to drizzle with the basil oil.

*Is your pan hot enough? Test it with a drop of water. If it sizzles, you're ready to cook.

PUFF PASTRY 101

Frozen puff pastry is one of the easiest, most versatile ingredients to work with. Made from layers of pastry dough, it bakes into a light, flaky treat that can be used in a variety of ways, including tasty appetizers, savory main dishes, or luscious dessert treats.

Puff pastry is called for in a number of recipes in Level 3, such as Blue Cheese Puffs with Avocado-Lemon Dip (page 160), Roasted Pepper, Brie and Tomato Tartlets (page 157), Shrimp Pot Stickers with Sweet Soy Sauce (page 164), and Chicken Pot Pie (page 176).

Here are some helpful hints on working with this delicate ingredient:

- Puff pastry is easiest to work with when it's neither too warm (extremely elastic, almost gooey) nor too cold (brittle), so be sure to thaw it thoroughly and properly according to the manufacturer's instructions.

- Wrap unused pastry sheets in plastic wrap or foil and store them in the freezer according to package directions.

- If your pastry is too warm, bring down the temperature by wrapping the pastry in plastic wrap and storing it in the freezer for 10 minutes.

- If your pastry is too cold, bring up the temperature by wrapping the pastry in plastic wrap and setting aside to warm up at room temperature for 10 minutes. Do not microwave the pastry.

- Use plenty of flour on your work surface so the pastry doesn't stick. Start with 2 tablespoons of flour per pastry sheet, then sprinkle on more as needed.

- Try not to over-handle the pastry so it remains tender and pliable.

- If the pastry begins to crack along the fold lines, dip your finger lightly in water and gently rub the pastry, pressing it together to form a tight seal. This is especially important for recipes that call for fillings, like the Shrimp Pot Stickers.

Gear

- Cutting board
- Chef's knife
- 2 small bowls
- Whisk
- Fry pan
- Wooden spoon
- Rolling pin
- Paring knife
- 2 pastry brushes
- Pizza cutter
- Baking sheet

Ingredients

PUFFS

- 1½ tablespoons olive oil
- 1 medium onion, peeled and finely diced
- ½ cup port wine (tawny or ruby)
- 3 tablespoons light brown sugar
- Cayenne pepper
- Kosher salt and pepper
- 2 tablespoons (¼ stick) butter, diced
- 2 eggs
- 2 tablespoons whole milk
- ¼ cup all-purpose flour, for dusting
- 1 package (2 sheets) frozen puff pastry, thawed in the fridge according to package directions
- ½ cup crumbled blue cheese
- 1 tablespoon melted butter, for the baking sheet

(continues)

Blue Cheese Puffs with Avocado-Lemon Dip

These golden brown cheesy puffs are light, yet satisfying. They pair wonderfully with Champagne, wine, or cocktails. Try experimenting with other fillings, like Butternut Squash Puree (page 195), aged cheddar and sage, or chicken, tomato sauce, basil, and mozzarella (about ½ cup each—use similar measurement ratios as below).

1. Preheat the oven to 375°F.

2. Place the fry pan over medium-high heat. When hot*, add the olive oil and onion. Sauté (page xxiv) the onions until golden brown, about 6 minutes.

3. Stir in the port wine, brown sugar, 2 pinches of cayenne, and kosher salt and pepper to taste. Allow to cook for 30 minutes, stirring occasionally. When the onion mixture is thick and syrupy, whisk in the diced butter until smooth. Remove from the heat and allow to cool for 5 minutes.

4. In a small bowl, whisk together the eggs and milk for egg wash and set aside. Lay out the puff pastry sheets on a flat, dry, well-floured surface. Coat the rolling pin with flour and gently roll out one sheet of puff pastry until flat and smooth. Set aside. Repeat with the second sheet, rolling it out an additional ½ inch in each direction.

5. Using the tip of a knife, lightly draw a grid of 1-inch square boxes on the smaller pastry sheet, about 30 boxes total. Brush egg wash along each grid line.

STEP 5

STEP 6 (A)

STEP 6 (B)

3

Ingredients (cont'd)

DIP

- 1 ripe avocado, peeled, pitted, and cubed
- 1½ teaspoons fresh lemon juice
- 1½ teaspoons olive oil
- ½ teaspoon granulated sugar
- Kosher salt
- Cayenne pepper

Kitchen FYI

• If you're preparing for a party and short on time and space, finish cooking these cheese puffs in the toaster oven, freeing up your main oven for other dishes.

• Not baking the puffs right away? Store the raw puffs in the refrigerator. Cover the baking sheet with plastic wrap and keep them cool until you're ready to bake.

6. Spoon ½ teaspoon of blue cheese in center of each square and top with ¼ teaspoon of port onions. Carefully lay the larger pastry sheet over the filling, covering the smaller pastry sheet completely. Use the back of a knife or the side of your pinky to gently apply pressure between each filled square to close the edges. Using the pizza cutter, cut out the squares in a slow, straight motion to create individual puffs. Use a fork to seal all four edges of each puff.

7. Lightly brush melted butter on the baking sheet to grease. Using your fingers or a small spatula, carefully transfer each puff onto the baking sheet, leaving enough space between so none are touching. Brush each puff with egg wash and lightly sprinkle with kosher salt. Bake for 10 to 12 minutes, until puffy and golden brown.

8. While puffs are baking, make the dip: In a small bowl, mash the avocado with the whisk while gradually adding the lemon juice, olive oil, and sugar, salt and cayenne to taste. Whisk until smooth. Cover with plastic wrap, pressing plastic onto the surface of the dip to prevent browning, and refrigerate until ready to use. The dip can be made up to 4 hours in advance.

9. To serve, arrange the warm cheese puffs on plate or platter, or in a small bread basket lined with a napkin. Put the avocado dip in a small bowl and set on the side.

Is your pan hot enough? Test it with a drop of water. If it sizzles, you're ready to cook.

③ LEVEL

MAKES 30 PIECES
PREP TIME 15 minutes
MARINATING TIME
20 minutes
COOK TIME 10 minutes

Gear

- Cutting board
- Chef's knife
- Microplane grater
- Medium bowl
- Small saucepan
- Whisk
- Fry pan or wok
- Tongs
- 30 decorative toothpicks or short wooden skewers, approximately 4 inches long
- Serving platter and dipping sauce dish

Ingredients

SKEWERS
- 1 cup Teriyaki Sauce (page 52)
- 1½ pounds beef filet mignon, cut into ¾- to 1-inch cubes
- 2 tablespoons vegetable oil

SAUCE
- 2 tablespoons sesame oil
- 1 teaspoon grated fresh ginger
- 3 tablespoons soy sauce
- 2 tablespoons sugar
- 1 tablespoon sesame seeds
- ¼ teaspoon hot Asian dry mustard or 2 pinches of cayenne pepper
- 1 tablespoon finely chopped fresh cilantro leaves, plus whole leaves for serving

Beef Teriyaki with Ginger Dipping Sauce

Like Satay Chicken Skewers (page 39), these delicious skewers simply need to be marinated in sauce, then cooked right before serving. The result is a sweet and savory beef bite with a ginger sauce dip that balances the flavors beautifully. Substitute chicken breast cubes or strips of top-grade sirloin or rib-eye for the beef.

① Pour the teriyaki sauce into the medium bowl and add the beef cubes. Cover with plastic wrap and refrigerate for 20 minutes.

② While the beef is marinating, make the sauce: Place the small saucepan over medium-high heat. When hot*, add 1 tablespoon sesame oil and the grated ginger and sweat (page xxiv) for 2 minutes, until ginger is soft and translucent.

STEP 2

STEP 4

STEP 5

Kitchen FYI

Don't leave the beef marinating in the refrigerator for too long. If meat sits in any salty sauce for too long, the salt will extract the meat's moisture and you run the risk of dehydrating. The result? Tough meat.

(3) Whisk in the soy sauce, sugar, the remaining sesame oil, and the sesame seeds. Reduce heat to low and allow to simmer (page xxiii) for 1 minute. Whisk in the mustard and chopped cilantro until well combined. Remove from heat and set aside until ready to use.

(4) Just prior to serving, cook the beef: Place the fry pan over high heat; when hot, add the vegetable oil. When smoking slightly, use tongs to transfer beef from marinade to hot oil. Sauté (page xxiv) the beef, tossing to cook on all sides, for about 1 minute, or longer if you prefer well-done. Using tongs, remove the beef from the heat. Discard the marinade.

(5) To serve, thread 2 or 3 cubes of meat per skewer, or 2 cubes per decorative toothpick. Place the skewers on a bed of cilantro leaves. Place dipping sauce in a small bowl on the side.

Is your pan hot enough? Test it with a drop of water. If it sizzles, you're ready to cook.

Gear

- Cutting board
- Paring knife
- Chef's knife
- Microplane grater
- Whisk
- Nonstick fry pan or wok
- Food processor
- Pastry brush
- Medium saucepan
- Slotted spoon
- Small saucepan
- Tongs

Ingredients

POT STICKERS

- 2 tablespoons sesame oil
- 1 small fresh red chile, trimmed, seeded, ribs removed, and minced
- 1 teaspoon grated fresh ginger
- 1 clove garlic, peeled, crushed, and minced
- ½ stalk lemongrass, white part only, very finely chopped
- 3 lime leaves, finely minced (leave out if you can't find)
- ½ pound raw small shrimp, peeled and deveined

(continues)

Shrimp Pot Stickers with Sweet Soy Sauce

Also known as wontons, these pot stickers are full of flavor, and easy to prepare. Serve them on a platter with the soy sauce to dip, or for more formal occasions, serve 4 or 5 pot stickers on a plate per person, with the soy sauce drizzled on top.

① Place the fry pan over medium-high heat. When hot*, add ½ tablespoon of the sesame oil. Add the chile, ginger, garlic, lemongrass, and lime leaves and sweat (page xxiv) for 2 minutes, until soft and translucent. Remove from the heat and allow to cool.

② Transfer the mixture to the food processor and pulse for 20 seconds, until well combined. Add the shrimp and pulse for an additional 30 seconds, until mixture is chunky and paste-like. Slowly add 1 egg white, half of the soy sauce, the cilantro, and salt and pepper to the food processor. Pulse for 30 seconds, until paste is thick and sticky.

③ Place 1 teaspoon of the shrimp mixture in the center of each wonton wrapper and brush egg white–water mixture around the top edge of the wrapper. Fold the wrapper in half, enveloping the mixture in the crease. Crimp well with your fingers or a fork, ensuring the edges are sealed. Set aside until ready to cook.

④ Place the medium saucepan ¾ full with salted water over high heat and bring to a boil. Using the slotted spoon, gently place each pot sticker in the water as space allows. Cook for 4 minutes, then transfer the pot stickers to a plate lined with paper towels to drain. Repeat with remaining batches as necessary.

STEP 3

STEP 4

STEP 6

Ingredients (cont'd)

- 1 egg white + 1 egg white whisked with 2 tablespoons water
- 3 tablespoons soy sauce
- 2 tablespoons chopped fresh cilantro leaves
- Salt and pepper
- 1 package wonton wrappers

SAUCE

- ½ cup soy sauce
- ¼ cup sugar

How Do I . . . ?

Test your shrimp filling for proper seasoning by placing a spoonful of the mixture in a fry pan with 1 teaspoon of vegetable oil. Fry until golden brown, remove from heat, and allow to cool before tasting. Add more garlic, salt, or pepper to the filling as desired.

⑤ While the pot stickers are cooking, make the sweet soy sauce: Place the small saucepan over high heat. When hot*, add soy sauce and sugar and bring to a boil. Allow to boil until liquid level reduces (page xxv) by ½ in the pan and mixture has thickened, about 8 minutes. Remove from heat and set aside.

⑥ Place a clean nonstick fry pan over medium-high heat. When hot*, add the remaining sesame oil. When bubbling, use tongs to gently place the pot stickers in the pan as space allows. Fry until the edges are golden brown, about 3 minutes on each side, then add the remaining soy sauce and fry for an additional minute. Remove from heat and set aside on a plate lined with paper towels to drain. Repeat with remaining batches as necessary.

⑦ To serve, place the pot stickers on a platter with a bowl of warm sweet soy sauce on the side for dipping.

Steamed Shrimp Pot Stickers   Instead of pan-frying (page xxiv) your pot stickers, try cooking them in bamboo steamer baskets. Use one large steaming basket or steam the pot stickers separately in smaller, individual baskets, cooking in batches as needed. Grease the baskets with nonstick cooking spray. For small baskets, place in a large stockpot; for a large basket, place in a wok. Add 2 inches of water around edges and place over high heat. When steaming, add the pot stickers and add lid to cover. Steam for 6 minutes, then carefully remove the pot stickers using tongs, and set aside. Repeat with remaining batches as necessary.

*Is your pan hot enough? Test it with a drop of water. If it sizzles, you're ready to cook.

Gear

- Cutting board
- Chef's knife
- Paring knife
- Mandolin
- Medium saucepan
- Ladle
- Plastic storage container with tight-fitting lid
- Small bowl
- Spreader

Ingredients

- ⅔ cup light brown sugar
- ⅔ cup white wine vinegar
- 3 large Asian pears, trimmed, peeled, and grated (or substitute Bosc pears or Fuji apples)
- Cheeses of your choice (opposite page)
- Crackers and/or bread, for serving

Assorted Cheeses with Pickled Asian Pear

Cheese is the perfect way to start (or end) a meal. Try some simple add-ins like bread, olives, figs, and grapes, to help bring out the assorted flavors and textures in your cheese assortment. For an extra-special treat, add Asian pears to your spread. Asian pears are a cross between an apple and a pear, and come into season in autumn. Crunchy and sweet, they are wonderful when pickled. You can also use this method with plain apples or pears.

1. Place the medium saucepan over medium-high heat. Add the sugar and vinegar and bring to a boil. Reduce the heat to low and simmer (page xxiii) for 4 minutes, until mixture begins to thicken.

2. Stir in the grated pears. Raise the heat to medium-high. Bring the mixture back to a boil, then reduce the heat to low and allow mixture to simmer for 1 minute. Remove from heat.

3. Using the ladle, transfer the mixture to the storage container, cover, and refrigerate until ready to use.

4. When ready to serve, arrange the cheeses and crackers on your chosen serving surface, from mildest to strongest, and put out the small bowl with the pickled pears and a spoon.

PREP

PREP

STEP 2

FINE CHEESES TO START (OR END) YOUR MEAL

Try to arrange an assortment with a variety of flavors and textures.

Here are some recommendations:

AMERICAN	IMPORTED	TYPE	TEXTURE
Great Hill Blue	Valdeon	Blue	Crumbly
Hudson Valley Camembert	St. André	Brie/Camembert	Soft
Aged Vermont Cheddar	Double Gloucester	Cow, Mixed	Firm
Coach Farm Chevrè	Le Chevrot	Goat/Chèvre	Soft
Domestic Swiss	Emmentaler	Swiss	Semifirm
Vella Dry Jack	Aged Gouda (18 months old)	Aged Cow's Milk	Firm

When selecting your cheese, take these key factors into consideration:

Texture: soft, hard, semisoft, crumbly

Flavor: strong, medium, sharp, stinky

Size: individual, small, medium, large

Color: blue, white, yellow, orange

Shape: wedge, slice, logs, pyramid

Milk: cow, goat, sheep, buffalo

What are you going to serve it with?

• Grapes, apples, pears, and fresh figs, cut into quarters and sliced
• Olives and sun-dried tomatoes
• Fruit jams and honeys
• Toasted nuts
• Crusty bread and mixed crackers

Elegant First Courses

Great meals start with great beginnings. As with the hors d'oeuvres, these first courses build on skills you've learned in earlier sections, but are executed with more detail. The recipes have more steps and require better timing, but they also reward you with dishes containing spectacular flavor.

The first course should complement the rest of the meal in terms of style, taste, and tone. The sample menus at the end of Level 3 offer suggestions on how to pair these first-course recipes with main dishes and desserts to create a well-rounded meal.

IN THIS CHAPTER

In this chapter, you'll find recipes for:
- Chicken Soup with Dumplings
- Shrimp and Lemongrass Soup
- Mussels in White Wine Sauce
- Potato Cakes with Mustard Sauce

And you'll develop the skills and know-how to:
- Buy and prepare lemongrass
- Properly clean and prepare fresh mussels
- Use leftover mashed potatoes to make elegant potato cakes

LEVEL

SERVES 4 TO 6
PREP TIME 30 minutes
COOK TIME 25 minutes

Gear

- Cutting board
- Chef's knife
- Paring knife
- Nonstick fry pan
- Silicone mixing spatula
- Food processor
- Pastry brush
- Slotted spoon
- Soup ladle

Ingredients

- 1 batch Chicken and Sweet Corn Noodle Soup (page 98), without noodles

DUMPLINGS
- 2 tablespoons sesame oil
- 6 shiitake mushrooms, stems removed coarsely chopped
- ¾ pound boneless, skinless chicken breasts, coarsely chopped
- 3 scallions, coarsely chopped
- 1 carrot, peeled, coarsely chopped
- One 8-ounce can whole water chestnuts, drained, coarsely chopped
- 1 tablespoon oyster sauce
- 1 tablespoon Thai sweet chili sauce
- 1 tablespoon soy sauce
- 1 tablespoon mirin (sweetened rice wine)
- 1 egg white, beaten
- 2 tablespoons cornstarch
- Salt and pepper
- Fresh cilantro leaves, finely chopped (about 2 tablespoons)
- 1 package wonton wrappers
- 2 egg whites whisked with 2 tablespoons water (egg wash)

Chicken Soup with Dumplings

Similar to pot stickers, these delicious dumplings are a hearty alternative to simple noodles in your chicken soup.

1. Make the chicken soup according to the recipe instructions on page 98. While soup is simmering (page xxiii), make the dumplings.

2. Place the fry pan over medium-high heat. When hot*, add the sesame oil and the mushrooms and sauté (page xxiv) for 2 minutes, until golden brown. Remove from the heat and set aside to cool.

3. Transfer the mushrooms to the food processor and add the chopped chicken. Pulse for 30 seconds, until the mixture thickens into a paste.

4. Add the scallions, carrots, and water chestnuts and pulse for 20 seconds. Add the oyster sauce, sweet chili sauce, soy sauce, mirin, egg white, and cornstarch and pulse until well blended. Add salt, pepper, and 1 tablespoon of cilantro, and pulse for an additional 3 seconds.

5. Place a wonton wrapper in the center of your palm. Place 1 teaspoon of the filling in the center of the wrapper, and brush egg wash around the edges. Gather the four corners of the wrapper to envelop mixture, and press together to seal.

6. About 10 minutes before serving, gently add the dumplings to the soup, using the slotted spoon. Allow to simmer for 5 to 7 minutes, then remove the soup from heat. To serve, ladle the soup into shallow bowls and garnish with the remaining chopped cilantro.

Is your pan hot enough? Test it with a drop of water. If it sizzles, you're ready to cook.

STEP 3

STEP 5

STEP 6

LEVEL

SERVES 4
PREP TIME 15 minutes
COOK TIME 40 minutes

Gear

- Cutting board
- Chef's knife
- Vegetable peeler
- 2 nonstick fry pans
- Blender
- Slotted spoon

Ingredients

- 6 tablespoons sesame oil
- 1 shallot, peeled and sliced
- 2 tablespoons fresh ginger, peeled and coarsely chopped
- 1 tablespoon chopped lemongrass
- 3 cloves garlic, peeled and diced
- 1 small red chile, seeded, ribs removed, and chopped
- 1 cup unsweetened coconut milk
- 1 cup homemade Chicken Stock (page 97) or store-bought
- 3 ounces fresh baby spinach (about 3 cups loosely packed)
- ⅓ cup chopped fresh cilantro leaves
- Salt and pepper
- 1 medium carrot, peeled and sliced ½ inch thick
- ½ medium yellow bell pepper, trimmed, seeded, ribs removed, and cut into ¼-inch-wide strips
- ½ medium red onion, peeled and sliced ¼-inch thick
- ½ cup sliced white mushrooms (trimmed, wiped clean)
- 1 pound extra-large shrimp, peeled and deveined
- ½ cup snow peas, ends trimmed, finely shredded into strips
- Grated zest of 1 lime

Shrimp and Lemongrass Soup

This soup is quick, easy, and powerful on the taste buds! Your local Thai restaurant will never get another call once you've made this dish. Lemongrass adds a citrusy flavor to the soup, which contrasts well with the shrimp. For variety, try substituting chicken or beef for the shrimp.

1. Place the nonstick fry pan over medium heat. When hot*, add 2 tablespoons of the sesame oil and the shallots, ginger, lemongrass, garlic, and chile. Sweat (page xxiv) for 5 minutes, until soft and translucent.

2. Stir in the coconut milk and chicken stock and bring mixture to a boil. Add spinach, cilantro, and salt and pepper to season. Remove from the heat and allow to cool for 15 minutes.

3. Once cooled, transfer the soup to a blender in batches (see Safety First, page 101) and blend until smooth and silky. Set aside until ready to use.

4. Place the clean nonstick fry pan over medium heat. When hot,* add the remaining ¼ cup sesame oil and heat until rippling. Add the carrots and sauté (page xxiv) for 3 minutes, then remove and set aside. Repeat with remaining batches of vegetables, cooking each separately until golden brown, about 3 minutes.

5. Add the shrimp and fry until browned, about 3 minutes each side. Transfer the cooked vegetables and the snow peas to the fry pan and cook 2 to 3 minutes more, stirring continuously.

6. Add the soup and bring the mixture to a gentle simmer (page xxiii). Stir the lime zest into the soup and add salt to season. Remove from heat and ladle the shrimp and vegetables into shallow bowls. Pour the soup over the top.

STEP 5

Is your pan hot enough? Test it with a drop of water. If it sizzles, you're ready to cook.

SERVES 4
PREP TIME 15 minutes
COOK TIME 10 minutes

Gear

- Cutting board
- Chef's knife
- Abrasive cleaning pad
- 8-quart stockpot
- Medium ladle

Ingredients

- 3 pounds mussels
- ½ cup white wine
- 3 garlic cloves, peeled and minced
- 3 stalks celery, trimmed and finely diced
- ½ fennel bulb, trimmed, cored, and finely sliced (about ⅛ inch thick)
- ½ cup homemade Chicken Stock (page 97) or store-bought, or 1 boullion cube dissolved in hot water
- 1½ cups heavy cream
- ½ bunch scallions, trimmed and finely chopped on an angle
- 2 tablespoons chopped fresh flat-leaf parsley
- 2 tablespoons chopped fresh tarragon
- 1 lemon, cut into wedges
- Crusty bread, for serving

Mussels in White Wine Sauce

Bring the oceanside right to your kitchen table with this delicious dish. Serve it with warm, crusty bread to soak up the extra sauce. And always have extra bowls handy for the empty shells.

1. Scrub the mussels with an abrasive pad to remove algae. Pluck off any beards (the fibers emerging from the mussel). Rinse several times to remove grit or sand.

2. Place the stockpot over medium-high heat. When hot*, add the mussels, wine, garlic, celery, and fennel. Cover the pot and steam for 3 to 4 minutes. Add the stock and cream and continue to boil (lid off) until liquid level reduces (page xxv) by ½ in the pan. Add the scallions and herbs and stir until well combined and open mussels are plump and juicy.

3. To serve, ladle the mussels into shallow bowls and add an extra ladle of sauce. Discard any empty shells before serving. Place 2 to 3 lemon wedges along each bowl rim and serve with crusty bread on the side.

*Is your pan hot enough? Test it with a drop of water. If it sizzles, you're ready to cook.

MUSSELS 101

- Mussels should be cooked while they are still alive. Purchase them fresh from your local market.
- Never purchase cracked or broken mussels.
- Discard any mussels that are open before they're cooked. Live mussels should remain closed in their shells. Gently tap on the shells of any open mussels; if the shells don't close easily, discard the mussels.
- Discard any mussels that remain closed after they're cooked.

STEP 1

STEP 2

STEP 3

SERVES 4
PREP TIME 35 minutes
COOK TIME 1 hour

Gear

- Cutting board
- Vegetable peeler
- Chef's knife
- 8-quart stockpot
- Colander
- Potato masher, food mill, or potato ricer
- Large bowl
- Wooden spoon
- 3-inch ring mold or ramekin
- Nonstick fry pan
- Medium spatula
- Baking sheet
- Small saucepan

Ingredients

CAKES

- 2 pounds medium Yukon Gold potatoes, peeled
- 8 tablespoons (1 stick) butter
- 2 egg yolks, beaten
- Salt and pepper
- 1 bunch scallions, ends trimmed, finely chopped
- ½ cup all-purpose flour, for dusting
- 2 tablespoons corn or vegetable oil
- 12 slices Baked Crisp Bacon (page 12)

SAUCE

- ¼ cup white wine
- 1 cup heavy cream
- 2 tablespoons (¼ stick) butter
- 1 tablespoon whole-grain mustard
- Salt and pepper

Potato Cakes with Mustard Sauce

The spring onions, or scallions, add a fresh kick to the hearty potatoes, and when paired with crisp bacon and a creamy whole-grain mustard sauce, they are a flavorful way to start a meal. Omit the sauce and serve the cakes alongside hearty dishes like Prime Rib of Beef (page 182) or Boneless Leg of Lamb (page 184). It's also a great way to use up leftover Buttery Mashed Potatoes (page 196).

1. Preheat the oven to 375°F.

2. Place the stockpot filled with salted water over high heat. Add the potatoes and bring to a boil. Once boiling, reduce heat to a simmer (page xxiii). Cook for about 35 minutes, until potatoes are soft (slide the tip of a knife into a potato to test).

3. Remove from heat and drain the potatoes in the colander in the sink, then return to the stockpot. Mash the potatoes in the stockpot, then transfer to the large bowl. With the wooden spoon, gently fold in the butter and egg yolks and add salt and pepper to season. Set mixture aside and allow to cool for 15 to 20 minutes. When cool, fold in the scallions.

4. Pour the potato mixture onto a well-floured surface so it doesn't stick. Using your hands, pat the mixture down until about 2 inches thick. Using the ring mold or an upside-down ramekin, cut out 4 round cakes. Dust the cakes with flour and set aside.

STEP 4

STEP 5

STEP 7

Kitchen FYI

• Have some leftover potato mixture? Make extra cakes, place them on a floured baking sheet, cover completely with a sheet of wax paper, and refrigerate for up to 2 days, until ready to cook.

• Be careful not to let the mustard sauce come to a boil. Mustard has a tendency to get bitter if overcooked.

5. Place the fry pan over medium-high heat. When hot*, add the oil. Using the spatula, gently add the cakes and fry until golden brown, 1 to 2 minutes on each side.

6. Transfer the cakes to the baking sheet, using the spatula. Place in the oven and bake for 8 to 10 minutes, until golden and crisp. Remove from the oven and set aside.

7. While potato cakes are baking, make the mustard sauce: Place the small saucepan over medium-high heat. When hot*, add the wine and allow the liquid level to reduce (page xxv) by ⅓. Add the cream and reduce liquid level by ⅓.

8. Mix in the butter and mustard and cook, stirring constantly, for 7 to 10 minutes, until sauce is thick and creamy (do not boil). Taste, and add salt and pepper to season.

9. To serve, place one potato cake at the center of each plate. Using a teaspoon, drizzle the mustard sauce on top and around the cake. Top each cake with 3 slices of bacon.

*Is your pan hot enough? Test it with a drop of water. If it sizzles, you're ready to cook.

Sophisticated Main Dishes

Here are eight main-dish recipes that will fine-tune your kitchen skills and result in sophisticated gourmet food to delight and impress your guests. Yet, true to *No More Takeout* style, you don't need a degree from a fancy culinary school to easily create these dishes right in your own kitchen.

There is something for everyone here, including rustic favorites like Chicken Pot Pie (page 176), and more sophisticated dishes like Boneless Leg of Lamb (page 184). Have fun and feel free to make them once my way, then, if you like, be adventurous and create your own variations. Don't forget to consult the menu section at the end of Level 3 for ideas on what first course or dessert might pair well with your main dish.

IN THIS CHAPTER

In this chapter, you'll find recipes for:
○ Chicken with Thai Green Curry
○ Chicken Pot Pie
○ Roast Turkey with Stuffing
○ Prime Rib of Beef
○ Boneless Leg of Lamb
○ Pan-Seared Striped Bass with Heirloom Tomato Salsa
○ Halibut with Peperonata and Pesto
○ Boiled Lobster with Warm Butter

And you'll develop the skills and know-how to:
○ Thaw, clean, and carve a turkey
○ Make homemade stuffing and gravy
○ Properly carve a roast, removing the bone
○ Substitute lobster meat in a variety of dishes
○ Fry delicate fish with ease
○ Make your own homemade pesto
○ Make and store clarified butter
○ Boil fresh lobster

SERVES 4
PREP TIME 15 minutes
COOK TIME 25 minutes

Gear

- Cutting board
- Chef's knife
- Paring knife
- Nonstick fry pan or wok

Ingredients

- 3 tablespoons sesame oil
- 1 pound boneless, skinless chicken breasts, cut into 1-inch chunks
- 2 tablespoons Thai green curry paste
- 1 medium red bell pepper, trimmed, seeded, sliced lengthwise into ¼-inch-wide strips
- 1 medium yellow bell pepper, trimmed, seeded, sliced lengthwise into ¼-inch-wide strips
- 1 medium red onion, peeled and thinly sliced
- ½ pound white mushrooms, trimmed and sliced ¼ inch thick
- 1 medium zucchini, trimmed and sliced into ¼-inch thick rounds
- 1 red apple, cored and cut into even cubes (peeled first, if desired)
- One 14-ounce can unsweetened coconut milk
- ½ cup heavy cream
- Salt and pepper
- Coconut Sticky Rice (page 141), for serving
- ¼ cup chopped fresh cilantro
- ¼ cup crushed unsalted peanuts
- 5 scallions, trimmed and finely chopped

Chicken with Thai Green Curry

For a quick, light meal full of flavor, this chicken curry recipe is one of my favorites. The fragrant green curry paste, a staple in Thai cuisine, adds a hint of spice to the chicken. Just be careful; the curry paste is strong, so taste it first to gauge how much you want to use: For a milder flavor, use 1 tablespoon; to spice things up, add as much paste as you can handle. Green curry also works well with beef, pork, or shrimp.

1. Place the fry pan or wok over medium-high heat. When hot*, add the sesame oil and sauté (page xxiv) the chicken until golden brown, about 5 minutes on each side.

2. Stir in curry paste. Add the peppers and onions, stir, and cook for 3 minutes. Then add the mushrooms and zucchini, stir, and cook for 2 minutes.

3. Fold in the diced apple, coconut milk, and cream. Cook for 6 minutes, or until liquid level reduces (page xxv) by ⅓ in the pan. Add salt and pepper to season, then remove from heat.

4. To serve, add a heaping spoonful of Coconut Sticky Rice to each plate. Ladle the chicken over the rice and garnish with cilantro, peanuts, and scallions.

Is your pan hot enough? Test it with a drop of water. If it sizzles, you're ready to cook.

PREP

STEP 3

STEP 4

③
LEVEL

SERVES 4

PREP TIME 30 minutes

COOK TIME 3 hours
(plus an hour refrigeration)

Gear

- Cutting board
- Chef's knife
- Vegetable peeler
- 8-quart stockpot
- Medium ladle
- Tongs
- Plate
- Slotted spoon
- 2 bowls (1 medium, 1 small)
- Whisk
- 4 individual 5-inch baking dishes or 1 large baking dish
- Rolling pin
- Pastry brush

Ingredients

- 1 whole chicken (4- to 5- pounds) or 4 quarters
- Salt and pepper
- 1 chicken bouillon cube
- 2 bay leaves
- 1 sprig of thyme
- 2 carrots, peeled and diced
- 1 large onion, peeled and diced
- 3 stalk celery, diced about ¼-inch thick
- 1 cup frozen peas
- 4 tablespoons (½ stick) butter, softened (page 14)
- ¼ cup all-purpose flour, plus more for dusting
- 1 cup heavy cream
- 1 egg
- 1 teaspoon milk or water
- 1 package (2 sheets) frozen puff pastry, thawed in the fridge according to package directions

Chicken Pot Pie

One of my favorite meals is pot pie and fries. Although I grew up on the frozen version, this is the real deal, straight from famed kitchens of County Cork, Ireland. When it's cold and wet outside, this hearty meal will warm you to the core. It's truly comfort food at its best. Because of the number of steps, this is a great dish to make the day before, then reheat to serve.

1. Place the stockpot over medium-high heat. Add the chicken, then add water until chicken is covered by 3 inches. Add salt, pepper, the bouillon cube, bay leaves, and thyme. Bring mixture almost to a boil, then reduce to a simmer (page xxiii) for approximately 2 hours. Watch carefully to maintain the simmer (mixture should not boil).

2. Using tongs, carefully transfer the chicken to a plate to cool. Bring the stock to a boil. Add the carrots, onions, and celery, then lower heat to a simmer for 10 to 12 minutes, until vegetables are soft and tender. Remove vegetables with the slotted spoon and set aside in a bowl. Discard the bay leaves and thyme stem. Add the peas to the stockpot and cook for 3 to 4 minutes. Remove with slotted spoon and add to the bowl.

3. Using a sharp knife, remove the chicken meat from the bones (page 180). Dice meat into 1-inch cubes and add to the vegetable mixture. Discard the skin and bones.

4. In the small bowl, mix the butter and flour until smooth. Whisk the butter-flour paste into the boiling stock and allow to thicken for 3 to 4 minutes. Whisk in the cream. Add salt and pepper to season. Carefully add the chicken and vegetables and continue to cook until mixture thickens (a gravy-like consistency, but not pasty).

STEP 1

STEP 3

(5) Remove mixture from heat and use a ladle to carefully pour it into individual baking dishes or one large baking dish. If mixture is too thick, stir in 1 tablespoon water before pouring it into baking dish. Cover with plastic wrap and refrigerate mixture for 1 hour.

(6) While the mixture is chilling, preheat the oven to 375°F. Make an egg wash by whisking the egg with milk. Set aside until ready to use.

(7) Lay out the puff pastry sheets on a flat, dry, well-floured surface. Coat the rolling pin with flour and gently roll out one sheet of puff pastry until flat and smooth. Using a knife, cut the pastry slightly larger than the size of your baking dishes. Set aside and repeat with remaining sheet.

(8) Remove chicken mixture from the refrigerator. Carefully drape the pastry sheets over dishes and brush with egg wash. Transfer dish to the oven and bake for 30 minutes, until pastry surface is puffy and golden brown. Remove from oven and serve immediately.

STEP 5

STEP 8

LEVEL

SERVES 8

PREP TIME 20 minutes

COOK TIME 4 hours plus 20 minutes for resting and making gravy

Gear

- Cutting board
- Chef's knife
- Vegetable peeler
- Large roasting pan
- Instant-read thermometer
- Medium saucepan
- Baking dish
- Large spoon
- Wooden spoon
- Fine-mesh sieve or strainer
- Small saucepan
- 2 bowls (1 medium, 1 large)
- Optional: baster; carving knife; gravy boat

Ingredients

TURKEY

- One 15-pound turkey (fresh is preferred, or thawed if frozen)
- 2 medium yellow onions, peeled and coarsely chopped
- 1 stalk celery, coarsely chopped
- 4 carrots, peeled and coarsely chopped
- 8 teaspoons (⅓ stick) butter
- 3 teaspoons kosher salt
- Pepper
- 1 tablespoon chopped fresh thyme leaves, stems reserved

(continues)

Roast Turkey with Stuffing

Whether served at a holiday feast or a casual dinner, a roasted turkey is a king among dishes. There are many ways to roast a turkey—and often nothing compares to Mom's—but this easy-to-follow recipe will help guide you when you're playing host or hostess for the holidays.

If it's your first time making a special meal with a roasted turkey, be sure to plan accordingly. Leave plenty of time not only for the turkey, but also to coordinate cooking other dishes to serve before, with, or after. I normally roast a 15-pound turkey, as shown here, but follow the guidelines in the Turkey Tips & Safety feature on page 181 to determine the proper roasting time for whatever size turkey you make.

1. Thaw turkey if frozen. Move a rack to the lower third of the oven; remove the other racks. Preheat the oven to 325°F.

2. Remove the giblets and discard. Place the onions, celery, and carrots in the bottom of the roasting pan, then place the turkey on top of vegetables, breast up.

3. Generously smear the butter on the turkey breast, then rub with salt and pepper to season, both inside and out (unless you are using a kosher turkey, which contains more salt). Sprinkle the thyme on the turkey right before it goes in the oven.

4. Place the roasting pan in the oven and roast the turkey for 4 hours (see Turkey Tips & Safety, page 181, for more information). About 30 minutes before it is done, slide the turkey out of the oven and baste it with the pan juices. Immediately return roasting pan to the oven. Test doneness by making a discrete slice between the leg and the breast (juice should run clear, not red). Using an instant-read thermometer (see Temperature Guide for an Instant-Read Thermometer, page xxvi) check that the internal temperature near the breast is 165 degrees.

STEP 2

STEP 5

STEP 9

Ingredients (cont'd)

STUFFING

- 1 tablespoon olive oil
- 1 large onion, peeled and diced
- 3 tablespoons chopped fresh thyme leaves, stems reserved
- 3 tablespoons chopped fresh sage leaves, stems reserved
- 3 tablespoons chopped fresh rosemary leaves, stems reserved
- ½ pound (2 sticks) butter
- 3 cups Bread Crumbs (page 48)
- 3 tablespoons chopped fresh flat-leaf parsley, stems reserved
- Salt and pepper

GRAVY

- 1 cup red wine
- All stems from the herbs for the turkey and stuffing
- 3 sprigs of fresh thyme
- 1 bay leaf
- 2 cups store-bought demi-glace or 2 packets brown gravy mix, prepared
- Salt and pepper

(5) While turkey is roasting, make the stuffing: Place the medium saucepan over medium heat. When hot*, add the olive oil and cook the onions, stirring, for 4 minutes or until soft and translucent.

(6) Stir in the chopped thyme, sage, and rosemary, then add the butter and mix well until melted. Stir in the bread crumbs and parsley. Taste and add salt and pepper to season. Remove from heat and transfer mixture to the baking dish. Set aside, covered, until the turkey is out of the oven. When ready to serve, reheat in the oven, as needed, until crisp.

(7) When done, transfer the turkey from the roasting pan to a platter or clean cutting board and allow it to rest for 20 minutes while you make gravy.

(8) Using a spoon, skim the fat off the juices in the roasting pan, leaving the vegetables and turkey drippings at the bottom. Place the roasting pan over medium-high heat. When hot*, add the wine and deglaze (pages xxiv–xxv) the pan, stirring with the wooden spoon.

(9) Mix in the herb stems, thyme, bay leaf, and demi-glace or gravy, and bring to a simmer (page xxiii) for 6 to 8 minutes, until thick. Remove the sauce from heat and strain into the small saucepan. Keep warm on the stove until ready to serve.

(10) Carve the turkey on the cutting board (see Carving a Turkey, page 180). Serve individual portions, or place the carved pieces on a serving platter. Spoon the stuffing into the large bowl and serve on the side. Pour the gravy in a gravy boat or a small bowl with a spoon and serve on the side.

*Is your pan hot enough? Test it with a drop of water. If it sizzles, you're ready to cook

continues

CARVING A TURKEY

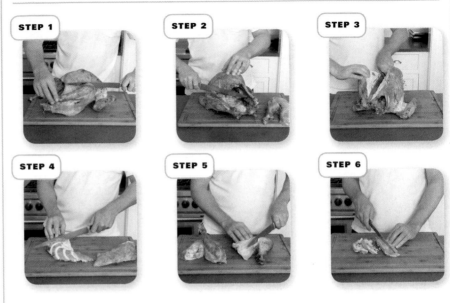

1 Slide a sharp knife between the breast and the leg.

2 Gently bend the leg back to remove it. Repeat with the other leg.

3 Slide the knife down on both sides of the breast bone. Remove the bone by sliding the knife between the breast bone and the meat. This will help you carve the whole turkey without obstruction.

4 Place whole breast pieces on the cutting board. Slice crosswise, against the grain, at a 45-degree angle.

5 Separate the drumstick from the thigh. Pull the center bone out of the thigh.

6 Carve the dark meat in slices.

TURKEY TIPS & SAFETY

Turkey Tips

- Allow about 1 pound of turkey per person.

- Make sure your turkey is fully thawed before cooking.

- Remove the giblets (including the heart, liver, gizzard, and neck) from the turkey before cooking and discard. Rinse the turkey well with water.

- Don't be shy with the seasoning. It may seem like a lot, but in the end, the amount per slice is fairly small.

- Pull back the neck skin of the turkey and fasten it with a skewer so it remains closed while cooking.

- Roasting time depends on the size of the turkey you're cooking. Allow 15 minutes per pound, plus an additional 15 minutes.

- Use an instant-read thermometer to test doneness. The internal temperature near the breast should be 165°F.

- Be sure not to place the thermometer too close to the bone, or you could get an incorrect temperature reading; the bones retain more heat than the meat, so your temperature reading will be misleading.

- If the turkey starts to brown too much while roasting, loosely cover the roasting pan with aluminum foil in a tent-like shape.

- Let the turkey rest for at least 15 to 20 minutes on a cutting board before carving. This allows the juices to settle back into the meat, keeping it moist and tender.

How to Thaw a Frozen Turkey

You can find prethawed turkeys in many stores, but if you buy your turkey frozen, there are many ways to thaw it safely and effectively. *Important reminder:* Use soap and water to wash your hands and any utensils in the kitchen that have come in contact with the raw turkey.

In the Refrigerator

This is the recommended way to thaw. While it takes a few days, it is the most thorough method. Place the turkey, still wrapped, in a pan to catch any juice drippings. Add 24 hours of refrigeration time for every 4 to 5 pounds of turkey.

Thawing Timetable

WEIGHT OF TURKEY	THAWING TIME (IN THE FRIDGE)
8 to 12 pounds	1 to 2 days
12 to 16 pounds	2 to 3 days
16 to 20 pounds	3 to 4 days
20 to 24 pounds	4 to 5 days

In Cold Water

Tightly wrap the turkey with plastic wrap and submerge it in a large bowl filled with cold water. Change the water every 30 minutes to keep temperature stable. Cook the turkey immediately when done thawing.

How to Store Fresh Turkey

If you've purchased a fresh turkey you can safely store it in the refrigerator for up to two days, until you're ready to use.

SERVES 4 PLUS LEFTOVERS
PREP TIME 15 minutes
COOK TIME 1½ hours

Gear

- Cutting board
- Chef's knife
- Vegetable peeler
- Roasting pan
- Fry pan
- Tongs
- Whisk
- Fine-mesh sieve or strainer
- Small saucepan
- Optional: carving knife; gravy boat

Ingredients

ROAST

- 3 to 4 pounds prime rib of beef (bone-in preferred)
- Salt and pepper
- 2 yellow onions, peeled and coarsely chopped
- 2 carrots, peeled and coarsely chopped
- 2 stalks celery, coarsely chopped
- 1 tablespoon olive oil
- 12 equal-size small-to-medium Yukon Gold potatoes, peeled
- 2 cloves garlic, peeled and coarsely sliced
- 1 tablespoon chopped fresh rosemary leaves

(continues)

Prime Rib of Beef

The ultimate splurge meal, prime rib is decadent yet satisfying on so many levels, and when paired with a robust red wine . . . wow! It always reminds me of holiday dinners, and my mother's Sunday roast.

Making the perfect gravy sometimes depends on the pan you've used to cook the roast. I recommend a standard heavy stainless-steel roasting pan or an enamel-coated cast-iron roasting dish. Both provide magnificent meat residue, which serves as the base of the gravy. (Nonstick roasting pans are not recommended.)

1. Preheat the oven to 425°F. Rub the beef generously with salt and pepper. Place the onions, carrots, and celery in the bottom of a roasting pan. Place the beef on top of the vegetables, fat side up.

2. Place the fry pan over medium-high heat. When hot*, add the olive oil and potatoes. Sear (page xxiv) all sides of the potatoes until golden brown, 4 to 6 minutes on each side. Add the garlic and rosemary and stir until potatoes are well coated. Using tongs, transfer the potatoes from the fry pan and arrange in the roasting pan around the beef.

3. Roast the beef in the oven for 20 minutes, then lower the oven temperature to 400°F and cook for 40 minutes more or until internal temperature reaches your desired doneness. (See Temperature Guide for an Instant-Read Thermometer, page xxvi for more information.) Remove the roasting pan from the oven and place on a heat-resistant surface. Using tongs, transfer the beef and potatoes to a serving platter. Allow to rest for 20 minutes.

4. While beef is resting, make the gravy: Place the roasting pan over medium heat. Sprinkle in the flour, add tomato paste, and whisk continuously until onions and carrots are well-coated and the mixture turns light brown.

STEP 1

STEP 3

Ingredients (cont'd)

GRAVY

- 2 tablespoons all-purpose flour
- 1 tablespoon tomato paste
- 1 cup red wine
- 1½ cups store-bought veal, beef, or chicken stock, or homemade Chicken Stock (page 97)
- Salt and pepper
- Pinch of cayenne pepper
- 2 tablespoons (¼ stick) butter, diced

⑤ Whisk in the red wine. Add 1 cup of the stock, mixing continuously. Whisk in any juices given off by the resting meat. Taste and adjust with salt, pepper, and cayenne. Continue whisking until gravy reaches your desired thickness (add remaining stock if gravy is too thick).

⑥ Remove gravy from heat and strain into the saucepan using the fine-mesh sieve. Add the butter and whisk until well combined.

⑦ Place beef on the cutting board, boneside down. Using a sharp knife, remove the bone by gently sliding the knife between the bone and the meat. To serve, cut meat downward in ¼- to ½-inch slices, laying them on the serving platter, with potatoes on the side. Serve the gravy in a small bowl or gravy boat on the side.

Is your pan hot enough? Test it with a drop of water. If it sizzles, you're ready to cook.

STEP 7 (A)

STEP 7 (B)

LEVEL

SERVES 4
PREP TIME 40 minutes
COOK TIME 2 hours

Gear

- Cutting board
- Chef's knife
- Paring knife
- Small bowl
- Roasting pan with rack
- Large spoon
- Instant-read thermometer

Ingredients

- 3 pounds boneless leg of lamb (preferably tied; ask your butcher)
- 4 cloves garlic, peeled and coarsely sliced
- 1 tablespoon chopped fresh rosemary and/or thyme
- 4 tablespoons (½ stick) butter, softened (see page 14)
- 2 tablespoons olive oil
- Salt and pepper
- 2 medium sprigs of fresh rosemary
- 2 pounds medium Yukon Gold potatoes, peeled and cut into ½-inch slices
- 1 medium yellow onion, peeled and thinly sliced
- 1 cup homemade Chicken Stock (page 97) or store-bought
- 2 bay leaves
- 1 tablespoon chopped fresh flat-leaf parsley

Boneless Leg of Lamb

Leg of lamb elevates meat-and-potatoes to an entirely new level. But don't let it intimidate you; slow and easy is key here. And the delicious seasonings give you a taste of Provence in every bite.

1. Move a rack to the middle of the oven. Preheat the oven to 375°F.

2. Using the tip of a knife, make ½-inch-deep cuts in the lamb and insert garlic slices. In the small bowl, mix the chopped herbs and butter. Stuff herb butter into the cuts. Drizzle the olive oil over the meat and season well with salt and pepper. Place the rosemary sprigs on top of the roast. Wrap the roast in plastic and refrigerate for 20 minutes, until ready to use.

3. Place the potatoes and onions in the bottom of the roasting pan, and toss with salt and pepper. Pour in the chicken stock and add bay leaves.

4. Place the rack over the roasting pan and put the lamb on the rack. Place the roasting pan on the middle rack in the oven and roast for 1 hour. Occasionally slide the roasting pan out of the oven and baste the lamb and potatoes with the pan juices and skim off excess fat. Immediately return the roasting pan to the oven. Check doneness using an instant-read thermometer (see page xxvi).

5. Remove the roasting pan in the oven and transfer the lamb to the cutting board. Remove and discard the rosemary sprigs and bay leaves. Return the roasting pan, with juices and vegetables, to the oven to cook for an additional 5 minutes. Remove and set aside.

6. Allow the meat to sit for 15 minutes, uncovered, before slicing. To serve, slice meat crosswise, across the grain, into ½-inch thick pieces. Place a spoonful of potatoes and onions in the center of each plate and top with 2 slices of lamb each. Spoon juices from the roasting pan over lamb and garnish with a sprinkle of chopped parsley on the potatoes.

STEP 2

STEP 3

STEP 4

SERVES 4
PREP TIME 15 minutes
COOK TIME 12 to 14 minutes

Gear

- Cutting board
- Chef's knife
- Small bowl
- Wooden spoon
- Pastry brush
- Nonstick fry pan
- Wide spatula

Ingredients

SALSA

- 3 medium heirloom tomatoes (preferably different colors), ½-inch dice
- 1 small red onion, peeled and minced
- 1 tablespoon purple basil cut into small squares (substitute regular green basil if you can't find purple)
- 2 tablespoons olive oil
- 1 tablespoon ketchup
- 1 teaspoon aged balsamic vinegar
- Smoked paprika
- Cayenne pepper
- Salt and pepper

FISH

- Four 6- to 7-ounce striped bass fillets (scaled and boned by the fishmonger)
- 1 tablespoon olive oil
- Salt and pepper
- Fennel Puree (page 194) or vegetable side of your choice, for serving

Pan-Seared Striped Bass with Heirloom Tomato Salsa

After a day of fishing off Montauk Point, Long Island, I stopped at a farm stand on the way home. The tomatoes were at their summer peak, and the basil was freshly picked. I was inspired by those fresh ingredients to create this dish for dinner that night. Let my inspiration be your guide more than my ingredient list: If a seasonal vegetable or fresh piece of fish looks irresistible, use it, and then make it work in the dish. I love using multicolored heirloom tomatoes here to add color and vibrancy to the dish. Serve it with Fennel Puree (page 194) for an extra punch of flavor.

1. Make the salsa: In the small bowl, combine the tomatoes, onion, basil, olive oil, ketchup, vinegar, and a pinch each of smoked paprika and cayenne. Taste and add salt and pepper to season. Cover with plastic wrap and refrigerate until ready to use.

2. Using the point of a knife, carefully score the fish, making 4 to 5 diagonal cuts on each side (about ½ inch apart) to allow for even heat distribution.

3. Brush the fish on both sides with the olive oil; add salt and pepper to season. Place the fry pan over high heat. When hot*, gently place the fish in the pan, skin side down. Fry for 6 minutes, putting constant pressure on the fish with the wide spatula to ensure even cooking. Carefully flip over and cook for 4 minutes more, until meat is white and tender.

4. To serve, place a spoonful of fennel puree on each plate and top with a piece of bass, skin side up. Spoon salsa on the center of each piece of fish.

Is your pan hot enough? Test it with a drop of water. If it sizzles, you're ready to cook.

STEP 1

STEP 2

STEP 3

SERVES 4
PREP TIME   15 minutes
COOK TIME   25 minutes

Gear

- Cutting board
- Chef's knife
- 2 nonstick fry pans
  (or 1 saucepan and 1 fry pan)
- Wooden spoon
- Wide spatula
- Roasting pan or baking sheet
- Small saucepan

Ingredients

- 1¾ pounds fresh halibut
  fillet (center cut) or 4 halibut
  steaks, 6 to 7 ounces each
  (center cut, skinless and
  boneless)
- 4 tablespoons olive oil
- 1 medium yellow bell pepper, trimmed, seeded, ribs
  removed, and cut into
  ¾-inch x ¾-inch squares
- 1 medium red bell pep-
  per, trimmed, seeded, ribs
  removed, and cut into
  ¾-inch x ¾-inch squares

(continues)

Change It Up

- Try using salmon or swordfish
  in place of the halibut.

- Ocean fish like halibut taste
  great grilled outside on a barbeque. Or skip the pan-frying
  altogether, and broil fish fillets
  for 8 to 10 minutes.

Halibut with Peperonata and Pesto

Halibut is a delicious mild-flavored white fish that is also forgiving to the new cook. Its thick flesh makes it easy to prepare, and it offers some flexibility in time. Combined with peperonata—a heavenly stew of sweet peppers—and the pesto counterpoint, this dish has serious star quality.

1. Preheat the oven to 375°F. Cut halibut fillet into 4 pieces (if not pre-cut).

2. Place a fry pan or saucepan over high heat. When very hot*, add 2 tablespoons of the olive oil, the peppers, and onions. Fry for 3 minutes, until golden brown. Reduce the heat to medium.

3. Add the tomato paste and cook, stirring, for 2 minutes. Mix in the vinegar, cook for 2 minutes, then mix in the brown sugar. Turn the heat up to medium-high. Cook for 6 minutes, stirring occasionally, until the peppers are glossy. Remove pan from heat and set aside.

4. Place a second fry pan over medium-high heat. When hot*, add the remaining 2 tablespoons olive oil. Gently add the halibut pieces to the fry pan and cook until lightly golden brown, 4 to 5 minutes on each side.

5. Remove from heat and transfer the halibut to the roasting pan. Top each piece with 1 tablespoon butter and add salt, pepper, and cayenne to season. Place the roasting pan in the oven and bake for 8 to 10 minutes, until fish is slightly flaky but cooked through (see page 67). Remove roasting pan from oven.

STEP 1

STEP 3

STEP 4

Ingredients (cont'd)

- 1 medium orange bell pepper, trimmed, seeded, ribs removed, and cut into ¾-inch × ¾-inch squares
- 1 large red onion, peeled and cut into ¾-inch × ¾-inch squares (discard odd-size pieces)
- 1 tablespoon tomato paste
- ½ cup balsamic vinegar
- ½ cup light brown sugar
- 4 tablespoons (½ stick) butter
- Salt and pepper
- Cayenne pepper
- ¼ cup Homemade Pesto (recipe follows) or store-bought

Kitchen FYI

If buying pesto, avoid the jarred grayish-green version on the shelf. Instead, look for the fresh bright green pesto in the refrigerated section. If it's too chilled, place the container in the microwave for 10 to 20 seconds on defrost, or add a few tablespoonfuls to a bowl or dish and allow it to come to room temperature. The pesto should be runny enough to drizzle over the fish.

6 To serve, reheat the peperonata in the small saucepan or a microwave-safe bowl. Add 1 tablespoon peperonata in center of each plate, place the fish directly in the center of the sauce, and drizzle pesto around the fish to finish.

Is your pan hot enough? Test it with a drop of water. If it sizzles, you're ready to cook.

MAKE YOUR OWN . . .

Homemade Pesto

MAKES ⅔ CUP

PREP TIME 8 minutes

INGREDIENTS

1 cup loosely packed chopped fresh basil leaves (about 1 medium bunch)
½ cup olive oil
2 large cloves garlic, peeled and coarsely chopped
3 tablespoons pine nuts
¼ cup freshly grated Parmesan cheese

Place all the ingredients in a blender or food processor and process until smooth and paste-like. Refrigerate, tightly covered, for up to 2 weeks.

FISH FRYING TRICKS

- Always use a nonstick pan.
- Make sure to use a sturdy, wide spatula.
- After pan-frying (page xxiv) until golden brown, transfer the fish to a roasting pan and finish cooking in the oven.

LEVEL

SERVES 4
PREP TIME 25 minutes
COOK TIME 10 minutes
ASSEMBLY TIME 10 minutes

Gear

- 8-quart stockpot
- Small saucepan
- Large spoon
- Fine-mesh sieve or strainer
- Small bowl
- Tongs
- Large bowl
- Colander
- Paring knife
- 4 small cups
- Claw crackers (or mallet or heavy hammer)
- Lobster forks or nut picks

Ingredients

- Sea salt
- Four 1¼- to 1¾-pound live lobsters

CLARIFIED BUTTER

- ½ pund (2 sticks) unsalted butter
- Optional: ½ teaspoon sea salt

Kitchen FYI

Use clarified butter immediately or store in an airtight container in the refrigerator for up to 2 weeks.

Boiled Lobster with Warm Butter

What's more alluring than sweet, delicate lobster dipped in warm butter? Served with Corn on the Cob (page 138), Roasted Rosemary Potato Wedges (page 72), and some warm, crusty bread, it's a sophisticated yet casual meal.

Lobster meat is quite versatile and can be used in everything from salad to sandwiches. See Lobster, Four More Ways (page 191) for creative serving suggestions.

1. Place the stockpot filled with well-salted water over high heat and bring to a vigorous boil. Reduce heat to medium and slowly drop in the live lobsters, one by one, head first. Partly cover and cook for 10 to 15 minutes, until shells are bright red.

2. While lobsters are cooking, make the clarified butter: In the small saucepan over low heat, melt the butter until it begins to break down into a golden yellow liquid and add sea salt, if using. Skim the top layer of foam using the spoon. Remove from heat and allow to cool. Strain the liquid through the sieve into the small bowl.

3. Using tongs, remove the lobsters from the stockpot, drain in the colander over the sink, and set aside until cool enough to handle. Remove rubber bands from claws and discard. Using the paring knife, slice the lobster in half, from head to tail. Then puncture small holes between the tail and body and between the claws and the body of the lobster.

4. To serve, place one lobster on the center of each plate and serve the melted butter in individual small cups for dipping. Place the large bowl to the side for discarding shells.

continues

STEP 1

STEP 2

CRACK IT OPEN: HOW TO CLEAN AND EAT A LOBSTER

When serving a boiled lobster whole, follow these easy steps to get the most meat (without much mess). If you plan to use lobster meat in other dishes, like salad (recipe follows), you'll need to extract the meat from the hard shells cleanly and carefully.

Claws

Twist off the claws at the point where they attach to the body. Disjoint the claws from the knuckles, removing meat as you proceed. Gently crack open the main claw, about 1 inch from the base. Slowly pull out the claw meat, trying to keep it intact. Discard cartilage (hard, flat, white pieces).

Tail

Twist tail with both hands to remove it from the body. Remove flipper fins. Using your thumb, push the tail meat through the base. Discard the green tomalley (liver). Using a paring knife, remove the digestive track that runs along the curved top part of the tail and discard.

Legs

Tear the legs away from the body and break them between the joints.

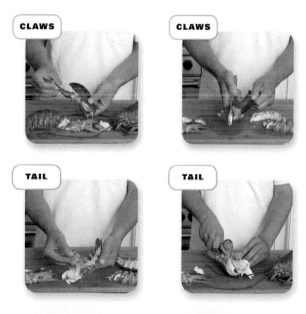

Gear
- Cutting board
- Chef's knife
- Paring knife
- Vegetable peeler
- Blender or food processor
- Medium bowl
- Small bowl
- Ring mold or ramekin
  (5 ounces)

Ingredients

SALAD
- Meat from 2 lobsters
- 1 large cucumber, peeled, seeded, and diced (¼-inch)
- 4 medium-size ripe tomatoes, ends trimmed, finely diced
- ½ medium red bell pepper, trimmed, seeded, ribs removed, and finely diced
- ½ medium yellow bell pepper, trimmed, seeded, ribs removed, and finely diced
- 1 avocado, peeled, pitted, and diced
- 1 cup finely diced romaine lettuce (inner leaves only), 6 to 8 leaves
- Salt and pepper
- 2 tablespoons olive oil

DRESSING
- Juice of 2 lemons
- 2 egg yolks
- 1 tablespoon Dijon mustard
- ½ teaspoon smoked paprika
- 1 tablespoon sugar
- ⅔ cup olive oil
- Salt and pepper

LOBSTER SALAD

SERVES 4
PREP TIME 25 minutes
COOK TIME 10 minutes
ASSEMBLY TIME 10 minutes

(1) Prepare the lobsters as directed in the recipe on page 188.

(2) While lobster is boiling, make the dressing: Add the lemon juice, egg yolks*, mustard, paprika, and sugar to the blender or food processor. Pulse on medium until well combined. While the blender is running, add the olive oil in a slow, steady stream.

(3) Taste and adjust the seasoning with salt and pepper, if needed. (If too tart, add more sugar. If you can taste egg, add more oil.) Continue mixing until dressing is creamy and smooth. Set aside until ready to use.

(4) In the medium bowl, toss the cucumbers, tomato, peppers, avocado, and lettuce with 5 tablespoons of the dressing, Taste and add salt and pepper to season. Set the salad aside until ready to use.

STEP 6 (A)

STEP 6 (B)

5. Once lobsters have cooled, place lobster on the cutting board. Cut the tails in half lengthwise. Carefully remove meat from the tail, chop it into 1-inch pieces, and transfer to the small bowl. Pick over the meat to make sure there are no bits of shell or cartilage still attached. Add olive oil and toss with lobster meat. Add salt and pepper to season. Continue mixing until meat is glossy and has a sheen.

6. To serve, place the ring mold in center of the first plate. Spoon a quarter of the salad mixture into the mold, then add the meat of a half lobster on top. Apply light pressure with a spoon and your fingers to hold mixture in place. Carefully lift the mold to remove. If using a ramekin, fill with salad mixture and lobster meat as directed above, then slowly turn it over onto a dish and carefully lift the ramekin to remove.

7. Place a lobster claw in the middle of each salad mold, and drizzle the remaining dressing around the outside of the salad. Repeat for each plate.

*See the warning on page 5 about using raw eggs.

LOBSTER, FOUR MORE WAYS

Lobster meat is actually quite delicate, so if you plan to add it to other dishes, be sure to do so at the end of cooking time, unless otherwise directed.

- Add lobster to Rigatoni with Red Pepper Sauce (page 45) in Step 4 for a hearty twist.
- For elegant hors d'oeuvres, use lobster salad as a crostini topping; or use lobster meat in place of the red peppers to make Lobster, Brie, and Tomato Tartlets (page 157).
- Add lobster chunks to Scrambled Eggs (page 4) or use as an omelet filling (page 9), topped with chopped fresh chives.
- Make Lobster Pot Stickers instead of shrimp (page 164).

Stylish Sides

Here are some more crowd-pleasing side dishes that will elevate your meal to a whole new level. Most of the sides here make perfect pairs with the Level 3 main dishes, but they'll work just as well with main dishes from Level 1 or 2, or any of your own creations.

Well-made sides are a subtle beauty—best enjoyed in harmony with, rather than overwhelming, their accompanying dishes. Feel free to make substitutions (when applicable) according to what looks the freshest at the market or what you're in the mood to eat.

IN THIS CHAPTER

In this chapter, you'll find recipes for:
- ○ Vegetable Puree, Three Ways
- ○ Buttery Mashed Potatoes
- ○ Sugar Snap Peas
- ○ Green Bean Parcels

And you'll develop the skills and know-how to:
- ○ Serve hearty vegetables as sophisticated purees
- ○ Spruce up basic mashed potatoes with a few simple flavor add-ins
- ○ Transform simple green beans into elegant packages

③
LEVEL

SERVES 4

Gear

- Cutting board
- Vegetable peeler
- Chef's knife
- Medium saucepan
- Wooden spoon
- Food processor

Ingredients

- 1½ pounds parsnips, peeled and coarsely chopped
- ¼ cup heavy cream
- ½ cup milk
- ½ cup water
- Salt and pepper
- 2 tablespoons (¼ stick) butter

Vegetable Puree, Three Ways

Serving vegetables as a puree is a novel way to dress up any main dish. The creamy, smooth texture of puree makes it the perfect pair to almost any meat or fish course.

PARSNIP PUREE

PREP TIME 5 minutes
COOK TIME 30 minutes

Sweeter than carrots, yet with a subtle earthiness, parsnips are an unsung hero of the root vegetable world. This slightly sugary yet rich light-colored puree is a wonderful complement to Pork Chops (page 58), steak, or any white fish.

1. Place the saucepan over medium-high heat. Add the parsnips, cream, milk, water, and salt and pepper to season. Bring to a boil, then lower the heat until simmering (page xxiii). Cook for 15 to 20 minutes, until the liquid has almost completely evaporated.

2. Stir in the butter and mix until well combined. Remove mixture from the heat and allow to cool for 5 minutes. Transfer mixture to the food processor and puree until creamy, thick, and smooth.

3. Wipe out the saucepan and add back the puree. Cover and place over low heat until ready to serve.

PREP

STEP 3

continues

Gear

- Cutting board
- Chef's knife
- Vegetable peeler
- Large fry pan
- Wooden spoon
- Food processor
- Small saucepan

Ingredients

- 2 tablespoons olive oil
- 1 medium red onion, peeled and diced
- 1 large fennel bulb with stalks, bulb quartered, cored, and thinly sliced; stalks peeled and finely chopped
- ¾ cup homemade Chicken Stock (page 97) or store-bought
- ½ cup milk
- 1 tablespoon sugar
- ¾ cup heavy cream
- 2 tablespoons (¼ stick) butter
- Salt and pepper

FENNEL PUREE

PREP TIME 10 minutes
COOK TIME 50 minutes

Fennel, whether raw or (in this case) cooked and pureed, matches perfectly with all types of seafood. I recommend you serve this as a side to Pan-Seared Striped Bass with Heirloom Tomato Salsa (page 185).

STEP 2

(1) Place the fry pan over medium-high heat. When hot*, add the olive oil, onions, fennel slices, and chopped stalks. Cook until soft and translucent, about 10 minutes.

(2) Stir in ½ cup of the chicken stock and bring to a simmer (page xxiii) until liquid level reduces (page xxv) by ⅓ in the pan. Reduce the heat to low, add the milk, sugar, and cream, and simmer for 35 minutes, until mixture is soft and creamy. Remove from heat and set aside to cool for 5 minutes.

(3) Transfer the mixture to the food processor and puree until creamy, thick, and smooth. Slowly add the remaining ¼ cup chicken stock if the puree is too thick. Add in butter and salt and pepper to season.

(4) Transfer mixture to the small saucepan. Cover and place over low heat until ready to serve.

*Is your pan hot enough? Test it with a drop of water. If it sizzles, you're ready to cook.

Gear

- Cutting board
- Chef's knife
- Vegetable peeler
- Roasting pan
- Aluminum foil
- Large bowl
- Large spoon
- Optional: potato masher
- Small saucepan

Ingredients

- 1 large or 2 small butternut squash (about 1¼ pounds), halved lengthwise, peeled, seeded, and chopped
- 2 tablespoons olive oil
- Salt and pepper
- 4 tablespoons (½ stick) butter

BUTTERNUT SQUASH PUREE

PREP TIME   10 minutes
COOK TIME   35 minutes

Butternut squash is the perfect accompaniment for any dish that has a savory or sweet undertone. Try serving this puree with Crispy Chicken Cutlets (page 122) or Veal Milanese (page 126).

1. Preheat the oven to 375°F.

2. Lay out the squash in the roasting pan, drizzle with the olive oil, and sprinkle with salt and pepper. Cover roasting pan with aluminum foil, place in the oven, and cook for 25 minutes. Check doneness by sliding a knife into the squash; if it slides through easily, the squash is done.

3. Remove the squash from the oven and transfer into the large bowl. Add the butter, and season well with salt and pepper. Mash mixture with a potato masher or fork until silky smooth.

4. Transfer mixture to the small saucepan. Cover and place over low heat until ready to serve.

STEP 2

STEP 3

3
LEVEL

SERVES 4
PREP TIME 10 minutes
COOK TIME 45 minutes

Gear

- Cutting board
- Vegetable peeler
- Chef's knife
- 8-quart stockpot
- Colander
- Potato masher, food mill, or potato ricer
- Wooden spoon

Ingredients

- 2 pounds medium Yukon Gold potatoes, peeled and halved
- Salt
- 8 tablespoons (1 stick) butter
- ½ cup milk
- ½ cup heavy cream
- White pepper

Buttery Mashed Potatoes

These buttery mashed potatoes create an elegant and silky side that pairs perfectly with Crispy Chicken Cutlets with Mushrooms (page 122) or Roast Turkey with Stuffing (page 178). To elevate humble potatoes to something creative, try serving a variety of flavor combinations in pretty bowls.

1. Place the stockpot filled with salted water over high heat and add the potatoes. Bring to a boil, then reduce to simmer (page xxiii) so water is gently bubbling. Cook for about 35 minutes, until potatoes are soft. Check doneness by sliding a knife into a potato; if it slides through easily, the potatoes are done.

2. Remove the potatoes from heat and drain in the colander over the sink. Return the potatoes to the stockpot and mash using a potato masher.

3. Using the wooden spoon, fold in the butter, milk, and cream. Add salt and pepper to season. Fold in optional add-ins, if using, as specified on the opposite page. Serve immediately.

STEP 2

STEP 3

Simple Herb Mashed Potatoes   Add 2 tablespoons coarsely chopped fresh flat-leaf parsley, 1 tablespoon finely chopped fresh sage, 1½ teaspoons coarse salt, and a pinch of freshly ground pepper in Step 3. Fold well.

Extra-Cheesy Mashed Potatoes   Add 3 ounces of your favorite cheese, such as cheddar (cubed), Gruyère, Parmesan (chopped), or blue cheese, in Step 3. Fold well.

Scallion and Roasted Garlic Mashed Potatoes   Preheat oven to 350°F. Place 4 peeled garlic cloves in a medium bowl and add 1 tablespoon of olive oil. Toss to coat evenly. Wrap garlic in a sheet of foil and bake in oven for 20 minutes, until golden brown. Mash garlic with a fork, then add to potatoes in Step 3. Fold well.

LEVEL

SERVES 4
PREP TIME 3 minutes
COOK TIME 4 minutes

Gear

- Cutting board
- Paring knife
- Medium saucepan
- Colander
- Slotted spoon

Ingredients

- ¾ pound sugar snap peas (ends and stringy edges removed)
- 1 tablespoon salted butter
- Salt and pepper

Sugar Snap Peas

When in season, fresh and plump sugar snap peas create a nice counter-point to a main dish that is rich in butter and cream, like Chilean Sea Bass with Leeks (page 133). This side dish should be made just before serving the main dish.

1. Place the saucepan filled with water over high heat and bring to a vigorous boil. Add the peas and cook until soft but still bright green, about 3 minutes. (See page 137 for more information on green-vegetable cooking.)

2. Remove from heat and drain in the colander over the sink, gently pressing down with the slotted spoon. Toss in the butter, and add salt and pepper to season. Serve immediately.

PREP

STEP 1

LEVEL

SERVES 4

PREP TIME 8 minutes

COOK TIME 12 minutes

Gear

- Cutting board
- Chef's knife
- Medium saucepan
- Slotted spoon
- Medium bowl
- Colander
- Baking dish

Ingredients

- Salt
- 1 pound haricots verts (French green beans), ends removed, trimmed to even lengths
- Ice water
- 1 small leek, including dark green part, trimmed, washed, and separated into leaves
- 2 tablespoons (¼ stick) butter, diced
- Salt and pepper

Green Bean Parcels

Sometimes a dish can look more delicious or special with a simple decorative or plating trick: These little tied bundles of string beans add a festive, formal look to any dish. They pair perfectly with Boneless Leg of Lamb (page 184) or Prime Rib of Beef (page 182).

1. Preheat the oven to 350°F. Place the saucepan ¾ full of salted water over medium-high heat. Bring to a boil.

2. Add the beans and blanch (page xxiii) until al dente (cooked but still crisp), 3 to 4 minutes. Using the slotted spoon, remove the beans and immediately plunge them into a bowl of ice water. Drain in the colander and set aside.

3. Add the leek leaves to the saucepan and blanch until al dente (cooked but still crisp), 2 to 3 minutes. Using tongs, remove the leek leaves and immediately plunge them into a bowl of ice water.

4. Drain the leaves on paper towels and place on the cutting board. Roll the leaves up in a large curl, then slice into ¼-inch-thick ribbons. Set aside.

5. Make 4 small bundles of beans. Tie each bundle around the middle with a leek ribbon. Place the bundles in the baking dish, distribute butter over the bundles, and add salt and pepper to season.

6. Immediately before serving, warm up the bean parcels in oven for 3 minutes.

PREP

STEP 5

Delectable Desserts

There is truly nothing more wonderful than a small, luxurious dessert to finish a splendid dinner party. And because it's the final course, desserts can also be the most memorable part of the meal. Dessert is also the perfect time to make some coffee, serve what's left of the wine, or even pull out a fine brandy or port. Here are some of my favorite ways to end a really good meal. These desserts are sophisticated and flavorful. Use the skills you've learned in Levels 1 and 2 to help guide you through the steps here, and get ready for the big smiles on your guests' faces.

IN THIS CHAPTER

In this chapter, you'll find recipes for:
○ Cinnamon-Roasted Pears
○ Lemon Tart
○ Sticky Toffee Pudding
○ Cake for Any Occasion

And you'll develop the skills and know-how to:
○ Core a pear
○ Make your own homemade tart crust
○ Make crème anglaise
○ Easily turn a basic yellow cake into a two-layer cake or cupcakes
○ Transform homemade whipped cream with flavorful add-ins
○ Make homemade frosting and decorate your own cake

SERVES 8

PREP TIME 10 minutes

COOK TIME 30 to 40 minutes, plus 1 hour cooling

ASSEMBLY TIME 3 minutes

Gear

- Cutting board
- Microplane grater
- Paring knife
- Vegetable peeler
- Melon baller or swivel vegetable peeler
- Medium saucepan
- Wooden spoon
- Baking dish
- Ice cream scoop

Ingredients

- 8 to 10 ripe Bartlett pears
- 5 cups water
- 2½ cups sugar
- 2 cinnamon sticks
- 1 teaspoon ground cinnamon
- Grated zest and juice of 1 orange
- Grated zest of 1 lemon
- 2 pints vanilla ice cream
- 2 cups Chocolate Sauce (page 77), warmed

How Do I . . . ?

To get a clean, perfectly round scoop of ice cream, remove the ice cream from the freezer about 5 minutes before serving. Warm the scoop in a bowl of boiling water, then gently glide the scoop through the ice cream. Dip into the hot water between scoops so each serving is clean.

Cinnamon-Roasted Pears

Roasted pears are warm, satisfying, and spicy. They always remind me of the harvest season. Use fresh ripe pears for the best flavor, but keep in mind that the ripeness of the pear will affect your baking time: The softer the fruit, the shorter the baking time.

1. Preheat the oven to 375°F. Peel the pears beginning ⅔ inch from the top and peeling down to the bottom, being careful to keep the stem intact. Remove the core with a melon baller and discard, being careful to leave the top of the fruit flesh intact. Set aside.

2. Place the saucepan over medium-high heat. Add the water, sugar, cinnamon sticks, ground cinnamon, orange juice and zest, and lemon zest, and bring to a boil. Continue stirring and cook until the sugar is dissolved.

3. Gently add the pears, immersing them completely, and simmer (page xxiii) for 10 minutes. Remove from the heat and transfer all contents of the saucepan, including the liquid, to a baking dish.

4. Bake for 15 to 30 minutes, depending on ripeness. Check doneness by sliding a knife into the pear; if it slides through easily, the pears are done. Remove from oven and set aside to cool for 1 hour.

5. Stand each pear up on cutting board. Using a sharp paring knife, gently slide the blade on a slight angle down the pear, starting about ¼ of the way down from the top. Turn pear slightly and make another diagonal slice. Repeat until pear is fully sliced into a fan-like pattern. Repeat with remaining pears.

6. To serve, place a scoop of ice cream onto a plate. Arrange each pear so it evenly falls over the ice cream, draped like a veil or a fan, but remaining upright. Drizzle warm chocolate sauce across the top.

STEP 1

STEP 3

STEP 5

SERVES 6 TO 8

PREP TIME 25 minutes, plus chilling/resting/cooling time for the dough

COOK TIME 45 to 50 minutes

Gear

- Cutting board
- Paring knife
- Microplane grater
- Rolling pin
- Parchment paper
- 9-inch tart pan with a removable bottom
- 2 bowls (1 medium, 1 large)
- Hand-held mixer
- Medium saucepan
- Silicone spatula
- Wire cooling rack
- Fine-mesh sieve or strainer

Ingredients

- Butter and all-purpose flour, for preparing the pan
- Store-bought frozen pie pastry for one 8-inch crust
- 1 cup dry beans or rice, for blind baking the crust
- 3 eggs plus 2 yolks
- ½ cup sugar
- Grated zest and juice of 3 large lemons (about 1 cup juice)
- 1 cup heavy cream
- ¼ cup confectioners' sugar
- Optional: Whipped Cream (page 79); ½ cup fresh raspberries or other fruit

Lemon Tart

A light, sweet finish to a long and luxurious dinner, this tart, graced with a dollop of whipped cream, goes perfectly with a cup of coffee. For added simplicity, I recommend using a frozen unbaked pie crust. Simply roll it out, and transfer to your tart pan. This will save you tons of time, but should still provide excellent results (and praise for making a homemade dessert).

1. Preheat the oven to 350°F. Coat the inside of the tart pan with butter, then sprinkle ¼ cup of sifted flour, turning pan from side to side until buttered surface is evenly coated with flour. Flip pan over to discard any loose flour.

2. Thaw the frozen crust until it pulls apart from the pan easily. Lay the dough on a flat, dry, well-floured surface. Coat the rolling pin with flour and gently roll out the dough until flat and smooth. Carefully lay it across the tart pan. Using your fingers, push the dough over the bottom of the pan and up the sides until pan is completely covered. Place tart pan in the freezer for 30 minutes.

3. Cut a piece of parchment paper into a circle about 2 inches larger than the diameter of the pan. Place the paper on top of the dough, then add dry beans to the top of the paper to keep the dough from rising. Place pan in the oven and bake for 20 minutes. Remove the pan from the oven, remove the beans and parchment paper, and return the pan to the oven for an additional 5 minutes.

4. While tart is baking, prepare the filling. In the medium bowl, place eggs and yolks and beat, using the hand-held mixer, until mixture is frothy. Add the sugar, lemon juice, and zest and mix for 1 minute.

5. Place the medium saucepan over medium-high heat. Add the cream and bring just to a boil. Remove from heat and slowly pour cream into the egg mixture. Reduce speed to low and mix for 1 minute, until thickened.

STEP 2

STEP 5

STEP 6

6. Pour the lemon custard into the tart shell. Immediately return the tart pan to the oven and bake for 20 minutes. Test doneness by shaking the pan gently; if the tart wobbles first, then settles, it's ready to remove; if the consistency is too liquidy, continue to bake for 5 minutes more, then test again. Remove from the oven and set aside on the wire rack to cool completely.

7. Gently slide a knife under the crust of the tart to loosen, and slide the tart onto a serving platter or cake plate. Dust the top with confectioners' sugar by pouring the sugar over the surface through the fine-mesh sieve. Place a dollop of whipped cream in the center and surround with fresh raspberries, if desired. Cut into 6 to 8 wedges and serve.

PASTRY PIE DOUGH 101

- Always roll out the pastry dough at least 2 inches wider than the diameter of the tart pan, so you have enough dough to cover the sides of the pan.
- Allow the dough to rest for at least 30 minutes prior to baking, to prevent it from shrinking.
- Tough pastry is caused by overhandling or overcooking. Don't overmix dough after each batch of flour is added.
- When blind baking the crust, watch carefully and remove it from the oven just as it turns golden brown.
- After baking, use a knife to cut along the outside of the pan for a perfect edge.

SERVES 6

PREP TIME 20 minutes

COOK TIME 50 minutes

Gear

- Hand-held mixer
- Medium bowl
- Medium saucepan
- Colander
- Food processor or blender
- Small bowl
- Flour sifter or fine-mesh sieve
- Silicone mixing spatula
- Six 2½-inch ramekins, or metal ring molds
- Baking sheet
- Cutting board
- Paring knife

Ingredients

- 6 tablespoons (¾ stick) butter
- ¾ cup light brown sugar
- 1 teaspoon vanilla extract
- 2 eggs
- 1 cup dried dates
- 2 cups water
- 1⅓ cups all-purpose flour
- 1 teaspoon baking powder
- 2 cups Toffee Sauce (page 78)
- Crème Anglaise (opposite page), for serving
- Optional: Whipped cream (page 79)

Sticky Toffee Pudding

In Ireland (where I'm from), *pudding* refers to a light, moist cake, not the creamy snack you eat out of a little container. And rarely will you find a version more enticing than this sticky toffee pudding. Make individual puddings using ramekins, ring molds, or even a muffin pan. The flavors of this pudding get better over time (especially when drenched in toffee sauce), so prepare it up to three days in advance and allow the flavors to steep.

1. Preheat the oven to 375°F. In the medium bowl, combine the butter and brown sugar using the hand-held mixer on medium speed, until just blended. Add the vanilla and beat until creamy. Slowly add 1 egg at a time, mixing on medium speed between additions.

2. Place the medium saucepan over medium-high heat and add the dried dates and water. Bring to a boil. Remove from heat and drain in the colander over the sink. Add mixture to the food processor or blender and pulse until smooth and paste-like, about 2 minutes.

STEP 5

STEP 6 (A)

STEP 6 (B)

③ Sift the flour with baking powder into the small bowl. Gradually add the dry mixture into the batter in three batches, mixing in between batches. Add in the date puree and mix until batter is thick and creamy.

④ Pour the batter into individual ramekins, filling only halfway. Place ramekins on the baking sheet, and bake for 30 to 35 minutes or until a toothpick inserted in the center comes out clean. Remove from oven and allow to cool for 10 to 15 minutes.

⑤ On the cutting board, gently turn ramekins over and remove puddings. Wash and dry the ramekins and return them to the cooled baking sheet.

⑥ Slice each pudding horizontally into three layers of equal thickness. Place the bottom slice back into the ramekin and coat with toffee sauce. Repeat with the middle and top layers of the pudding, finishing with sauce on top. Cover the baking sheet with plastic wrap and refrigerate. Remove 30 minutes before serving.

⑦ Preheat the oven to 200°F. Remove the plastic wrap, place the baking sheet in the oven, and bake for 15 minutes, until puddings are warm. To serve, gently turn the ramekin over onto a plate, or serve individually in ramekins. Drizzle with crème anglaise (below) or with a dollop of whipped cream.

Gear

- Paring knife
- Medium saucepan
- 3 bowls (1 small, 1 medium, 1 large)
- Whisk
- Wooden spoon
- Sieve

Ingredients

- ½ cup heavy cream
- ½ cup milk
- 3 egg yolks
- 3 tablespoons vanilla sugar (page 147) or 2 drops vanilla extract added to 3 tablespoons sugar
- Seeds scraped from ½ split vanilla bean (page 147)
- Ice water

CRÈME ANGLAISE

MAKES 1¼ CUP

COOK TIME   10 minutes

① Place the medium saucepan over medium-high heat and add the cream and milk. Bring to a boil, then remove from the heat.

STEP 3

② In the small bowl, combine the egg yolks, vanilla sugar, and vanilla bean seeds and whisk until well combined and mixture is pale yellow. While whisking, slowly add the hot milk mixture.

③ Return mixture to saucepan, and place over medium heat. Stir continuously in a figure-eight pattern using the wooden spoon, until custard thickens. Test mixture by coating the back of the wooden spoon, then running your finger through it—if it leaves a clean line, the mixture is ready.

④ Prepare an ice water bath in the large bowl. Strain the hot custard through the sieve into a clean medium bowl and cool the bowl in the ice bath. Refrigerate in a covered container.

LEVEL

SERVES 6 TO 8

PREP TIME 20 minutes

COOK TIME 1 hour including cooling time

Gear

- One 9-inch round springform cake pan
- Wax paper
- Flour sifter
- 2 bowls (1 medium, 1 small)
- Whisk
- Hand-held mixer
- Silicone mixing spatula
- Ruler
- Wire cooling rack
- Round serving plate

Ingredients

- 1⅔ cups all-purpose flour
- ⅓ cup cornstarch
- 2 teaspoons baking powder
- ½ teaspoon salt
- 1½ cups sugar
- ½ pound (2 sticks) unsalted butter, softened (page 14), plus more for greasing pan
- ½ cup milk, room temperature
- 3 eggs, room temperature
- 2 teaspoons vanilla extract

Cake for Any Occasion

A basic yellow cake should be a staple in every cook's repertoire. This super-simple dessert can transform from a light treat with fresh fruit to a flavorful birthday cake with buttercream or cream cheese frosting. The possibilities are endless (you can flavor the buttercream with extracts or by adding melted chocolate, for example, or decorate it any way your creativity leads you). You can even make delicious cupcakes using the same batter.

1. Position the rack in the middle of the oven and preheat the oven to 350°F. Grease the cake pan with butter.

2. In the medium bowl, sift together the flour, cornstarch, baking powder, and salt. Add the sugar. Cut the butter into small pieces, add to the dry ingredients, and mix until well combined.

3. In the small bowl, whisk together the milk, eggs, and vanilla. Make a well in the center of the dry ingredients. Gradually pour the liquid into the well. Use the hand-held mixer on medium speed to beat the liquid and dry ingredients together until well combined and smooth, about 3 minutes.

4. Pour the batter into the cake pan, filling about ¾ full, using the silicone mixing spatula to get all the batter out of the bowl and smooth the top. Use the clean ruler to measure that the batter fills ¾ of the pan and is distributed evenly throughout. Place the pan in the oven and bake for 25 to 30 minutes, or until a toothpick inserted in the center just comes out clean.

5. Using oven mitts, remove the cake pans from the oven and set aside on the wire rack to cool for 30 minutes. When cake is cool and firm, gently run a butter knife between the cake and the sides of the pan to loosen. Unclip the sides of the pan and remove (make sure the cake is not clinging to the sides when you release the clip; if it is, it has not cooled enough).

STEP 3 (A)

STEP 3 (B)

STEP 4

Cupcakes for Any Occasion Use the same batter to make 24 cupcakes. Fill paper-lined cupcake pan cups about ⅔ full and bake for 20 to 25 minutes. Decorate as desired.

Two-Layer Cake Looking for an elegant upgrade? Try making a layer cake. Slice a single-layer cake in half, or distribute the batter evenly between two cake pans instead of one. Add a layer of toppings (jam, fruit, frosting, or as desired) between the two cake layers.

AN ARRAY OF ADD-INS

It's simply impossible to list the many ways to spruce up your basic yellow cake. Be creative: Mix and match your favorite dessert flavors to create your own unique decoration. Following are three simple options to get you started.

Additional toppings or enhancements include shredded coconut; bittersweet chocolate chips; mint chocolate, peanut butter, or other small candies; chopped nuts, such as hazelnuts or walnuts; sprinkles; jelly beans; dried fruit; cocoa powder; and confectioners' sugar.

FRESH FRUIT TOPPING

PREP TIME 5 minutes

1 cup each blueberries, strawberries, raspberries, and blackberries

Arrange fresh berries across the top of the cake in any pattern desired. For an elegant (and patriotic) presentation, place one row of strawberries around the outer edge of the cake. Next, add a row of blackberries, then add blueberries to the center of the cake.

continues

FLAVORED WHIPPED CREAM TOPPING

PREP TIME   10 minutes

1 cup heavy cream, chilled
1 teaspoon sugar
2 tablespoons Cointreau or flavored liqueur of choice
Optional: zest of 1 lemon or 1 orange; 1 cup fresh berries

1. Pour the chilled heavy cream, sugar, and liqueur into a chilled bowl. Using the hand-held mixer or whisk, whip until stiff peaks form.

2. To serve, place a large dollop on top of the cake and spread with the silicone spatula across the top until smooth, or add a dollop to each slice. Sprinkle with lemon or orange zest and top with fresh berries, if desired.

STEP 1

COCONUT BUTTERCREAM FROSTING

PREP TIME   5 to 10 minutes

3 cups confectioners' sugar
1 cup unsalted butter, softened (page 14)
1 teaspoon vanilla extract

2 teaspoons coconut extract
6 tablespoons heavy cream
Optional: 1 cup shaved bittersweet or dark chocolate;
    1 cup shredded coconut

1. In a medium bowl, mix the sugar and butter using a hand-held mixer on low speed. Mix until well blended, then increase speed to medium and beat for 3 minutes, until smooth.

2. Add vanilla, coconut extract, and cream to butter and sugar mixture, and beat together on medium for 1 minute, until thick and creamy.

③ Place the cooled cake on a large flat plate or cake plate. Using the silicone spatula, spread the frosting onto the cake and then evenly across the top, to the edges. When smooth, spread the remaining frosting along the sides of the cake, slowly turning the plate until cake is completely and evenly frosted. Serve immediately, or cover cake with plastic wrap and store in the fridge.

④ To enhance the frosting decoration, sprinkle chocolate shavings and/or shredded coccnut across the top and on the sides, if desired.

STEP 2   STEP 3 (A)   STEP 3 (B)

MENUS

You've made some casual meals and done some simple entertaining. Why stop there? You are clearly ready throw your own cocktail party, have some close friends over for an elegant dinner party, or even (gasp) take on the holidays! **I know you can do it,** you really can. As I've mentioned so often, it's about being organized and building upon the tips and tricks you've learned along the way. That, and enjoying yourself too!

When **planning** to host a large crowd, or even just preparing a romantic meal for your date, try to choose a day when you have time to spare. Leave plenty of time to plan, to shop, and to do prep work early so **everything is ready** to just pop in the oven. Think of it as a TV cooking show; there's a stage crew (although you'll be a crew of one unless you request help) to get everything ready so that when the chef begins cooking, everything only takes a few minutes to complete. This is what you're aiming for.

One of the first things I learned in culinary school was the importance of being organized so that everything comes together at just the right time. Level 1 provided some simple solutions to getting ready ahead of time; Level 2 gave you uniform Plan of Work ideas that focused on what to do the day before and what should be **accomplished** right before your guests arrive. I've added more tips in Level 3, specific to each menu, to really keep you organized.

Cocktail Party

Antipasto Platter (page 89) • Satay Chicken Skewers (page 39) • Blue Cheese Puffs with Avocado-Lemon Dip (page 160) • Shrimp Pot Stickers with Sweet Soy Sauce (page 164)

When planning your party menu, be mindful of which items will pair best with the theme of the event, the season, or even the weather. Most important: Don't be too ambitious. Make two or three hors d'oeuvres, set out some basic munchies, and keep the bar well stocked. The beauty of hors d'oeuvres is that you can make some well in advance and keep them stored in the freezer.

Prep

The day before—allow four hours, plus shopping time

- ○ Plan your menu.
- ○ Do an inventory of your bar—do you have all the drinks and mixers you need? Add what's missing to your shopping list.
- ○ Go shopping, but save the fresh bread to purchase the day of the party.
- ○ Get cleaning! Set up a food table with linens and clean serving platters.
- ○ Prepare (*but don't cook*) your appetizers: If using recipes that call for puff pastry, store appetizers in the freezer. Sauces or dips can also be made the day before, unless the recipe includes avocado (save that for day of). Cover tightly and keep refrigerated. Prep and marinate the chicken; cover and refrigerate. Make the pot stickers, lay out on a tray, cover with plastic, and refrigerate.

Prep

Same day, at least 4 hours ahead

- ○ Pick up last minute ingredients and fresh bread.
- ○ Gather all needed gear.
- ○ Set up the bar. Chill the wines.
- ○ Move cheese puffs from freezer to fridge. Make avocado dip, if using.
- ○ Skewer the chicken, ready to cook.

Okay, You're On!

Begin 1 hour before guests arrive

- ○ Pop the cheese puffs into the oven.
- ○ Fry the pot stickers. Heat the dipping sauce.
- ○ Serve the cheese puffs and pot stickers.
- ○ Cook the chicken skewers. When ready, serve on a platter.

Antipasto Platter (page 89)

Satay Chicken Skewers (page 39)

Blue Cheese Puffs with Avocado-Lemon Dip (page 160)

Shrimp Pot Stickers with Sweet Soy Sauce (page 164)

Elegant Dinner for Four

Goat Cheese Crostini with Caramelized Red Onions (page 90) • *Lobster Salad (page 190)* • *Crispy Chicken Cutlets with Mushrooms (page 122) with Buttery Mashed Potatoes (page 196) and Sugar Snap Peas (page 198)* • *Lemon Tart (page 202)*

Thinking like a pro includes *timing your prep work* and *being detailed in your execution* of the dishes. Remember, you're a confident cook now!

Elegant Menu Plan of Work

This plan is based on a simple idea: Start with what time you'd like to serve your meal, consider the unexpected things that may come up (like finding a missing ingredient), figure out *prep*, *cook*, and *serve* times, then work backward.

**Goat Cheese Crostini with
Caramelized Red Onions
(page 90)**

**Lobster Salad
(page 190)**

**Crispy Chicken Cutlets with
Mushrooms (page 122)**

**Lemon Tart
(page 202)**

PLAN AND ORGANIZE: THE DAY OF THE DINNER

Step 1—Figure out how long everything will take

	PREP TIME	COOK TIME	SERVE TIME	TOTAL
Crostini	15 minutes	35 minuts	2 minutes	= 52 minutes
Lobster	25 minutes	10 minutes	10 minutes	= 45 minutes
Chicken	14 minutes	14 minutes	2 minutes	= 30 minutes
Potatoes	20 minutes	38 minutes	2 minutes	= 1 hour
Peas	8 minutes	5 minutes	2 minutes	= 15 minutes
Sauce	n/a	13 minutes	2 minutes	= 15 minutes

Note: Some of these actions will be accomplished simultaneously.

Step 2—Do the math, then count backward from meal time

• Working backward, add **serve** times together: 2 + 10 + 2 + 2 + 2 + 2 + 2 = 22 minutes
• Then add **cook** times together: 35 + 10 + 14 + 38 + 5 + 13 = 1 hour, 55 minutes
• Then add all your prep times together 15 + 25 + 14 + 20 + 8 + 10 = 1 hour, 32 minutes

MEAL TIME: 8 P.M.

Serve Time	22 minutes
Cook Time	1 hour, 55 minutes
Prep Time	1 hour, 32 minutes
Total	3 hours, 49 minutes

So, if you count back from your 8 p.m. meal time, you should plan to begin your meal prep no later than **4 p.m.**

Holiday Get-Together

Roasted Pepper, Brie, and Tomato Tartlets (page 157) • Spinach Salad with Honey-Mustard Dressing (page 26) • Prime Rib of Beef (page 182) with Roasted Potatoes Slices (page 71) • Medley of Vegetables, Roasted or Grilled (page 136) • Sticky Toffee Pudding with Crème Anglaise (page 204)

Roasted Pepper, Brie, and Tomato Tartlets (page 157)

Holiday meals can be tricky. Be flexible during your holiday party—instead of requiring everyone to show up at the same time, consider offering up a sumptuous buffet your guests can enjoy as they arrive. For you, the hardest part is getting everything out onto the table. After that, you can enjoy the festivities like everyone else.

A holiday get-together does require a good bit of planning. This Plan of Work suggests a basic timeline (in which you are doing all the prep work the same day) that will help you get your meal ready on time and still have fun.

Spinach Salad with Honey-Mustard Dressing (page 26)

Holiday Get-Together Plan of Work

TIMELINE: 7 HOURS

Noon	Have shopping *completed* (try to do as much as possible the day before).
1:00	Begin prep process: Collect all ingredients and needed gear. Set tables and organize (better yet, do it the night before so you can save yourself the time).
2:00	Chop and slice all veggies, measure out ingredients, etc. Make dessert (or, do this one the day before). Make salad and dressing (but do not dress); cover and refrigerate. (Salad dressing can also be made the day before.)
4:00	Clean workspace after main prep—discard peelings, wash dishes you've used. You'll feel a lot more organized and in control.
4:30	Begin cooking process. Put roast in the oven. Grill the vegetables.
5:15	Put in potatoes to roast. Then clean up and get dressed.
6:30	Check roast, put final touches on gravy and side dishes.
6:50	Cooking crunch time—this is when it all comes together. Put hors d'oeuvres in the oven. Finish cooking and serve everything. Get someone to help you take the dishes to the table. Make sure dessert is ready to go.
7:00	Okay, you're on!

Prime Rib of Beef with Roasted Potatoes Slices (page 182)

Sticky Toffee Pudding with Crème Anglaise (page 204)

Index

A

aïoli, Crab Cakes with Smoked Paprika Aïoli, *94,* 94–95, *95, 152*

alcoholic beverages. *See* wine and spirits

Antipasto Platter, 89, *89, 211*

appetizers, 156. *See also* starters

apples
    Apple Spice Muffins, 21
    Grape, Walnut, and Apple Salad, 25

aromatics, xiv

arugula
    Arugula and Parmesan with Balsamic Dressing, 28, *28*
    Arugula with Crisp Salami and Taleggio Croûtes, 107, *107*
    in Insalata Tricolore, 28
    moistening dry, 127

asparagus
    Asparagus, Pecorino, and Pea Risotto, *118,* 118–19, *119, 152*
    cooking time, 137
    Medley of Vegetables, Roasted or Grilled, *136,* 136–37, *137*

Assorted Cheeses with Pickled Asian Pear, *166,* 166–67

avocados
    Blue Cheese Puffs with Avocado-Lemon Dip, *160,* 160–61, *161, 211*
    in Lobster Salad, *190,* 190–91, *212*
    Nachos with Guacamole and Fresh Salsa, *34,* 34-35, *35, 85*
    preparation, xix

B

bacon. *See also* pancetta
    Bacon, Two Ways, *12,* 12–13, *13*
    crumbling, 13
    in Potato Cakes with Mustard Sauce, 172–73, *173*
    Potato Skins with Bacon and Cheese, *36,* 36–37, *85*
    in Spaghetti with Meat Sauce, 42, *42*
    warming up, 12

Baked Frittata, 10–11, *11, 84*

Baked Fusilli with Chicken, Mushrooms, and Pesto, 49, *49*

Baked Lasagna, *114,* 114–15, *151*

Baked Potatoes, 73, *73*

baking gear/utensils, xxv, 80, 158

bananas
    Banana Cream and Toffee Pie, *148,* 148–49, *153*
    Banana-Walnut Muffins, 21

Basic Basics, The (Level 1), 1

basil
  basil oil, 90, 91
  in Homemade Pesto, 187, *187*
  Tomato and Basil Soup, 99, *99*
  Tomatoes with Fresh Mozzarella and Basil, 29, *29*
  Tortellini with Peas, Basil, and Italian Sausage, *112*, 112–13
beans
  in Fish Tacos, *68*, 68–69
  in Quick Chili, 64, *64*
beef. *See also* hamburgers; meat; sausages; veal
  Beef and Cheddar Bake, 115
  Beef Teriyaki with Ginger Dipping Sauce, *162*, 162–63
  cuts, xv
  Fajitas with Beef, 54, *54*, *85*
  Four-Finger Firmness Guide, xxvi
  Hearty Beef Stew, *102*, 102–3
  marinating, 163
  in Meatballs, 59, *59*
  Prime Rib of Beef, *182*, 182–83, *183*, *213*
  in Rustic Meatloaf, *62*, 62–63, *83*
  in Spaghetti with Meat Sauce, 42, *42*
  Steak, Four Ways, *55*, 55–57, *56*, *57*
  steak browning, 55
  steak cooking times, 57
  steak seasoning, 55
  temperature when done, xxvi
  testing for doneness, xxvi, 58, 125
  Traditional Pot Roast, 125, *125*
bell peppers
  in Chicken Cacciatore, 124, *124*
  in Chilled Pasta Salad, 31, *31*
  cooking time, 137
  Decadent Red Pepper Sauce, 46
  in Fajitas with Chicken, Beef, or Shrimp, 54, *54*, *85*
  in Halibut with Peperonata and Pesto, *186*, 186–87
  in Lobster Salad, *190*, 190–91, *212*

  Medley of Vegetables, Roasted or Grilled, *136*, 136–37, *137*
  in Potato Skins with Grilled Chicken, Monterey Jack Cheese, and Red Pepper, 37
  preparation, xxi
  Rigatoni with Red Pepper Sauce, *45*, 45–46, *83*
  Roasted Pepper, Brie, and Tomato Tartlets, 157–58, *158*, *213*
  shopping tips, xvi
berries
  Berry Blast Muffins, 21
  Blueberry Muffins, 20, *20*
beverages, Fruit and Yogurt Smoothie, 23
black bean sauce, Vegetable Stir-Fry with Black Bean Sauce, 50, *50*
blanching technique, xxiii
Blueberry Muffins, *20*, 20–21
Blue Cheese Puffs with Avocado-Lemon Dip, *160*, 160–61, *161*, *211*
Boiled Lobster with Warm Butter, 188, *188*
Boiled Long-Grain White Rice, 74, *74*
boiling technique, xxiii
Boneless Leg of Lamb, 184, *184*
bread
  in Antipasto Platter, 89, *89*, *211*
  Arugula with Crisp Salami and Taleggio Croûtes, 107, *107*
  Bread Pudding, *146*, 146–47, *151*
  croutons, 99, 101
  Goat Cheese Crostini with Caramelized Red Onions, *90*, 90–91, *212*
bread crumbs, 48, *48*
  in Meatballs, 59, *59*
  Roast Turkey with Stuffing, *178*, 178–79
breakfast dishes, 2–23
broccoli
  cooking time, 137
  preparation, xx
  shopping tips, xvi
Broiled Pork Chops, 58, *58*
broiling technique, xxv

Brownies, 81, *81*

Brussels sprouts, Roasted Brussels Sprouts with Almonds, 140, *140*

Buffalo Chicken Wings, 38, *38*

butter
Boiled Lobster with Warm Butter, 188, *188*
clarified, 188
preparation tips, xxvii
Salmon Steaks with Champagne Butter, *130,* 130–31
softening, 14
to thicken soup, 103
Whole Chicken Roasted with Herb Butter, *120,* 120–21, *121*

butternut squash
Butternut Squash and Ginger Soup, *100,* 100–101, *151*
preparation, xxi–xxii
Vegetable Puree, Three Ways, *193,* 193–95, *194, 195*

Buttery Mashed Potatoes, 196, *196*

C

cabbage, in Coleslaw, 30, *30*

cakes
add-ins, 207
Cake for Any Occasion, *206,* 206–7
Chocolate Truffle Cake, *144,* 144–45
Cupcakes for Any Occasion, 207
removal from cake pan, 145
Sticky Toffee Pudding with Crème Anglaise, *204,* 204–5, *205, 213*
toppings, *207,* 207–9, *208, 209*
Two-Layer Cake, 207

Candied Walnuts, 27

capers
Chicken with Capers and Lemon, 123
Sole with Capers and Lemon, *66,* 66–67

carrots
Pan-Roasted Carrots, 139, *139*
preparation, xx
in Rustic Meatloaf, *62,* 62–63, *83*
savory/sweet holiday side dish, 139

casseroles
Baked Fusilli with Chicken, Mushrooms, and Pesto, 49, *49*
Baked Lasagna, *114,* 114–15, *151*
Beef and Cheddar Bake, 115
Chicken Parmesan, 117
Eggplant Parmesan, *116,* 116–17, *153*
Macaroni and Cheese, *47,* 47–48, *48*

Casual Dinner for Four (or Eight), 153, *153*

celery
in Mussels in White Wine Sauce, 171, *171*
in Rustic Meatloaf, *62,* 62–63, *83*

celery root, 103
in Hearty Beef Stew, *102,* 102–3

cheese
accompaniments, 167, *167*
in Antipasto Platter, 89, *89, 211*
Arugula and Parmesan with Balsamic Dressing, 28, *28*
Arugula with Crisp Salami and Taleggio Croûtes, 107, *107*
Asparagus, Pecorino, and Pea Risotto, *118,* 118–19, *119, 152*
Assorted Cheeses with Pickled Asian Pear, *166,* 166–67
Beef and Cheddar Bake, 115
Blue Cheese Puffs with Avocado-Lemon Dip, *160,* 160–61, *161, 211*
Chicken Parmesan, 117
in Classic Caesar Salad, 105, *105, 153*
Eggplant Parmesan, *116,* 116–17, *153*
Extra Cheesy Mashed Potatoes, 197, *197*
Goat Cheese Crostini with Caramelized Red Onions, *90,* 90–91, *212*
Grilled Cheese Sandwiches, 33, *33*
Macaroni and Cheese, *47,* 47–48, *48*

Mushroom and Swiss Omelet, 8, *8*
in Outta-the-Bag Salad, 25, *25, 83*
Parmesan, xxvii
Potato Skins with Bacon and Cheese, *36*, 36–37, *85*
Potato Skins with Chili and Cheddar Cheese, 37
Potato Skins with Grilled Chicken, Monterey Jack Cheese, and Red Pepper, 37
Potato Skins with Scallops, Parmesan, and Shallots, 37
recommendations, 167, *167*
Roasted Pepper, Brie, and Tomato Tartlets, 157–58, *158, 213*
shopping tips, 167
Tomato, Feta, and Olive Salad, 25
Tomatoes with Fresh Mozzarella and Basil, 29, *29*
chicken
Baked Fusilli with Chicken, Mushrooms, and Pesto, 49, *49*
Buffalo Chicken Wings, 38, *38*
Chicken and Sweet Corn Noodle Soup, 98, *98*
Chicken Cacciatore, 124, *124*
Chicken Milanese, 127
Chicken Parmesan, 117
Chicken Pot Pie, *176*, 176–77, *177*
Chicken Soup with Dumplings, 169, *169*
Chicken Stock, 97, *97*
Chicken with Capers and Lemon, 123
Chicken with Thai Green Curry, 175, *175*
Crispy Chicken Cutlets with Mushrooms, *122*, 122–23, *151, 212*
Fajitas with Chicken, 54, *54, 85*
Pan-Fried Chicken Breasts, 53, *53*
Potato Skins with Grilled Chicken, Monterey Jack Cheese, and Red Pepper, 37
pounding a cutlet, 123
Satay Chicken Bites, 39
Satay Chicken Skewers, 39, *39, 211*
Sesame Noodles with Teriyaki Chicken, *51*, 51–52

temperature when done, xxvi, 121
Whole Chicken Roasted with Herb Butter, *120*, 120–21, *121*
Chilean Sea Bass with Leeks, 133, *133*
chile peppers, 98
chili
Potato Skins with Chili and Cheddar Cheese, 37
Quick Chili, 64, *64*
Chilled Pasta Salad, 31, *31*
chocolate
in Banana Cream and Toffee Pie, 149
in Brownies, 81, *81*
Chocolate Chip Cookies, 80, *80, 85*
Chocolate Pots, 143, *143, 152*
Chocolate Sauce, 77, *77, 83*
Chocolate Truffle Cake, *144*, 144–45
melting, 144
White Chocolate Sauce, 77
Cinnamon-Roasted Pears, 201, *201*
clams
Linguine with Clams, 111, *111*
preparation, 111, *111*
shopping tips, xv
Classic Caesar Salad, *105*, 105–6, *106, 153*
Cocktail Party, 211, *211*
coconut
Coconut Shrimp with Pineapple Salsa, 132, *132*
Coconut Sticky Rice, 141, *141*
Pineapple Coconut Muffins, 21
coconut milk
in Chicken with Thai Green Curry, 175, *175*
in Shrimp and Lemongrass Soup, 170, *170*
Coleslaw, 30, *30*
cookies and bars
batter storage, 80
Brownies, 81, *81*
Chocolate Chip Cookies, 80, *80, 85*
cooking gear/utensils, x
cooking methods, xxiii–xxv
corn
Chicken and Sweet Corn Noodle Soup, 98, *98*

corn *(continued)*
    Corn on the Cob, 138, *138*
    Grilled Corn on the Cob, Two Ways, 138
Couscous, 75, *75*
crab, shopping tips, xvi
crab cakes
    coleslaw topping for, 30
    Crab Cakes with Smoked Paprika Aïoli, *94,*
        94–95, *95, 152*
    frying tips, 95
cream
    in Chocolate Sauce, 77, *77, 83*
    Fresh Fruit with Whipped Cream, 79, *79, 84*
    heating, 143
    to thicken soup, 103
    in Toffee Sauce, 78, *78*
    whipping, 79, 149, 208
cream cheese, in Stuffed Mushrooms, *92,* 92–93, 153
Crispy Chicken Cutlets with Mushrooms, *122,*
    122–23, *151, 212*
croûtes, Arugula with Crisp Salami and Taleggio
    Croûtes, 107, *107*
croutons, 99, 101
cucumber, in Lobster Salad, *190,* 190–91, *212*
Cupcakes for Any Occasion, 207
cuts, basic types, xix
cutting techniques, xviii–xxii

D

dates, in Sticky Toffee Pudding with Crème An-
    glaise, *204,* 204–5, *205, 213*
Decadent Red Pepper Sauce, 46
deglazing technique, xxiv–xxv
desserts, 76–81, 142–49, 200–209
dips, Blue Cheese Puffs with Avocado-Lemon Dip,
    160, 160–61, *161, 211*
dredging technique, 66, *66*
dumplings, Chicken Soup with Dumplings, 169, *169*

E

eggplant
    cooking time, 137
    Eggplant Parmesan, *116,* 116–17, *153*
    Medley of Vegetables, Roasted or Grilled, *136,*
        136–37, *137*
eggs. *See also* frittatas; omelets
    avoiding cracked, 6
    cooking times, 3, 6, 7
    cracking, 3
    emulsion in salad dressing, 105
    Fried Eggs, 3, *3*
    Healthier Scrambled Eggs, 5
    in Niçoise Salad with Fresh Tuna, *108,* 108–9
    Poached Eggs on Toast, 7, *7*
    safety, 5
    Scrambled Eggs, *4,* 4–5
    separating, xxii, 5
    shopping tips, xvii
    Soft or Hard "Boiled" Eggs, 6, *6*
Elegant Dinner for Four, 212, *212*
endive, Belgian, in Insalata Tricolore, 28
entertaining. *See* meal planning and entertaining
entrées. *See* main dishes
equipment. *See* gear; *utensils*
Extra Cheesy Mashed Potatoes, 197, *197*

F

Fajitas with Chicken, Beef, or Shrimp, 54, *54, 85*
fennel
    in Mussels in White Wine Sauce, 171, *171*
    Vegetable Puree, Three Ways, *193,* 193–95, *194, 195*
first courses, elegant, 168–73
fish. *See also* shellfish; *specific fish*
    Chilean Sea Bass with Leeks, 133, *133*
    Fish Tacos, *68,* 68–69
    frying, 67, 187
    Halibut with Peperonata and Pesto, *186,* 186–87

Niçoise Salad with Fresh Tuna, *108,* 108–9
Pan-Seared Striped Bass with Heirloom Tomato
    Salsa, 185, *185*
Salmon Steaks with Champagne Butter, *130,*
    130–31
shopping tips, xvi
Sole with Capers and Lemon, *66,* 66–67
food handling, xvii. *See also* safety
Four-Finger Firmness Guide, xxvi
French Toast, 17, *17*
Fresh Fruit with Whipped Cream, 79, *79, 84*
Fried Eggs, 3, *3*
frittatas
    Baked Frittata, 10–11, *11, 84*
    basic fillings, 9
fruits. *See also specific fruits*
    to accompany cheeses, 167, *167*
    citrus, zesting, xxvii
    Fresh Fruit with Whipped Cream, 79, *79, 84*
    Fruit and Yogurt, 23, *23*
    Fruit and Yogurt Smoothie, 23
    shopping tips, xvi

G

Game Day Munchies, 85, *85*
gadgets. *See* gear; utensils
garlic
    in Homemade Pesto, 187, *187*
    Jumbo Shrimp with Lemon, Garlic, and Tar-
        ragon, 65, *65*
    preparation, xx
    Scallion and Roasted Garlic Mashed Potatoes,
        197, *197*
    shopping tips, xiv
gear
    baking, xi, 80 158
    cooking, x
    kitchen gadgets, viii
    kitchen tools, ix

knives, xii, xviii–xxii
    measuring, xi, xxii
ginger
    Beef Teriyaki with Ginger Dipping Sauce, *162,*
        162–63
    Butternut Squash and Ginger Soup, *100,*
        100–101, *151*
Goat Cheese Crostini with Caramelized Red Onions,
    90, 90–91, *212*
Grape, Walnut, and Apple Salad, 25
gravy separator, 121
green beans
    cooking time, 137
    Green Bean Parcels, 199, *199*
    in Niçoise Salad with Fresh Tuna, *108,* 108–9
greens. *See* arugula; spinach
Grilled Cheese Sandwiches, 33, *33*
Grilled Corn on the Cob, Two Ways, 138
grilling technique, xxv

H

Halibut with Peperonata and Pesto, *186,* 186–87
Ham, Two Ways, 16, *16*
hamburgers
    cooking alternatives, 61
    freezing, 61
    Hamburger Deluxe, *60,* 60–61
    sides and toppings, 30, 61
Healthier Scrambled Eggs, 5
Hearty Beef Stew, *102,* 102 3
Hearty Lamb Stew, 103
herbs
    adding to soup, 96
    fresh *vs.* dried, xiv, xxvii
    preparation, xx, xxvii
    shopping tips, xvi
    Simple Herb Mashed Potatoes, 197, *197*
    Whole Chicken Roasted with Herb Butter, *120,*
        120–21, *121*

Holiday Get-Together, 213, *213*
Homemade Pesto, 187, *187*
honey, Spinach Salad with Honey-Mustard Dressing, *26*, 26–27, *213*
hors d'oeuvres, 156–67

I

ice cream
    with Chocolate Sauce, 77, *77*, *83*
    scooping, 201
ingredients
    aromatics, xiv
    cooking methods, xxiii–xxv
    preparation, xviii–xxii
    shopping tips, xv–xvii, 167, 187
    spice rack, xiv
    staples, xiii
Insalata Tricolore, 28

J

Jumbo Shrimp with Lemon, Garlic, and Tarragon, 65, *65*

K

knives
    cutting techniques, xviii–xxii
    types and care, xii

L

lamb
    Boneless Leg of Lamb, 184, *184*
    Hearty Lamb Stew, 103
    temperature when done, xxvi

leeks
    Chilean Sea Bass with Leeks, 133, *133*
    in Green Bean Parcels, 199, *199*
    preparation, xiv
lemongrass, Shrimp and Lemongrass Soup, 170, *170*
lemons
    Blue Cheese Puffs with Avocado-Lemon Dip, *160*, 160–61, *161*, *211*
    Chicken with Capers and Lemon, 123
    Jumbo Shrimp with Lemon, Garlic, and Tarragon, 65, *65*
    Lemon Tart, *202*, 202–3, *203*, *212*
    Sole with Capers and Lemon, *66*, 66–67
levels
    Level 1 (The Basic Basics), 1
    Level 2 (Raising the Bar), 87
    Level 3 (Now You're Cooking!), 155
Linguine with Clams, 111, *111*
lobster
    added to other dishes, 191
    Boiled Lobster with Warm Butter, 188, *188*
    cleaning and eating tips, 189, *189*
    Lobster Salad, *190*, 190–91, *212*
    shopping tips, xv

M

Macaroni and Cheese, *47*, 47–48, *48*
main dishes, 40–69, 110–33, 174–91
mayonnaise, in Smoked Paprika Aïoli, *94*, 94–95, *95*, *152*
meal planning and entertaining
    Casual Dinner for Four (or Eight), 153, *153*
    Cocktail Party, 211, *211*
    Elegant Dinner for Four, 212, *212*
    Game Day Munchies, 85, *85*
    Holiday Get-Together, 213, *213*
    organization tips, 44, 82, 150
    Romantic Meal for Two, 152, *152*
    Sunday Brunch, 84, *84*

Weekend Cooking, 151, *151*
Weeknight Dinner, 83, *83*
measuring gear, xi
measuring techniques, xxii
meat. *See also specific meats*
    in Antipasto Platter, 89, *89, 211*
    cooking temperatures, xxvi, 57
    Meatballs, 59, *59*
    Rustic Meatloaf, *62,* 62–63, *83*
    shopping tips, xv
    testing for doneness, xxvi, 58, 121, 125, 128
Medallions of Pork, *128,* 128–29
Medley of Vegetables, Roasted or Grilled, *136,*
    136–37, *137*
milk, sweetened condensed, in Banana Cream and
    Toffee Pie, *148,* 148–49, *153*
mise en place, xviii
muffins
    Apple Spice Muffins, 21
    Banana-Walnut Muffins, 21
    Berry Blast Muffins, 21
    Blueberry Muffins, *20,* 20–21
    mixing, 21
    Pineapple Coconut Muffins, 21
mushrooms
    Baked Fusilli with Chicken, Mushrooms, and
        Pesto, 49, *49*
    in Chicken Cacciatore, 124, *124*
    cooking time, 137
    Crispy Chicken Cutlets with Mushrooms, *122,*
        122–23, *151, 212*
    in Fajitas with Chicken, Beef, or Shrimp, 54, *54, 85*
    in Medallions of Pork, *128,* 128–29
    Medley of Vegetables, Roasted or Grilled, *136,*
        136–37, *137*
    Mushroom and Swiss Omelet, 8, *8*
    preparation, xx
    in Rustic Meatloaf, *62,* 62–63, *83*
    shopping tips, xvi
    in Spaghetti with Meat Sauce, 42, *42*
    Stuffed Mushrooms, *92,* 92–93, 153

mussels
    cooking tips, 171
    Mussels in White Wine Sauce, 171, *171*
    shopping tips, xv
mustard
    cooking tips, 173
    Potato Cakes with Mustard Sauce, 172–73, *173*
    Spinach Salad with Honey-Mustard Dressing,
        26, 26–27, *213*

N

Nachos with Guacamole and Fresh Salsa, *34,* 34–35,
    35, 85
Niçoise Salad with Fresh Tuna, *108,* 108–9
noodles. *See also* pasta
    Chicken and Sweet Corn Noodle Soup, 98, *98*
    Sesame Noodles with Teriyaki Chicken, *51,* 51–52
Now You're Cooking! (Level 3), 155
nuts
    Banana-Walnut Muffins, 21
    Grape, Walnut, and Apple Salad, 25
    Roasted Brussels Sprouts with Almonds, 140, *140*

O

oils
    basil oil, 90, 91
    emulsion in salad dressing, 105
    extra-virgin olive oil, xxvii
olives
    in Niçoise Salad with Fresh Tuna, *108,* 108–9
    Tomato, Feta, and Olive Salad, 25
omelets. *See also* frittatas
    bacon topping, 13
    basic fillings, 9
    Mushroom and Swiss Omelet, 8, *8*
onions
    in Chilled Pasta Salad, 31, *31*

onions *(continued)*

in Fajitas with Chicken, Beef, or Shrimp, 54, *54, 85*

Goat Cheese Crostini with Caramelized Red Onions, *90,* 90–91, *212*

preparation, xx–xxi

shopping tips, xiv

Outta-the-Bag Salad, 25, *25, 83*

P

pancakes

add-ins, 19

Super-Simple Pancakes, *18,* 18–19

pancetta, Ravioli with Peas and Pancetta, 113

Pan-Fried Chicken Breasts, 53, *53*

pan-frying technique, xxiv

Pan-Roasted Carrots, 139, *139*

Pan-Seared Striped Bass with Heirloom Tomato Salsa, 185, *185*

paprika, Crab Cakes with Smoked Paprika Aïoli, *94,* 94–95, *95, 152*

parsley, in Whole Chicken Roasted with Herb Butter, *120,* 120–21, *121*

parsnips, Vegetable Puree, Three Ways, *193,* 193–95, *194, 195*

parties. *See* meal planning and entertaining

pasta. *See also* noodles; wonton wrappers

Baked Fusilli with Chicken, Mushrooms, and Pesto, 49, *49*

Baked Lasagna, *114,* 114–15, *151*

Beef and Cheddar Bake, 115

Chilled Pasta Salad, 31, *31*

cooking, 31

Linguine with Clams, 111, *111*

Macaroni and Cheese, *47,* 47–48, *48*

and Meatballs, 59, *59*

Pasta with Basic Basics Tomato Sauce, 41, *41*

Ravioli with Peas and Pancetta, 113

Rigatoni with Red Pepper Sauce, *45,* 45–46, *83*

Seasonal Pasta, *43,* 43–44, *44*

Spaghetti with Meat Sauce, 42, *42*

Tortellini with Peas, Basil, and Italian Sausage, *112,* 112–13

pastry, puff. *See* puff pastry

pastry dough

blind baking, 203

rolling and baking tips, 203

pears

Assorted Cheeses with Pickled Asian Pear, *166,* 166–67

Cinnamon-Roasted Pears, 201, *201*

in Outta-the-Bag Salad, 25, *25, 83*

peas

Asparagus, Pecorino, and Pea Risotto, *118,* 118–19, *119, 152*

cooking time, 137

Ravioli with Peas and Pancetta, 113

Sugar Snap Peas, 198, *198*

Tortellini with Peas, Basil, and Italian Sausage, *112,* 112–13

pepper mill, xxvii

peppers. *See* bell peppers; chile peppers

pesto

Baked Fusilli with Chicken, Mushrooms, and Pesto, 49, *49*

Halibut with Peperonata and Pesto, *186,* 186–87

Homemade Pesto, 187, *187*

shopping and serving tips, 187

pies and tarts, savory

Chicken Pot Pie, *176,* 176–77, *177*

Roasted Pepper, Brie, and Tomato Tartlets, 157–58, *158, 213*

pies and tarts, sweet

Banana Cream and Toffee Pie, *148,* 148–49, *153*

Lemon Tart, *202,* 202–3, *203, 212*

producing a clean slice, 149

pineapple

Coconut Shrimp with Pineapple Salsa, 132, *132*

Pineapple Coconut Muffins, 21

planning. *See* meal planning and entertaining
Poached Eggs on Toast, 7, *7*
pork. *See also* bacon; ham; meat; pancetta; salami;
    sausages
    Broiled Pork Chops, 58, *58*
    in Meatballs, 59, *59*
    Medallions of Pork, *128,* 128–29
    Pork Chops, 58, *58*
    in Rustic Meatloaf, *62,* 62–63, *83*
    temperature when done, xxvi
    testing for doneness, 58, 128
potatoes. *See also* potato skins
    Baked Potatoes, 73, *73*
    baking ahead of time, 37
    Buttery Mashed Potatoes, 196, *196*
    Extra Cheesy Mashed Potatoes, 197, *197*
    in Hearty Beef Stew, *102,* 102–3
    in Niçoise Salad with Fresh Tuna, *108,* 108–9
    Potato Cakes with Mustard Sauce, 172–73, *173*
    preparation, xx
    Prime Rib of Beef with Roasted Potatoes, *182,*
        182–83, *183, 213*
    Roasted Potato Slices, 71, *71*
    Roasted Rosemary Potato Wedges, 72, *72*
    Scallion and Roasted Garlic Mashed Potatoes,
        197, *197*
    shopping tips, xvi
    Simple Herb Mashed Potatoes, 197, *197*
    storage of leftovers, 173
    toppings, 13, 135
    Twice-Baked Potatoes, 135, *135*
potato skins
    Potato Skins with Bacon and Cheese, *36,* 36–37,
        85
    Potato Skins with Chili and Cheddar Cheese, 37
    Potato Skins with Grilled Chicken, Monterey
        Jack Cheese, and Red Pepper, 37
    Potato Skins with Scallops, Parmesan, and Shal-
        lots, 37
pots and pans, x
poultry, xv. *See also* chicken; turkey

preparation of ingredients, xviii–xxii
Prime Rib of Beef with Roasted Potatoes, *182,*
    182–83, *183, 213*
produce, xvi. *See also* fruits; vegetables
puddings
    Bread Pudding, *146,* 146–47, *151*
    Chocolate Pots, 143, *143, 152*
    liqueurs to flavor, 143
puff pastry
    Blue Cheese Puffs with Avocado-Lemon Dip,
        160, 160–61, *161, 211*
    Chicken Pot Pie, *176,* 176–77, *177*
    cooking and refrigeration tips, 161
    Roasted Pepper, Brie, and Tomato Tartlets,
        157–58, *158, 213*
    working with, 159

Q

Quick Chili, 64, *64*

R

radicchio, in Insalata Tricolore, 28
Raising the Bar (Level 2), 87
Ravioli with Peas and Pancetta, 113
reducing technique, xxv
rice
    amount of water to add, 74
    in Asparagus, Pecorino, and Pea Risotto, *118,*
        118–19, *119, 152*
    Boiled Long-Grain White Rice, 74, *74*
    Coconut Sticky Rice, 141, *141*
Rigatoni with Red Pepper Sauce, *45,* 45–46, *83*
risotto
    Asparagus, Pecorino, and Pea Risotto, *118,*
        118–19, *119, 152*
    tips for creamy texture, 119
Roasted Brussels Sprouts with Almonds, 140, *140*

Roasted Pepper, Brie, and Tomato Tartlets, 157–58, *158, 213*

Roasted Potato Slices, 71, *71*

Roasted Rosemary Potato Wedges, 72, *72*

roasting technique, xxv

Roast Turkey with Stuffing, *178,* 178–79

Romantic Meal for Two, 152, *152*

rosemary

    Roasted Rosemary Potato Wedges, 72, *72*

    in Whole Chicken Roasted with Herb Butter, *120,* 120–21, *121*

Rustic Meatloaf, *62,* 62–63, *83*

S

safety

    blending hot soup, 101

    egg, 5

    food handling, xvii

    frozen foods, xvii

    oiling pans, 80

    refrigeration, xvii

    stirring caramel, 78

    turkey, 181

salad dressings

    applying, 29

    Arugula and Parmesan with Balsamic Dressing, 28, *28*

    Spinach Salad with Honey-Mustard Dressing, *26,* 26–27, *213*

salads, 24–31, 104–9

    Arugula and Parmesan with Balsamic Dressing, 28, *28*

    Arugula with Crisp Salami and Taleggio Croûtes, 107, *107*

    Chilled Pasta, 31, *31*

    Classic Caesar Salad, *105,* 105–6, *106, 153*

    Coleslaw, 30, *30*

    Grape, Walnut, and Apple Salad, 25

    Insalata Tricolore, 28

    Lobster Salad, *190,* 190–91, *212*

    Niçoise Salad with Fresh Tuna, *108,* 108–9

    Outta-the-Bag Salad, 25, *25, 83*

    rules, 106

    Tomato, Feta, and Olive Salad, 25

    Tomatoes with Fresh Mozzarella and Basil, 29, *29*

    toppings, 13, 106

salami, Arugula with Crisp Salami and Taleggio Croûtes, 107, *107*

Salmon Steaks with Champagne Butter, *130,* 130–31

salsa

    Coconut Shrimp with Pineapple Salsa, 132, *132*

    Fresh Salsa, 34, *34*

    Pan-Seared Striped Bass with Heirloom Tomato Salsa, 185, *185*

sandwiches

    Grilled Cheese Sandwich, 33, *33*

    Hamburger Deluxe, *60,* 60–61

    Meatball Sandwich, 59, *59*

Satay Chicken Bites, 39

Satay Chicken Skewers, 39, *39, 211*

sauces. *See also* pesto; salsa

    Beef Teriyaki with Ginger Dipping Sauce, *162,* 162–63

    Chocolate Sauce, 77, *77*

    Crab Cakes with Smoked Paprika Aïoli, *94,* 94–95, *95, 152*

    Decadent Red Pepper Sauce, 46

    Mussels in White Wine Sauce, 171, *171*

    pan juice tips, 121, 125

    Pasta with Basic Basics Tomato Sauce, 41, *41*

    Potato Cakes with Mustard Sauce, 172–73, *173*

    preparation tips, xxv

    Rigatoni with Red Pepper Sauce, *45,* 45–46, *83*

    Shrimp Pot Stickers with Sweet Soy Sauce, *164,* 164–65, *165, 211*

    Spaghetti with Meat Sauce, 42, *42*

    Teriyaki Sauce, 52

    thinning, 41, 125, 131

    Toffee Sauce, 78, *78*

    Vegetable Stir-Fry with Black Bean Sauce, 50, *50*

White Chocolate Sauce, 77
White Sauce, 48, *48*
sausages
    Sausage, Two Ways, *14*, 14–15, *15*
    Tortellini with Peas, Basil, and Italian Sausage, *112*, 112–13
sautéing technique, xxiv
scallions
    in Coconut Sticky Rice, 141, *141*
    in Potato Cakes with Mustard Sauce, 172–73, *173*
    Scallion and Roasted Garlic Mashed Potatoes, 197, *197*
scallops, Potato Skins with Scallops, Parmesan, and Shallots, 37
Scones, 22, *22*
Scrambled Eggs, *4*, 4–5
searing technique, xxiv
Seasonal Pasta, *43*, 43–44, *44*
Sesame Noodles with Teriyaki Chicken, *51*, 51–52
shallots
    Potato Skins with Scallops, Parmesan, and Shallots, 37
    preparation, xiv
shellfish, xvi. *See also* clams; lobster; mussels; shrimp
shrimp
    Coconut Shrimp with Pineapple Salsa, 132, *132*
    cooking tips, 65
    Fajitas with Shrimp, 54, *54, 85*
    Jumbo Shrimp with Lemon, Garlic, and Tarragon, 65, *65*
    shopping tips, xvi
    Shrimp and Lemongrass Soup, 170, *170*
    Shrimp Pot Stickers with Sweet Soy Sauce, *164*, 164–65, *165, 211*
    Steamed Shrimp Pot Stickers, 165
side dishes, 70–75, 134–41, 192–99
simmering technique, xxiii
Simple Herb Mashed Potatoes, 197, *197*
snacks, 32–39
Soft or Hard "Boiled" Eggs, 6, *6*
Sole with Capers and Lemon, *66*, 66–67

soups and stews, 96–103
    bacon topping, 13
    blending hot, 101
    Butternut Squash and Ginger Soup, *100*, 100–101, *151*
    Chicken and Sweet Corn Noodle Soup, 98, *98*
    Chicken Cacciatore, 124, *124*
    Chicken Soup with Dumplings, 169, *169*
    Chicken Stock for, 97, *97*
    Hearty Beef Stew, *102*, 102–3
    Hearty Lamb Stew, 103
    options for mixing and finishing, 103
    Quick Chili, 64, *64*
    reheating, 103
    Shrimp and Lemongrass Soup, 170, *170*
    Tomato and Basil Soup, 99, *99*
soy sauce, Shrimp Pot Stickers with Sweet Soy Sauce, *164*, 164–65, *165, 211*
Spaghetti with Meat Sauce, 12, *42*
spice rack, essentials, xiv
spinach
    in Shrimp and Lemongrass Soup, 170, *170*
    Spinach Salad with Honey-Mustard Dressing, *26*, 26–27, *213*
squash. *See also* butternut squash; zucchini
    preparation, xxi–xxii
    shopping tips, xvi
staples, everyday, xiii
starters, savory, 88–95, 156
Steak, Four Ways, *55*, 55–57, *56, 57*
steak, testing for doneness, xxvi
Steamed Shrimp Pot Stickers, 165
Sticky Toffee Pudding with Crème Anglaise, *204*, 204–5, *205, 213*
stir-fries
    Sesame Noodles with Teriyaki Chicken, *51*, 51–52
    Vegetable Stir-Fry with Black Bean Sauce, 50, *50*
stock
    Chicken Stock, 97, *97*
    in risotto, 119

Stuffed Mushrooms, *92,* 92–93, 153
sugar
    brown, measuring technique, xxii
    safety, 78
    Toffee Sauce, 78, *78*
    vanilla-flavored, 147
Sugar Snap Peas, 198, *198*
Sunday Brunch, 84, *84*
Super-Simple Pancakes, *18,* 18–19
sweating technique, xxiv

T

tarragon, Jumbo Shrimp with Lemon, Garlic, and
    Tarragon, 65, *65*
tarts. *See* pies and tarts
Teriyaki Sauce, 52
thyme, in Whole Chicken Roasted with Herb Butter,
    120, 120–21, *121*
tomatoes
    in Chicken Cacciatore, 124, *124*
    in Chilled Pasta Salad, 31, *31*
    in Lobster Salad, *190,* 190–91, *212*
    Pan-Seared Striped Bass with Heirloom Tomato
        Salsa, 185, *185*
    Pasta with Basic Basics Tomato Sauce, 41, *41*
    in Pineapple Salsa, 132, *132*
    preparation, xxi
    Roasted Pepper, Brie, and Tomato Tartlets,
        157–58, *158, 213*
    shopping tips, xvi
    Tomato, Feta and Olive Salad, 25
    Tomato and Basil Soup, 99, *99*
    Tomatoes with Fresh Mozzarella and Basil, 29,
        29
tools, kitchen, ix. *See also* gear; utensils
Tortellini with Peas, Basil, and Italian Sausage, *112,*
    112–13
tortilla chips, in Nachos with Guacamole and Fresh
    Salsa, *34,* 34–35, *35, 85*

tortillas
    in Fajitas with Chicken, Beef, or Shrimp, 54, *54,*
        85
    in Fish Tacos, *68,* 68–69
    heating, 69
Traditional Pot Roast, 125, *125*
turkey
    carving, 180, *180*
    in Meatballs, 59, *59*
    Roast Turkey with Stuffing, *178,* 178–79
    tips and safety, 181
Twice-Baked Potatoes, 135, *135*
Two-Layer Cake, 207

U

utensils
    baking, xi, 80 158
    cooking, x
    kitchen gadgets, viii
    kitchen tools, ix
    knives, xii, xviii–xxii
    measuring, xi, xxii

V

vanilla beans, 147, *147*
veal. *See also* meat
    in Meatballs, 59, *59*
    in Rustic Meatloaf, *62,* 62–63, *83*
    temperature when done, xxvi
    Veal Milanese, *126,* 126–27, *152*
vegetables. *See also specific vegetables*
    adding to soup, 96, 103
    in Antipasto Platter, 89, *89, 211*
    cooking times, 137
    cooking tips for green, 137
    Medley of Vegetables, Roasted or Grilled, *136,*
        136–37, *137*

preparation, xix–xxii

in Seasonal Pasta, *43*, 43–44, *44*

shopping tips, xvi

Vegetable Puree, Three Ways, *193*, 193–95, *194*, *195*

Vegetable Stir-Fry with Black Bean Sauce, 50, *50*

vinegar, Balsamic, Arugula and Parmesan with Balsamic Dressing, 28, *28*

W

walnuts, Candied Walnuts, 27

Weekend Cooking, 151, *151*

Weeknight Dinner, 83, *83*

White Chocolate Sauce, 77

White Sauce, 48, *48*

Whole Chicken Roasted with Herb Butter, *120*, 120–21, *121*

wine and spirits

liqueurs in chocolate pots, 143

Mussels in White Wine Sauce, 171, *171*

Salmon Steaks with Champagne Butter, *130*, 130–31

wonton wrappers

Chicken Soup with Dumplings, 169, *169*

Shrimp Pot Stickers with Sweet Soy Sauce, *164*, 164–65, *165*, *211*

Steamed Shrimp Pot Stickers, 165

Y

yogurt

Fruit and Yogurt, 23, *23*

Fruit and Yogurt Smoothie, 23

in Rigatoni with Red Pepper Sauce, *45*, 45–46, *83*

Z

zucchini

cooking time, 137

Medley of Vegetables, Roasted or Grilled, *136*, 136–37, *137*